Content-Area Writing

Content-Area Writing

Every Teacher's Guide

**Harvey Daniels,
Steven Zemelman,
and Nancy Steineke**

Heinemann
Portsmouth, NH

Heinemann

361 Hanover Street
Portsmouth, NH 03801–3912
www.heinemann.com

Offices and agents throughout the world

The authors and publisher wish to thank those who have generously given permission to reprint borrowed material:

Excerpts from *A Teacher's Guide to the Multigenre Research Project* by Melinda Putz. Copyright © 2006 by Melinda Putz. Published by Heinemann, Portsmouth, NH. Reprinted with permission.

Excerpts from *Subjects Matter* by Harvey Daniels and Steven Zemelman. Copyright © 2004 by Harvey Daniels and Steven Zemelman. Published by Heinemann, Portsmouth, NH. Reprinted with permission.

Library of Congress Cataloging-in-Publication Data
Daniels, Harvey, 1947-
    Content-area writing : every teacher's guide / Harvey Daniels, Steven Zemelman, and Nancy Steineke.
      p. cm.
    Includes bibliographical references and index.
    ISBN-13: 978-0-325-00972-8
    ISBN-10: 0-325-00972-4   1. Composition (Language arts)—Study and teaching—United States.
    2. Language arts—Correlation with content subjects—United States.
    3. English language—Composition and exercises—Study and teaching—United States.
    I. Zemelman, Steven. II. Steineke, Nancy. III. Title.
LB1576.D233 2007
808'.042071—dc22   2006037120

Acquisitions editor: Leigh Peake
Production: Patricia Adams
Typesetter: Technologies 'N Typography
Interior design: Joyce Weston and Jenny Jensen Greenleaf
Interior chapter opening photographs: Robb Hill
Cover design: Judy Arisman
Cover photograph: Gabrielle Keller
Manufacturing: Steve Bernier

Printed in the United States of America on acid-free paper

11 10   VP   4 5

Contents

PART TWO   Public Writing

Acknowledgments

At the Academy Awards, if you try to thank everyone who helped you win that Oscar, the orchestra will start "playing you off" after about thirty seconds. They will drown you out and make you shut up. That can't happen in books, but maybe it should.

Between us, we have written nineteen books, and after nineteen sets of acknowledgments, we have already thanked virtually every person on the planet, including our spouses, children, parents, siblings, cousins, and ancestors; our current and former students; our own teachers from back in elementary school; our camp counselors, sports coaches, and Scout leaders; our current colleagues, principals, deans, department heads, and bosses; and our increasingly crucial personal support crews, the hardworking acupuncturists, yoga instructors, masseuses, and physical therapists who keep our bodies together so we can still think. In one book, Smokey even acknowledged the musicians whose tunes he listens to while writing (thanks again, Steven Tyler, Ted DeMille, and JT).

So this time around we'll just say: **You know who you are, and we love you all! Goodnight!**

Well . . . maybe *just a few* specific thanks. For us, it all comes down to kids, teachers, and our wonderful publisher.

- ☞ Our gratitude to all the students who contributed samples of their writing and stories about their writing experiences. We are in awe of what you can do with words. As our Colorado colleague Charles Coleman says: "Often the beauty of student writing is the freshness of its voice." Thanks, kids—without your voices, this book would definitely not be "fresh," with all that means today.

- ☞ Thanks to all the teachers who invited us into their classrooms to coteach, observe, and steal their best ideas. With some of you, we came in the flesh and spent many days together; with others, we talked on the phone and communicated by email. Whatever the delivery system, we hope that your teaching ideas and assignments appear here fully and accurately. Your professional generosity is a much-needed example in these hard times, when so many forces turn teachers into competitors instead of colleagues.

- ☞ Steve and Smokey published their first book with Heinemann in 1985. As we now enter our third decade as Heinemann authors, we can testify better than anyone (except maybe Don Graves, Nancie Atwell, and Lucy Calkins) why this is the premier publisher in education and why the strongest voices in our field are on Heinemann's list. Lesa Scott leads a team that's second to none. Thanks to savvy editor Leigh Peake, le supervisor du production Abby Heim, marketing maestro Pat Carls, overall guru Maura Sullivan, the left side of our brains, Melissa Wood, back cover concoctor Eric Chalek, and Marissa DuPont, who can actually decipher Smokey's handwriting. Special hero-category thanks go to our production editor, Patty Adams. She received the worst kind of manuscript you can get in this business—late and long—and whipped it into a beautiful and, we hope, coherent book. Finally, when we take our books and ideas on the road, the way is paved by the redoubtable Vicki Boyd, Angela Dion, Cherie Bartlett, Karen Belanger, money wizard Kristine Giunco, and everyone else up in "the balcony."

We really *do* love you all.

———

Come to think of it, we'd also like to thank each other. In this book, we recommend that students should sometimes write *together*, coauthoring texts just as people in American workplaces do every day. On this topic, at least, we are certainly no hypocrites. We've just found out that if two's company, three's a delight.

Though each of us has previously written a fair amount, this is our first book together. And there's never been a smoother, more seamless process than this one. Whether Steve was walking the Great Wall in China, or Smokey was packing to move to New Mexico, or Nancy was trying to grade 150 student papers, somebody always stepped in and took up the slack. Writing books is never easy or stress free, but this one was a joy to work on—together.

—Smokey, Steve, and Nancy
December 4, 2006

[*Music swells.*]

Oops, we almost forgot to thank our families—Elaine, Nick, and Marny; Susan, Mark, and Daniel; [*louder music*] and Bill—for their constant support and unfailing . . . *FADE TO BLACK*

CHAPTER ONE

Writing in the Content Areas

Is There a Writing Crisis?

A worrisome Associated Press story appears in scores of newspapers and quickly jumps to Yahoo! News. "Poor writing costs taxpayers millions," blares the headline. The article goes on to detail the staggering costs of ineffective writing instruction in our schools, as measured by graduates who come into the workforce unable to communicate clearly on paper or even in emails (Pope 2005). It is estimated that state governments spend upward of a quarter of a billion dollars per year remediating the writing skills of their employees—and that number is vastly exceeded by the expenditures of private employers. All the officials interviewed concurred that writing is a critical criterion in hiring and shook their heads over how hard it is to recruit skillful writers these days.

Just as this book was going to press, the Carnegie Commission issued a stirring report called *Writing Next* that made no bones about the gravity of this situation. As the document's introduction explains:

> . . . . American students today are not meeting even basic writing standards, and their teachers are often at a loss for how to help them. In an age overwhelmed by information. . . . we should view this as a crisis because the ability to read, comprehend, and write—in other words, to organize information into knowledge—can be viewed as tantamount to a survival skill. (Graham and Perin 2006, p. 4)

The report goes on to prescribe eleven specific treatments for the potentially "devastating consequences" of this new writing gap.

The worry about declining writing achievement has been echoing in every corner of the media. "Poor scores for writing alarm state" announced the *Chicago Tribune*. Four of ten Illinois kids, it turned out, "can't put together an organized, detailed essay that follows basic grammar and spelling rules." Passing rates on the state's writing exam were down "drastically" from the previous year, ranging from 59 percent in fifth grade to 62.5 percent in eighth (Rado 2002). Yikes! Panic! Terror!

Or Not?

On the other hand, we can see plenty of reasons for confidence, or at least calm, about our young people's ability to make sense with words. To begin with, worry about the deteriorating writing skills of young people is hardly unique to our times. For millennia, grown-ups have bemoaned the "sudden drop-off" in the literacy abilities of their offspring. Indeed, during America's last "writing crisis," back in the 1980s, coauthor Harvey "Smokey" Daniels wrote a whole book on this topic. In *Famous Last Words* (1983), he showed that there is an eternal human propensity to decry the language of the younger generation, and this worry recurs without reference to any particular facts. He dubbed this universal human tendency the Paul Lynde principle, in honor of the actor in *Bye Bye Birdie* who sings the comedic tune "What's the Matter with Kids Today?" ("Why can't they be like we were, perfect in every way . . .")

And we also know that every standardized exam has imperfections and prejudices built into its DNA. That student writing test that so "alarmed" the people of Illinois? It actually required many kids to write an essay about in-line skating. Got that? In-line skating? Ready to write your essay? We weren't either. Turns out that the test makers meant what we in the Midwest call roller-blading. And need we point out that this sport is virtually unknown in the Chicago housing projects, where the lowest writing scores were concentrated?

So, hype and headlines aside, what are the real trends in student writing achievement? When kids spend twelve years in school, and when we send them forth from our science classes, our math programs, our history courses, and our English lessons, how well can they write? Can they make sense on paper? Write a letter to the editor? Explain a process or write clear directions? The National Assessment of Educational Progress is probably the only consistent long-term measure of American education. And NAEP says that our young writers are doing *just OK*. Since it began evaluating writing in 1975, NAEP's score trend has been essentially flat (NAEP 2006). There have been transient ups and downs at different grade levels, some of them big enough for a few pundits to rev up the hand-wringing. But the main, inarguable, long-term picture is one you might call stable. Or, you might call it stagnant. Kids may not be getting any worse at school-based prose, but they're not getting any better either. But the world of text moves on, further and further beyond the writing found in school.

Teachers often say that kids hate writing. But maybe what they hate is the kind of writing we make them to do. You gotta admit, answering the questions at the end of the chapter isn't going to be the highlight of any teenager's weekend. But when kids are done slogging through *our* assignments, look at what today's adolescents are doing on their own! They are doing more *authoring* than any young people in the history of the world. Just look at your students. They are texting their friends on cell phones, writing and receiving instant messages, maintaining robust email correspondences, blogging, creating websites, updating their MySpace pages, publishing their poems or stories online, creating labyrinthine fantasy tales and games, composing songs and lyrics with software like GarageBand, making and sharing video clips, hanging in chat rooms, or joining threaded discussions.

Some young people are even writing on *paper,* for crying out loud—keeping a diary, writing notes to friends (maybe during your class), and using lists to keep themselves organized. Far from being writing averse, today's students are the most writing-ready kids we have ever seen. As author William Zinsser says, "All those people who say they hate writing and can't write and don't want to write can write and do want to write. In fact, they can't be turned off. Never have so many Americans written so profusely and with so few inhibitions" (in National Commission on Writing 2006, 14).

But school is all about inhibitions! In the old days, we used to scold kids for ending a sentence with a preposition—now we lash them for using emoticons or

---

One of the things writers do is try to imagine what their readers might be thinking. Here are the three of us, Nancy, Steve, and Smokey, imagining our conversation with you as you read this opening chapter.

You: So, I really have to have my students write?

Us: Yep.

You: Even in my science class, my history course, my math program?

Us: You bet.

You: But why can't the English teachers take care of the writing stuff and let me cover my content?

Us: Well, English teachers actually have some content to teach, too—like literature, and lots of it. And they *are* doing plenty with the kids' writing: basic composing skills, organizational patterns, vocabulary, usage, and mechanics. But that's not enough to ensure superior writing in your class.

You: Hey, tell me about it!

Us: See, kids don't need to learn just writing in general—they need to learn how to write *history,* write *science,* write about *math,* the *arts,* and every other subject in the curriculum. They need to learn how to use writing to learn content more effectively in your classroom.

You: I still don't think you understand my situation. At my school, I have a huge mandated curriculum to teach, and it is enforced with a tough state test. Our classes are bigger than ever, and we've got more special ed and ELL (English language learner) kids in every class. So many of my kids have special needs these days. And now you want to add on another job? Make me into a writing teacher?

Us: No way—you have your hands full with the curriculum you've got and the kids in front of you. But we do want to help you become a content-area teacher who *uses writing activities*

continued next page

continued from previous page

to help students to learn your subject quicker, better, and deeper. And the diversity of kids in your room? Writing is the best tool we know of to help differentiate instruction for all of their needs. We'll promise you this—if you try the strategies and structures outlined in this book, more of your kids will understand and remember more of your content than they would otherwise.

You: I suppose you have research to back this up?

Us: Oodles. Would you like to hear some of it now?

You: Maybe not—but put it down later in the book, will ya?

Us: Too late. We've got to tell you about this study done by Fred Newmann and his colleagues here in Chicago called *Authentic Intellectual Work and Standardized Tests: Conflict or Collaboration?* (Pretty good title for an academic study, eh?) Newmann found that kids scored higher on the Iowa Test of Basic Skills (ITBS) when their teachers lectured less, when classes were more interactive, and when kids did lots of well-structured and challenging *writing* (Newmann et al. 2001). In a separate study, he and his co-researchers found that students also scored higher when their teachers lectured less and classes were more interactive (Smith et al. 2001).

You: OK, OK. [*sigh*]. But here's the problem. I still don't know where I am supposed to find the *time* for more writing in my classes.

Us: What, is time a problem? Gosh, in our schools in Chicago, we have tons of extra time that we aren't even using! Like between 10:15 and 11:00 and between 1:45 and 2:30, we all just kinda lay around—we call it fallow time. It's just like rotating crops—you have to leave some of the fields unplowed every year.

You: Very funny. Not.

continued next page

email shorthand in their schoolwork.☹ Sure, assessment is vital and appropriateness of language is, too—and we'll deal forthrightly with those issues throughout this book. But for now, we need to admit: We are not tapping kids' vast out-of-school authoring experience. The kids are composing and publishing with us or without us, and we are not building a bridge from what they are writing to what we know and can share.

We understand that not every kid in your classes—or in this country—is already practicing this kind of tech-driven writing fluency. The digital divide is real, and access to the tools of the new literacy is unequal. But even the poorest teenagers in our society are gaining experience—and *competence*—with tools that never existed when most of us teachers were kids. Perhaps you saw the recent research from Canada showing that kids who played video games extensively were better problem solvers and could focus their attention more effectively than kids who didn't? And that these tech-head kids were outperformed only by kids who also happened to be bilingual? ("Better Living Through Video Games?" 2006). The notion of multiple intelligences is not just a cute little Harvard theory anymore; it is real. The definition of smarts is changing every day.

So Is There a Writing Crisis or Not?

As you can tell, we are a little wary of crisis mongering and sudden predictions of doom. We think that helping young people learn to write has always been a tough job, and that teachers have always felt torn between all the discipline knowledge they'd like to impart and the time constraints they face.

But we're not laid back about today's student writing either, no matter how familiar the current furor may seem. Something is definitely up. Kids are not writing well for academic purposes in school, and that can make a big difference now and later in life. Just look at the chain of implications:

1. Writing helps students *get more actively engaged in subject matter,* understand information and concepts more deeply, make connections and raise questions more fluently, remember ideas longer, and apply learning in new situations. (Other than that, it isn't much help!) If we say that reading helps us *take in* knowledge, with writing, we *make it our own.*

2. Writing helps students meet state standards and *pass high-stakes standardized tests.* And that doesn't just mean essay tests or the constructed-response sections of state exams. When kids have been steadily making their thinking visible in writing, they are likely to score better on all kinds of tests.

3. Writing helps students *gain access to further education.* Skillful writing helps kids score well on the essay sections of the ACT and SAT exams (and the other sections, too). Writing also helps kids get good grades in their high school classes and write successful application essays, so they get admitted to college. Once there, writing skill helps students succeed in college courses, where papers typically replace multiple-choice tests for the assessment of high-order intellectual work. Indeed, virtually all colleges now require students to pass multiple writing-intensive classes in order to graduate—or even to move on to upper-division classes.

---

continued from previous page

Us: OK, OK. The point is: *You* don't have any extra time, *we* don't have any extra time, and *nobody else* teaching in any American school feels like they have a single free second to wedge in one more topic, one more mandate, one more sliver of curriculum. After all, there's so much to cover, right? And with those state governments laying on more and more curriculum mandates and standardized tests, time gets tighter every year.

You: You can say that again.

Us: Don't tempt us. But we're "out of time" only if we insist on teaching in the old, s-l-o-w ways. The strategies we are going to cover in this book move fast, but they will actually *save you time* and *raise kids' achievement* in your class.

You: For real?

Us: Yes. That's because the twenty-five activities we recommend are *not added content,* but alternate *processes;* they substitute for other uses of time but don't add minutes. We think of the activities in this book as teaching methods. You've got to teach your subject matter somehow; these are just different ways of doing the instruction.

You: OK, but I'm going to hold you to all these promises as I read this book.

Us: Fair enough. And thanks—nice talking to you.

---

4. Writing *paves the way to fulfilling employment.* Remember all those bosses decrying the lack of good writers in their corporate workforce? Those HR department heads are clear: they want to hire young people who come out of schools and colleges ready to use words well, on paper or in the digital ether. The specific job-related text might be emails, or engineering reports, or budget narratives, or grant proposals, or job performance reports on other employees, but the underlying skill is clear, strong writing.

5. Writing prepares young people for *involved, active citizenship*. Every school mission statement says it somewhere: "P. T. Barnum Middle School is preparing young people for vigorous participation in a democratic society" and blah, blah, blah. But if you look at how Barnum is run and how the classes are taught, citizenship usually means quiet compliance, not active participation. We think schools should graduate people who can raise hell when it is necessary and possess the tools to do so, particularly writing. Our country has been established, gradually improved, and today moves toward its ideals largely through the pen, the word, the text. We need fellow citizens who can write and be heard.

> *American schools should graduate people who can raise hell when it is necessary and possess the tools to do so.*

6. Writing is *part of a better life*. Just when people say that writing is a lost art, or that nobody writes letters anymore, somebody invents email, and we are all writing to people we would never lick a stamp for. In fact, a recent study at the Rochester Psychiatric Center ("Positive Health Effects of Expressive Writing, New Research" 2005) showed that writing is good for you and can make you feel better. "Researchers have known for some time that expressive writing can have a positive effect on the writer's health, such as illness recovery," the report begins. But investigators were surprised to find that this effect works not just for people suffering illness but for everyone. The new study found that writing has many beneficial outcomes, including fewer feelings of stress, better performance on a working memory test, and a reduction of psychological symptoms. But we have known for ages that writing can keep you from going nuts. That's what diaries and journals are for, right? Remember Robinson Crusoe?

But more broadly, making words come alive on paper—or on a computer screen—whether or not we share them with others, can be one of life's greatest pleasures. All our graduates have a right to feel competent and comfortable with writing, perhaps the greatest gift language has to give.

But the Test Scores! The Test Scores!

Chicken Little, give it a rest. Whew, those *tests*, those ubiquitous "No Child Left Intact" tests. These federally mandated, state-administered exams are probably the single biggest exaggerators of the writing "crisis," as well as the more widespread panic about *everything* in our schools. In another book, we might ask: Is this frenzy of distrust of public schools an accident, or is it exactly the mindset that these tests were designed to create? But for now, we accept as reality that most states have developed separate writing assessment tests and we must prepare our kids for them. And many other high-stakes tests in science, math, and social studies are adding constructed-response questions. On these items, students cannot just darken the right bubble; they must write some phrases or sentences that provide an answer or elaborate their thinking. Without fluent, clear, concise writing, kids will be sunk on tests like these.

Even parents are freaking out about their kids' writing. Agitated by headlines like the *New York Times*' "Writing in Schools Found Both Dismal and Neglected" (Lewin 2003) and their own youngsters' sometimes incomprehensible scores on mysterious statewide tests, parents are getting concerned. In a recent study, nearly 70 percent of adult Americans thought that writing should be *taught across all subjects and grade levels* (National Writing Project 2006). And plenty of enterprising companies are eager to turn composition insecurity into cash. AOL has just introduced parents to its new Writing Wizard, some software with big promises:

> Help your kids improve their homework. AOL Writing Wizard is like having a private writing tutor for your child 24/7. See dramatic improvement in grammar, spelling, punctuation, content, organization, language usage and style. And you can expect higher test scores, better homework, and improved classroom assignments. ("Sign Up for AOL Writing Wizard Today" 2006)

If they opt for the free thirty-day trial, Mom and Dad can get a taste of the "fun drills and exercises" that are included in the program. What kid wouldn't roll his eyes with delight when the folks handed over a subscription to *this* video game!

The College Board is pushing hard for more writing too. Its own National Commission on Writing reported that "the difficulty is that [students] cannot systematically produce writing at the high levels of skill, maturity and sophistication required in a complex modern economy. The Commission [noted] the inability of most students to create prose that is precise, engaging and coherent" (2003, 16). Among other solutions, the commission suggested that schools "double the amount of time most students spend writing, require a writing plan in every school district, [and] insist that writing be taught in all subjects and at all grade levels" (3). And, of course, being an arm of the College Board and the Educational Testing Service, the commission endorsed yet another *standardized test* to make sure college-bound kids can write. Today, both the SAT and its rival ACT test, the gatekeeper exams for American college entrance, feature a newly designed essay-writing section that's prominently figured into each student's score.

So here we are, back from our brief tour of the writing crisis. What, then, is the take-away, the bottom line, the moral of the story? There's a mismatch between school writing and real-world writing, and it's widening every day. There's ample evidence that not just the demand for but also the nature of skillful writing are changing fast.

And we teachers aren't connecting with kids. What a shame, because we have so much to offer them. We can show them writing processes and strategies. We can show them how good writing works in our discipline, what stands as evidence, how we support a point, how we establish proof.

This is not so much a crisis as an opportunity, a turning point, even an auspicious moment. We have smart kids who are eagerly authoring their lives already, using a variety of tools that all depend on words, stories, and the structures of language. But they are missing a lot, too. Without the coaching, modeling, feedback, and reflection we teachers can offer, their writing is limited and growth in the subject areas will be incomplete. All of us working in middle and high schools have an extraordinary opportunity to teach our subjects better than ever by using writing and by equipping our kids for the most exciting and creative world of authorship ever imagined.

An Emerging Consensus

All of our national content-area organizations have endorsed the drive for more and better writing in every subject across the curriculum. Math educators have been sounding the cry since 1988, when the National Council of Teachers of Mathematics mandated writing as a tool of mathematical thinking and problem solving in its groundbreaking national standards report. Through a number of ensuing revisions, the NCTM standards continue to call for more student writing, along with drawing and making representations (both forms of writing). As today's NCTM website says: "There are many different ways to encourage students to think and talk about mathematics; informal writing activities can help students reflect on their understanding of mathematical concepts and encourage them to make connections among topics" (2006).

In its own national standards report, the National Council for the Social Studies concurs: "The social studies program should be designed to increase the student's ability to use the writing process and to classify, interpret, analyze, summarize, evaluate, and present information in well-reasoned ways that support better decision-making for both individuals and society" (1994). The American Association for the Advancement of Science (AAAS) puts it succinctly: "Learning requires the student's engagement in four activities, all intended to result in thinking: reading, listening, doing, and writing" (2006, 192).

And secondary students, according to our National Science Education Standards, should be able to "communicate the problem, process, and solution. Students should present their results to students, teachers, and others in a variety of ways, such as orally, in writing, and in other forms—including models, diagrams, and demonstrations" (National Research Council 1996, 192).

The Coverage Problem

So all the experts agree that students need more writing instruction and more writing practice in every class. But there's one problem that just won't go away, and you know what it is. Time! We all complain about it. It is a consuming issue in our work. But let's take a minute and consider the perennial teacher time crunch in a new light.

In a recent *New Yorker* cartoon, a smiling, prosperous businessman strides up a city avenue, thinking silently: "I've forgotten everything I learned in high school." Maybe it's because we are teachers, but we didn't think this was funny at all. And we couldn't even imagine the cartoon editors at the magazine reviewing this submission, slapping their knees with mirth, and stopping the presses to speed this hilarious work of art to a school-abused public. But the fact is, most American adults have said roughly the same thing, at one time or another, with the same kind of weird pride as the guy in that cartoon.

But maybe our students forget everything because *we teach them too much stuff.*

All of us toil in an educational system where *covering* the material—*all* the material—is the watchword in all subjects. We have a set body of knowledge, often a huge one, embedded in textbooks, codified by district curriculum guides, and enforced by the power of state-made standardized tests. If we don't cover everything, we are shamed and embarrassed and maybe even in trouble. In U.S. history, what if June comes and we are still on Reconstruction? What if my students flunk the state test? Have I shirked my duty, shortchanged young people? Will I, in this era of hard-core teacher accountability, have my salary lowered or find a pink slip in my mailbox?

At the same time, we all realize that this ideal of coverage is a total fantasy, a lie we all agree to tell each other for the sake of—what? Tradition? There's way too much content and far too little time to do intellectual justice to everything. In the faculty lounge, we freely admit this to each other. We know that when we cover every name, date, place, and battle in history, kids won't remember most of it. Maybe until the test on Friday, maybe not, but definitely not afterward. It all gently disperses like vapor. If we are covering all this material, we are covering it like a painter covers a wall with paint—a thousandth of an inch thick—and it's starting to peel the minute it goes on. This isn't a curriculum of ideas, it is a curriculum of mentioning.

> *This isn't a curriculum of ideas, it is a curriculum of mentioning.*

Is this what our mothers raised us to do: to teach teenagers things that they'll immediately forget? What kind of calling is that? We got into this work because we are in love with history, dazzled by science, smitten by literature, fascinated by numbers, captivated by language. And isn't that what we want to pass along? The awe and the big ideas? We *can* break out of this ancient cycle of superficiality and still give kids what they need to jump the hurdles that face them, in school and in life (and keep our jobs, too). The key is a *selective thinking curriculum* with *active, engaged learning activities*. We have to teach less and teach it better. We need to take kids deeper into a smaller number of topics.

This less-is-more approach is not fringe thinking; on the contrary, it is a principle clearly enunciated in virtually all of our national curriculum standards documents, from the subject-matter experts in each of the disciplines taught in school. But you must recognize that there are now two standards movements in America, and your *state* standards may totally contradict the wisdom of the NCTM or the AAAS. They probably reflect the accountability version of standards and focus on tests and punishments for kids and schools. The state "standards" may require you to cover every square inch of world history, every cell of botany, every tributary of mathematics. But that is the state's curriculum, driven by office-seeking politicians and profit-driven textbook companies, not the considered judgments of the reputable mainstream experts in your discipline.

Deeper, not wider, is an old idea; strong research support for it has been around for decades and is constantly being replicated. The three of us certainly didn't make up this idea (we are not *that* old), but we have written about it quite a bit (Daniels and Bizar 2005; Daniels and Zemelman 2004; Zemelman, Daniels, and Hyde 2005; Steineke 2002). If you want to learn more about the progressive, deeper-not-wider recommendations in your own field's standards documents, visit the national organization's website. Even if you are not an active member of the National Council of Teachers of English (NCTE) or the National Science Teachers Association (NSTA), you'll be able to review the standards and see if we are giving it to you straight. For a summary of all the main subjects' standards, Steve and Smokey's *Best Practice: Today's Standards for Teaching and Learning in American Schools* (Zemelman, Daniels, and Hyde 2005) summarizes them all and gives teaching implications, K–12.

We've told the following story in the last couple of books we've written, but it always bears repeating. A few years ago, the social studies faculty at Stagg High School, in a blue-collar suburb of Chicago, got fed up with the mandated, overstuffed, and superficial curriculum of U.S. history. They went on a weekend retreat, determined, as former chair Wayne Mraz reports, to boil U.S. history down to twelve big ideas that would then become the focus of the curriculum instead of the usual broad-

Want to Jump Around?

Tired of all these preliminaries? Want a dose of kids' work and teacher talk? Go directly to Chapter 3, 4, 7, or 9. Worried about the writing assessments in your district or state? Check out Chapter 10. Want to hear about how a content-area teacher can be a mentor for young writers in her discipline? See Chapter 6.

spectrum, scattershot delivery of factoids, elections, wars, and great and near-great personages. After what the teachers agreed was the longest two days of their lives, they emerged with sixteen "fenceposts of history" and went home to build a new course around this finite set of big ideas. Now, if you're a history teacher—or any U.S. citizen—you might want to quibble with some entries on this list, or some omissions. But the teachers now had enunciated sixteen big ideas and given themselves "rails" of about eleven school days each to tackle these crucial issues in the development of the United States.

That's what we all need to do, as individual teachers and as departments: decide what the really big ideas are—the key concepts, the major skills, the habits of mind— in each discipline. But then what happens when our deeper-not-wider kids collide with those broad and shallow state tests or the ACTs? What happens when a question pops up on one of those topics we omitted while delving into something else? What we find is that well-schooled deep-study kids do fine. They're immediately able to knock out two of the multiple choices, because they know how to think like a historian, a scientist, a mathematician, a writer. They can grapple with the question or problem because they are strong readers and thinkers. When information or data is given, they can work with it, using the intellectual tools they have acquired through challenging and sustained inquiry.

Going Deeper—into What?

If you agree with the national curriculum standards that teaching a smaller number of topics more thoroughly is a good idea, how do you know *which topics* to delve into? What are the truly crucial ideas in algebra, chemistry, art history, French literature? Happily we have help from Grant Wiggins and Jay McTighe, whose deservedly acclaimed book *Understanding by Design* (2005) sets out four criteria for determining the big ideas to teach—and the ones to discard. Wiggins and McTighe offer these screens for identifying the "keeper content" in any course:

1. Does the topic reside at the heart of the discipline? Is it a concept without which the whole field cannot be truly understood?

2. Does the topic require "uncovering"? Is it vulnerable to misconceptions? Is it something that, without teaching, students are likely to continue misunderstanding?

3. Does the topic have applications and connections to real life outside of school?

4. Is the topic potentially engaging to students? (2005, pp. 10–11)

We find it wonderful and helpful that Wiggins and McTighe are implicitly saying: If there is curricular toss-up, keep the topic that might interest the kids.

Why Content Teachers Care About Writing (and Reading)

In an earlier book, *Subjects Matter* (2004), Steve and Smokey spoke from the heart about content teaching:

> Most of us middle and high school teachers chose our profession mainly because we loved a *subject*—physics, mathematics, art, history, biology, science, literature. Elementary teachers, on the other hand, most commonly say they elected teaching because they "like being with children." That's a big difference. It doesn't mean we secondary types don't like young people (most of us are quite fond of them, actually), but we have another quite powerful dynamic going in our heads: we care deeply about a particular field, a body of knowledge, a special set of tools and procedures, an intellectual tradition, a heritage.
>
> Looking back over our careers, we can feel the truth of this. We didn't sign up for this occupation, go to school for four or five years, get ourselves certified, and agree to this pitiful pay scale, just to push some state assessment score up a half a percent. Our imagination wasn't fired by some list of 3000 state standards to be met in the first semester of 9th grade. We got into this job because we were hooked on a field, usually our college major, and we wanted to transmit that excitement to young people. We wanted students to share our enthusiasm, our fascination, our wonder at the beauty and importance of the ideas in our field. We had something powerful and precious to share: knowledge.
>
> The way we usually talk about school subjects is so wimpy. We typically say that students "take" Biology, "take" Geometry, or "take" Art History. "Take" sounds so passive, so limp—like when you "take a pitch" in baseball, or when you decide, with resignation, to "just take it." Well, when we went expectantly off to student teaching, when we landed our very first teaching job, when we called our first real class to order—we weren't hoping the kids would just "take" a subject from us. We wanted them to engage it, explore it, like it—maybe even love it.
>
> We imagined students catching our fever of ideas. We pictured them exploring a Civil War battlefield on a summer vacation, or looking through a telescope in their back yards, or writing their own software on a home computer, or sketching a great artwork in a museum gallery, or authoring their own collection of sonnets. After having us as teachers, after we had lit the fire, we saw our students moving on to take more courses in math, in science, in literature, in art. We envisioned them going on to major in our subject in college—the greatest compliment a secondary teacher can get. They would make this special subject a part of their own lives, just like we did; some would join the field, make a contribution, become fellow-travelers, our colleagues and peers.
>
> But even in these professional fantasies, we were realistic. We knew we'd never get them all; not every student would commit their working life to our subject area. But we expected every kid to grasp the big ideas, to respect the field, to remain

Who Are We?

Glad you asked. Let us answer that with a surprising and depressing statistic: between the three of us, we have 110 years of teaching experience. Dear reader, we're not sure if you should see this as a credential or a sign of imminent senility. But it seems like only yesterday that we were beginning our careers, meeting and teaching young people on the west side of Chicago, in its blue-collar suburbs, and in the woods of northern Massachusetts.

In this book, with the greatest delight, we turn our attention to writing across the curriculum, a topic that all three of us have treasured, pursued, and studied since we got our first classrooms back in the dinosaur days. Two years ago, Steve and Smokey wrote a book called *Subjects Matter: Every Teacher's Guide to Content-Area Reading*. Shortly after the book was published, schools, districts, and individual teachers began clamoring for a companion text on content-area *writing*. We knew that any such book could work only if Nancy "The Engine Room" Steineke (ask Steve or Smokey what this means) came on board.

Between us, we have taught a few zillion classes in English, history, and science, and for shorter periods, mathematics, art, business, foreign language, and animal husbandry (thanks to Federal Hocking High School for that experience). Today, Nancy continues to teach full-time at Victor J. Andrew High School, where she has taught English and American Studies since 1977. Steve works with networks of progressive schools in Chicago, as well as writing and consulting around the United States. Smokey is on leave from National-Louis University, working full-time as a writer, speaker, and acquisitions editor for Heinemann, the publisher of this book.

All three of us have had mostly joyful and privileged careers. We've not only taught in our own classrooms year in and year out but also visited and guest taught with scores of other teachers around the country—a humbling and energizing experience. Although we are old friends who hang out and often teach together, this is the first time we three have written together (so far so good, but the book is young). We also laugh a lot as we exchange notes on our latest teaching innovations, most recently involving our common commitment to get more music into our school and nonschool lives. Oh, and by the way, we're not nearly done with those long careers. We're aiming for a joint 150 before we call it a day.

The "we" of this book most definitely includes the generous classroom teachers from Chicago; Houston; Saline, Michigan; Rome City, Indiana; Stewart, Ohio; Woonsocket, Rhode Island; and a dozen other corners of the country, who provided stories, samples, materials, and experiences about the writing strategies in this book. When we say that these ideas are classroom tested and proven, that doesn't just mean by us. And let's all hope that this kind of generous and open sharing continues in our profession, even as policies like merit pay drive wedges between teachers and, at worst, make us competitors instead of colleagues.

curious about it through life. When our ex-students read the daily paper, they'd scan for stories about the subject and understand the basic issues. Perhaps they'd subscribe to *Scientific American, American Heritage,* or *Harper's.* Maybe they'd read popular books in the field: *Zero: Biography of a Dangerous Idea, Founding Brothers: The Revolutionary Generation, Salt: A World History, The Future of Life, Into the Wild,* or *The Lovely Bones.* And who knows? Maybe our alumni might be the kind of people who join in monthly book discussion groups, meeting with friends to talk about the latest novels or nonfiction trade books. Or even become teachers themselves.

Of course, between our long-term dreams and the immediate realities, things can intrude. Here sit our students before us, first period, today. Before they can become lifelong learners and pillars of their intellectual communities, there might be a few obstacles to overcome. Maybe these kids aren't ready to explore genetics at the level that excites us. Maybe, right at this moment, they are grappling with personal or developmental issues that override their being awed by the majesty of the Pythagorean Theorem. Perhaps their previous experience in school has delivered them to our classrooms too licked to tackle the Stamp Act. And quite possibly, state standards, mandated curricula, departmental exams, and tests, tests, tests, are undermining our own ability to teach with passion and personality.

Yes, there are a lot of obstacles to young people falling in love with math, science, history, language, the arts. But that doesn't mean that our idealism is sentimental and misplaced, or that we should give up the dream that binds us to this profession. It is right and reasonable to hope that kids can have a lifelong engagement with at least one, hopefully several fields of knowledge. (8–10)

And, we might add, writing is a crucial part of creating and maintaining this engagement.

What's in the Book?

The book is organized around two equally important and valuable kinds of writing, *writing to learn* and *public writing.* We'll define these two types right at the start of the next chapter, but for now let us give you a taste of the differences.

Writing to Learn	Public Writing
notes	research papers
brainstorming	lab reports
jottings	mathematical proofs
lists	proposals
pro-con lists	biographies
to-do lists	historical accounts
sketches	legal analyses
doodles	articles

Writing to Learn	Public Writing
diagrams	editorials
concept mapping	reviews
clustering	essays
journaling	literary criticism
response logs	speeches
outlines	persuasive essays
instant messages	letters
plans	poems
free writes	plays
	novels
	short stories

In the next couple hundred pages, we show how your kids can master both types of composing, and become powerful writers and thinkers, in your content-area classroom and in the rest of their lives.

In Chapters 3 through 4, we offer fifteen specific writing-to-learn activities for any content area and provide step-by-step instructions on how to use each one. We also share stories and samples of real kids using these strategies in math, English, science, social studies, and other classes. The first set of these WTLs, in Chapter 3, are quick and easy activities that require no teacher preparation and take up as little as two to five minutes of class time, but pay big dividends in engagement and understanding. The next group of activities, in Chapter 4, require a bit of setup and a little more writing time, but they can change the dynamic in the classroom and put the responsibility for thinking squarely on kids' shoulders.

Chapters 5 through 9 take up the perhaps more familiar topic of formal or public writing. Here we want students to develop longer, more substantial, carefully polished texts. But instead of just giving better instructions for those same-old term papers, lab reports, and book reviews, we offer ten different writing projects you probably *haven't* already tried. We think one reason that teenagers' school writing is so often disappointing—and why we teachers often become discouraged and go back to multiple-choice tests—may be that we have been using the wrong assignments. The other big problem is that nobody ever showed us how to support kids *while they are writing.* So, to help you successfully coach your students through these longer, more ambitious projects, Chapters 6 and 8 provide specific tools for mentoring young writers at work and setting up temporary writing workshops in your classroom.

As in the WTL section, we've divided public writing into two sections; Chapter 7 features six substantial but time-limited formal writing projects, while Chapter 9 shares just four ambitious, longer-range projects—ones that might well replace the term paper or research paper of old.

All twenty-five of these writing activities, from shortest to longest, from most personal to most public, can be used over and over. None of them is a gimmick or a one-day wonder. On the contrary, each structure is generative and reusable. You cannot wear out a cognitive tool like making lists, writing letters, or rewriting information into another genre. As the year rolls on and your curriculum content changes, all these writing tools are constantly at hand, always fresh, ready to help kids engage subject matter and to energize classroom conversations. Once these *teaching strategies* are installed in your teaching repertoire, they're yours to keep.

> *Never add a new activity to your teaching schedule before you subtract something else.*

Finally, we close the book with a chapter on essay tests, on how to improve the quality of students' writing on tests that you design yourself as well as the ones imposed by the state, the SATs, and other outside authorities.

While we of course recommend all the activities in this book, we do not recommend them *all at once.* As you test them out, please follow the cardinal rule of instructional change: Never add a new activity to your teaching schedule before you subtract something else. First, cast a critical eye over your current teaching plans and find the one most questionable or weak activity you have planned—study questions at the end of the chapter, a worksheet, whatever. Then delete that borderline activity before you add the new element. Then you can decide if it is a better use of your time.

⇒ Want to Jump Around?

While writing this book, we three noticed how much our writing style is being influenced by the websites that we use every day, both for work and for our personal interests. Like the young writers we teach, we are becoming more accustomed to documents that are truly interactive, unlike the gray, linear print we grew up on. One aspect of this new text is that readers can jump ahead or back to locate information they need right now. Inside this definitely nonelectronic book, we cannot offer true web-style navigation. But as surrogate Back and Forward keys, we've installed what we call Jump Around buttons, one of which you just encountered. Anywhere that we imagine a curious reader might need different information right away, we'll put a suggestion of how to travel forward or loop back to pick up some just-right text. Sorry, but without any plugged-in power, you'll still have to flip the pages by hand.

We always think that reading a book, even a professional book like this one, should be a bit of an adventure. So let us end by forecasting some things that we hope will surprise, provoke, puzzle, or amuse you over the next two hundred pages:

- ⇒ Content-area teachers should *not* mark all the errors in kids' papers.
- ⇒ Writing activities can actually *save* classroom time while deepening kids' understanding of your subject.
- ⇒ Taking class notes is a weak learning tool.

- Traditional class discussions should often be replaced by silent conversation.

- Students, not teachers, should be the main audience for each other's writing.

- Textbook study questions are not challenging enough for your students.

- Teacher-assigned writing topics too often encourage fake writing.

- Most student plagiarism is innocent and can be easily cured.

- Traditional research papers waste everyone's time but can be replaced with four better models.

- Writing is the key to differentiation in diverse classrooms.

- Writing is the best preparation for high-stakes tests in all subjects.

- Today's kids are the most experienced authors we have ever taught.

- You are a much better writer than you think, no matter how discouraging your own school experience might have been. You are ready to coach young writers.

- Writing can be fun. It can bring out the best in kids: curiosity, voice, craftsmanship, and playfulness.

Works Cited

American Association for the Advancement of Science. 2006. *Project 2061*. Accessed August 30, 2006 at www.project2061 .org/publications/rsl/online/COMPARE/NRC/BSL2NRC/CH12/B_NRC827.HTM.

"Better Living Through Video Games?" 2006. *Toronto Globe and Mail*. Accessed September 5, 2006, at www.theglobeandmail.com/servlet/Page/document/v4/sub/Marketing Page?user _URL=http://www.theglobeandmail.com%2Fservlet%2Fstory %2FRTGAM.20060209 .wxbrains09%2FBNStory%2FScience%2Fhome&ord= 1157543494581&brand=theglobeandmail&force_login=true.

Daniels, Harvey. 1983. *Famous Last Words: America's Language Crisis Reconsidered.* Carbondale: Southern Illinois University Press.

Daniels, Harvey, and Marilyn Bizar. 2005. *Teaching the Best Practice Way: Methods That Matter, K–12*. Portland, ME: Stenhouse.

Daniels, Harvey, and Steven Zemelman. 2004. *Subjects Matter: Every Teacher's Guide to Content-Area Reading*. Portsmouth, NH: Heinemann.

Graham, Steve, and Dolores Perin. *2006. Writing Next: Effective Strategies to Improve Writing of Adolescents in Middle and High Schools*. New York: The Carnegie Commission. Accessed October 23, 2006, at www.all4ed.org/publications/writingnext/writingnext.pdf.

Lewin, Tamar. 2003. "Writing in Schools Found Both Dismal and Neglected." *New York Times,* April 26, 15.

National Assessment of Educational Progress. 2006. "NAEP Writing Achievement Levels." Accessed October 20, 2006, at http://nces.ed.gov/nationsreportcard/writing.

National Commission on Writing. 2003. *The Neglected "R": The Need for a Writing Revolution.* New York: College Board. Accessed August 30, 2006, at www .writingcommission.org/prod_downloads/writingcom/neglectedr.pdf.

———. 2006. *Writing and School Reform.* New York: College Board. Accessed September 6, 2006, at www.writingcommission.org/prod_downloads/writingcom/writing-school-reform-natl-comm-writing.pdf.

National Council for the Social Studies (NCSS). 1994. *Expectations of Excellence: Curriculum Standards for Social Studies.* Silver Spring, MD: NCSS. Accessed August 30, 2006, at www.socialstudies.org/standards/execsummary/.

National Council of Teachers of Mathematics (NCTM). 2006. *Principles and Standards for School Mathematics.* Reston, VA: NCTM. Accessed August 30, 2006, at illuminations .nctm.org/reflections/912/facilitating_communication/part2.html.

National Research Council. 1996. "Content Standard E: Science and Technology: Abilities of Technological Design." In *National Science Education Standards.* Washington, DC: National Academy Press. Accessed August 30, 2006, at www.nap.edu/readingroom/books/ nses/overview.html.

National Writing Project (NWP). 2006. *The American Public Wants Writing Taught in All Grades and Subjects. And They Want It Now.* Brochure. Berkeley, CA: NWP.

Newmann, Fred, et al. 2001. *Authentic Intellectual Work and Standardized Tests: Conflict or Co-existence?* Chicago: Consortium on Chicago School Research.

Pope, Justin. 2005. "Poor Writing Skills Cost Taxpayers Millions." Yahoo! News. Accessed August 28, 2005, at news.yahoo.com/s/ap/20050704/ap_on_re_us/government _bad_writing_&printer=1;_y.

"Positive Health Effects of Expressive Writing, New Research." 2005. *Medical News Today,* August 21. Accessed August 30, 2006, at www.medicalnewstoday.com/medical news.php?newsid=29433.

Rado, Diane. 2002. "Poor Writing Scores Alarm State." *Chicago Tribune,* August 4.

"Sign Up for AOL Writing Wizard Today." Accessed August 30, 2006, at free.aol.com/ tryaolfree/index3.adp?promo=755469&service=psww.

Smith, Julia et al, 2001. *Instruction and Achievement in Chicago Elementary Schools.* Chicago: Consortium on Chicago School Research.

Steineke, N. 2002. *Reading and Writing Together: Collaborative Literacy in Action.* Portsmouth, NH: Heinemann.

Wiggins, Grant, and Jay McTighe. 2005. *Understanding by Design.* New York: Prentice Hall.

Zemelman, Steven, Harvey Daniels, and Arthur Hyde. 2005. *Best Practice: Today's Standards for Teaching and Learning in America's Schools.* 3d ed. Portsmouth, NH: Heinemann.

CHAPTER two

Writing to Learn

Remember the last time you went to the grocery store? Did you bring a list with you? We sure hope so, because whenever we go shopping listlessly, we always forget the bread and the milk while piling up the cart with unplanned purchases, costly treats, and calorific impulse buys. That's why we need a list: to help us remember things, to plan and organize our shopping behavior, and, perhaps, to stick to the budget and the diet, no matter how tempting the treats might be in aisle 6.

The humble grocery list is an example of *writing to learn* (WTL). You probably use more of this kind of writing in your everyday life than you realize. Maybe you leave notes around the house for yourself or other family members, make holiday card or gift lists, jot reminders on a calendar or in a Palm Pilot, and dash off emails that take care of assorted everyday chores. If you are trying to make any kind of decision—how to balance the household budget, what to name the new baby, how to remodel the attic—you are probably using some form of writing, scratching, or noodling with paper (or the computer). Recently, while hunting for a new house, coauthor Smokey Daniels and his wife, Elaine, found themselves using a pro-and-con list to decide whether to make an offer on a particular property:

27 Tall Tree Drive

Pluses	*Minuses*
lots of square footage	far from town
great views	high maintenance costs
outdoor areas	kitchen appliances old
vaulted ceiling	bathroom fixtures ugly
huge kitchen	office space very small
satellite TV antenna installed	dialup internet access

And no, the Danielses didn't buy the house on Tall Tree. Using this little bit of writing to learn, they were able to examine both sides of the available information more carefully. (And, after all, who wants to go back to dialup Internet access now?)

What we are doing in all these modest, everyday instances is using writing as a tool of thinking. We are using writing to find out what's inside our heads, to dump ideas down on a page so we can play with them, move them around, make connections, figure out what's important, cross some out, and highlight others. In other words, we are *thinking*. And this kind of thinking, using writing as a kind of torque wrench of the mind, is officially called *writing to learn*.

Hearing this, you might say, "Aw shucks, that scratching I do? That's not really writing." (Well, you probably wouldn't literally say "aw, shucks," but you get the idea.) Don't be so modest. Denying that your jotting is really writing is like saying that, for example, skimming a document isn't really reading. Hey, skimming is a vital thinking strategy that proficient, literate people know how to use when it's the right tool for the job. Just think how cumbersome life would be if we had only one approach, one rate, one all-purpose form of reading in our cognitive repertoires. Same for writing; there are different types for different tasks.

A story: Among the women in Harvey's family, there is an old joke that when you copy down a cooking recipe for a friend, you always leave out one crucial ingredient. That way, no matter how earnestly Marge tries to duplicate your lemon chiffon cheesecake, hers will never taste quite as good. We do the same thing in our classrooms every day—we leave out key ingredients when we give kids the recipes for reading, writing, and thinking. (Unlike the omissions of the diabolical Daniels women, ours are inadvertent.) Writing to learn is a great example of one of these missing ingredients.

If we competent adults use writing-to-learn activities in our lives, maybe it is not just an "aw, shucks" throwaway, but a window into how smart people think. Maybe using a wide variety of casual writing and graphic representations is actually one of the keys to our success. Maybe our little writing to learns (or WTLs), among other factors, have helped us cope with college, become an expert in a complex discipline of knowledge, get ourselves a job and a life, and call ourselves a grown-up and a teacher. And maybe all the personal, informal writing that we have done for our own purposes over the years has also paved the way for us to create larger, more public documents when the time came for that. In fact, if we look back at our own writing lives with more than the usual scrutiny, we can probably notice that when we wrote successful big pieces in life or in school, they often began with or grew out of some humbler jottings, lists, or scratched outlines.

Writing to Learn in School

In the next two chapters, we will show you fifteen ways to use writing to learn in your classes. As you choose to implement these, you will be showing your students some of the tricks of the thinking trade, giving them new tools for delving into your subject matter.

We want to be crystal clear: WTLs are different from the more formal or *public* writing tasks teachers commonly assign students—like term papers, research reports, and critical essays. It's important to understand the differences and to handle each type appropriately. In graphic form, the contrast looks like this:

WRITING TO LEARN	PUBLIC WRITING
short	substantial
spontaneous	planned
exploratory	authoritative
informal	conventional
personal	audience centered
one draft	drafted
unedited	edited
ungraded	assessable

To elaborate a little:

Short: Unlike a term paper or major project, WTLs—whether lists, notes, or instant messages—tend to be brief in length on a page and in composing time. They are bits of writing that we do in quick bursts, not in extended composition. They don't take up much of a page or a screen. Often, we write them on index cards or small pads of paper, or in a little box on a web page.

Spontaneous: A WTL is done off the top of our heads, just to get things down. We don't go rent a garret apartment in Paris and wait for the muse to strike. We don't *plan* lists, notes, or jottings the way you might carefully map out a longer, more formal and public piece of writing. They come to us quickly, and often *while* we write, more ideas arrive and go down on the page.

Exploratory: In writing to learn, we use writing as a tool to help us figure stuff out, not as a way of announcing with certainty what we already know. WTL is writing in process, along the way—it's writing that doesn't necessarily know where it is going when it begins. When we start a grocery list, we don't know everything we need to buy. That's why we list! We use writing as a tool to help us develop a set of possibilities or goals for future action.

Informal: WTL is casual language, dressed down, relaxed and ready to spend a quiet evening at home. On a grocery list, we don't need to write *Hellmann's Mayonnaise*; *mayo* may be all we need. And when dashing off an instant message, we can use all the emoticons and shorthand we want. BTW, don't 4GET that so-called Internet jargon like ASAP, R&R, and FYI had already entered the standard language B4 the first silicon chip was ever cooked. KWIM?

Personal: Mostly, WTL pieces are *for us*, the writers, not someone else. When we are done with that grocery list, we don't mail it off to the editors of *The New Yorker* magazine, hoping they'll publish it and launch our literary careers. WTLs are not mainly concerned with reaching, pleasing, or informing an audience—they are created to help us think, to get some work done, to plan, to collect our thoughts. Occasionally, WTLs may be shared with other people, as with instant messages and notes around the household, but the audience is usually very small, safe, and uncritical.

One Draft: Almost a defining characteristic of WTLs is that, in keeping with their nature as brief, spontaneous, utilitarian jottings, they are not revised. You wouldn't go back and create a second draft of your grocery list. Hey, if it helped you to shop effectively, it has done its work. Nor would you do a second edition of an IM to a friend or a note left for your spouse on the kitchen table. Not to say we all haven't written a few quick notes we regret, but still.

Unedited: Correcting errors and editing grammar have little role to play in WTLs. What's the difference if you misspell catsup (or is it ketchup?) on your grocery list? If you get the red stuff, you're good to go. No one is going to see it anyway, unless you (like everyone else) leave the list in the bottom of the shopping cart. Even so, whoever finds it probably won't be an English teacher with a red pen in hand.

Ungraded: Speaking of red pens, they have no place in writing-to-learn activities. That's a big difference between WTL and public writing. In formal writing, kids' products may be reviewed, ranked, scored, rated, or otherwise evaluated. But just

Shouldn't Kids' Writing Always Be Graded and Corrected?

The idea of unedited and ungraded writing can make teachers nervous. We've been acculturated to mark up with red ink whatever kids write, without thinking much about it. In fact, to be honest, this labor-intensive kind of grading is one of the main reasons we don't assign more writing in our classes—it takes so darned long to circle all the errors! And that's when we start cursing the English teachers under our breath: *Why haven't they cured this?*

For now we'll just tell you flatly: the intensive correction of student papers does not work; it has never worked and it never will work. Kids' writing does not improve when teachers cover their papers with corrections, no matter how scrupulous and generous that kind of feedback may seem. There's voluminous research showing this, going back decades (Zemelman and Daniels 1988, 20–30). And still we teachers do it. And our departments require it. And the parents expect it. We are all trapped in this dysfunctional, unscientific, and staggeringly time-consuming tradition. The problem is, it doesn't grow better writers.

So, with writing to learn, we break with this tradition. But still you might wonder, if we allow unedited and ungraded writing, won't students' errors and bad habits take root? How are they going to write a decent term paper if we don't correct their mistakes and demand accuracy every time they write? To put it another way, do we impede kids' growth as formal, public writers by encouraging less-crafted writing some of the time?

Well, do you lose your ability to give a formal speech by shooting the bull with the gang at the bowling alley? Do you lose your ability to run if you walk a little bit? The point is that there is a sliding scale of language use that *all* speakers, kids and adults alike, use.

Formal ←————————————————→ Informal

Speaking or writing informally on one occasion doesn't undermine your capacity to use language formally later. But we all need balanced opportunities to operate across the whole spectrum of language uses, contexts, and levels. If we have students do only short, unedited noodling, we are doing them a big disservice. At the same time, if we have them write *only* big, abstract, third-person research papers, we are depriving them of a vital dimension of writing—indeed one that is often a building block of bigger public texts.

A great feature of WTLs is the way they can grow from something small, private, and embryonic into something bigger, more developed, and public. WTLs are often the seeds, nuggets, or kernels of longer, more polished pieces of writing. When we noodle ideas on a pad, or jot down a diary entry, or chart some pros and cons, we may be building the outline of something more. As you work through this book, you'll see how often smart teachers use quick WTLs as prewriting activities to help launch students on inquiries that end up with big formal, public texts.

Even if you still feel uncomfortable about leaving students' informal writing unmarked up, think of the *time* it would take you to grade it all. It's unthinkable!

We want you use lots of short, spontaneous writing activities in your class—maybe even every day. If you start dragging all those things home to grade, your personal life will be over. What's that you say? You work in a school where the department (or the kids themselves) demands that points be assigned for every piece of work? Fine! Just use all-or-nothing grading. Ten points for doing the WTL activity; zero for not doing it. This is over-the-shoulder grading—you should be able to walk by and assess by glancing at a kid's paper. All you have to keep track of is the four kids who didn't do the work. Everyone else automatically gets ten points in the grade book each time you do a WTL exercise. If you think kids will fake WTLs, announce that you will randomly collect one kid's piece from each lesson. Good deterrent.

like its out-of-school counterparts, writing to learn doesn't get graded. That's not to say that WTLs don't get lots of feedback. We will use them to start discussions, feed small-group work, or review key ideas, right during class.

So those are the traits of this special species of text called writing to learn: free, loosely structured writing with few rules and no penalties.

The intensive correction of student papers does not work; it has never worked and it never will work.

Why WTL Is So Powerful

OK, how can this quick and casual writing help your kids learn physics? Or photosynthesis, World War I, abstract expressionism, the past-perfect tense, or *To Kill a Mockingbird*?

Well, what does teaching consist of? What, exactly, are we doing—and what are the students doing—with the subject matter? How do we arrange the variables of learning: content, time, space, materials, and people? For starters, we usually assign some reading and ask students to write answers to questions about it. And we offer presentations, either a lecture or a lecture-discussion, during which students are required to take notes. These major modes of instruction, both using writing, are time-honored and ubiquitous, but do they really work? Do students engage with the material? Do they understand and remember the content? Are they acquiring knowledge?

We know from learning research that in order for learners to understand and remember ideas, they must *act upon them*. Just hearing or reading words is not enough. We are all intimately familiar with students who truthfully tell us, "I don't remember anything," after reading a chapter or sitting through a presentation (even a great one!), and we have a whole lexicon of teacher jargon to describe this: tuned out, fast asleep, out of the loop, on Neptune, and so on.

You've probably run across Edgar Dale's classic cone-of-experience model. Though his concept was probably more intuitive than scientific, Dale's formulation has stuck around for sixty years. Briefly, it states that people generally remember

10 percent of what they read
20 percent of what they hear
30 percent of what they see
50 percent of what they hear and see
70 percent of what they say and write
90 percent of what they say as they do a thing

Well, it turns out that the old saw remains true to this day. Research from every branch of learning science—from the behaviorists, the cognitive science people, the schema theorists—all concurs: learners must *act* on information in order to *understand, remember, and use it* (Hyde 2006). Hence, writing to learn.

So isn't taking class notes a good example of writing to learn? Usually not. However traditional and familiar, note taking rarely requires listeners to *act on the material*. Unless the teacher has specifically trained students differently, most young people taking class notes act like automatons, uncritically copying down words as they fly by. With a little practice, you can do this completely unconsciously, while simultaneously texting that cute junior three rows back. A well-trained monkey could do this job, and would probably remember about as much (OK, a monkey that knew English).

To get learning power, kids need to grapple with ideas, transform them, and put them in *their own words*. When we flip through our mental file of students' faces, we are reminded of countless students whose notes included all the key words but who couldn't pass the simplest quiz. This should warn us: note taking is not enough to guarantee solid learning.

You might protest: "Well, my students will have to take lecture notes in college someday, so we might as well start having them take lecture notes here in middle school." (Of course, we all know that on every major campus in America there is a thriving class-notes co-op that sells the daily goods for a couple of bucks. For higher education to proceed, that's all that's needed. You just need one student with good handwriting who doesn't mind going to class, and everyone else can sleep in. Sis boom bah!) But seriously, giving kids some practice with college-style note taking is definitely a great idea, and we should do that *some* of the time, especially later on in

To get true learning power, kids must put ideas into their own words.

school. But right now, most of the time, we have far more powerful kinds of subject-matter writing that can help kids learn.

Well, how about having kids write answers to the questions at the end of a textbook chapter? Isn't that good writing-to-learn practice? Let's take an example and talk about the limitations. But before we do, let us stop and stipulate: some textbooks are better than others, way better, and a few textbooks have richer, better questions than this one. But nevertheless, this sample end-of-the-chapter question is the essence, the very meat and potatoes of the genre.

> 15. Congress passed the tax relief Act of 1986 in order to reduce or end a confus-ing variety of tax _____, tax _____, and tax _____, as well as the number of tax _____.

Whew, got that? So, what's wrong with this item and the writing task it poses? First of all, this question requires, at best, factual recall, one of the lowest levels of thinking on anybody's taxonomy of cognition. But even worse is the nature of the task itself. The giveaway is right in the instructions: "Use the information in your textbook to complete these sentences." A kid with any sense is going to glide over the text and pluck the answers from the chapter, where they'll probably appear right in order, handily presented in bold type, ready for quick and thoughtless transposition to the answer sheet. It is entirely possible for a student to glance through a textbook and copy down these answers without ever reading the chapter, doing any thinking, or, ul-timately, having a glimmer of recollection—of anything. This is not nearly enough cog-nitive work for students to do! This isn't *acting on ideas*, grappling with them, putting them into one's own words. This isn't *thinking*.

A perplexing sidelight to question 15 is that someone very knowledgeable about tax law in the United States, even one of the economists who helped concoct President Reagan's famed supply-side tax cuts, would have no way of answering this question. None. Only a kid in school who had the textbook right in front of him could possibly determine what goes into each of these blanks. That's because blanks do not repre-sent knowledge about taxation, but merely a frame into which adolescent readers are supposed to copy certain words from somewhere else.

Yes, we know wonderful teachers who instruct their students in the art of note tak-ing, and we know others who replace textbook quizzes with their own open-ended, in-ferential study questions. We applaud those hardworking colleagues. But in their stan-dard forms, both lecture notes and end-of-the-chapter questions are essentially forms of *transcription*, of writing down other people's words. They don't ask enough of learn-ers. Copying is not strong enough writing for kids to learn from. There are so many better tools.

Putting the Writing to Work

As you'll see in the next couple of chapters, writing-to-learn activities are not products or artifacts like the term papers or lab reports we discuss later on. Instead of collecting and grading these quick writes, we *put them to work in the classroom*—we use them to advance the learning.

WTLs give us starting points for new units: we have kids write to surface their prior knowledge, including their misconceptions, to activate their thinking, to set class and individual goals for an upcoming unit. Along the way, we use WTLs to help students stop and collect their thoughts, sort out ideas, notice and hold their thinking, review and readjust goals, and get ready to move ahead. Later in a unit, we use different kinds of short writings to help kids synthesize what they have learned, connect with others, compare notes, or plan projects or outlets for their learning.

Some writing-to-learn strategies can significantly improve or even replace whole-class discussions. Now, all of us would probably agree that large-group discussions too often involve teachers pulling teeth in the form of eliciting relevant comments from reluctant kids. Some have dubbed this very common teaching structure as the *gentle inquisition*, which leaves both kids and teachers frustrated. And why not? With one person talking and twenty-seven others waiting for a turn they either don't want or never get, this certainly isn't engaged learning at its finest.

And yet, discussion is very important. Kids need to talk to learn too, no doubt about it. Remember Dale's classic model: learners remember much more of what they say and do than what they hear other people yapping about. But if students can talk *only* one at a time and only when called on by the teacher, they'll never get enough talk time to learn anything. When we stick to the whole-class, out-loud discussion format, we marry ourselves to a bottleneck. We limit each kid's airtime to, if we are fair, one-thirtieth of a class period. Not enough! That's why, in the best practice classroom, we do lots of this valuable topic-talk in *kid-to-kid writing*, either used on its own or as a prelude to stronger but shorter whole-class discussions.

What's Coming Up

Between them, the next two chapters describe fifteen different writing-to-learn strategies and how to use them in any class. The first batch are true quick writes, activities that require no teacher planning and take as little as two minutes of class time but can give kids whole new opportunities to think about a subject. Our sentimental favorite is the elementally simple *writing break*. All this strategy entails is the teacher stopping, in the middle of any class, and giving the students two minutes to jot down whatever is in their heads at that moment: words, phrases, questions, confusions, connections, distractions, whatever. And then you carry on with the lesson. That's it. Now there are a million other things you could do with those quick writings: have kids discuss them in pairs, have them hand their papers back three rows and write comments to each other, have volunteers read a few aloud.

But stopping to write is enough. You give students something we almost never offer them as we relentlessly cover the material—a chance to take a breath, pull their thoughts together, reflect on their thinking, and appraise their own level of understanding. This, all by itself, is a powerful gift and a masterly teaching strategy.

The second set of WTL activities, in Chapter 4, includes the slightly more complex strategies that need a little more class time and teacher setup—and which have an even richer range of possible uses and applications in the classroom. Needless to say, there's plenty of overlap between the two chapters; you can do a much longer and more involved writing break, and you can shorten up some of the usually longer activities.

So adapt, adjust, and enjoy.

Works Cited

Hyde, Arthur. 2006. *Comprehending Math: Adapting Reading Strategies to Teach Mathematics K-6*. Portsmouth, NH: Heinemann.

Zemelman, Steven, and Harvey Daniels. 1988. *A Community of Writers: Teaching Writing in the Junior and Senior High School*. Portsmouth, NH: Heinemann.

CHAPTER
three

Quick Writes
Easy Writing-to-Learn Strategies

In This Chapter

1. Writing Break

2. Exit Slip

3. Admit Slip

4. Brainstorming

5. Drawing and Illustrating

6. Clustering

7. Mapping

Got two minutes? That's how little class time some of these activities will take, and yet they can deepen students' thinking, create more engagement, and spark lively discussion in your classroom. Is time tight in your teaching day? Got lots to cover? These simple ideas are the place to start. Try a few strategies and see if writing to learn helps students understand, remember, and use the content you are teaching this week.

Writing Break

What It Is

A teacher friend of ours puts it bluntly: "Writing breaks are a reminder to me to just shut up every once in a while and let the kids think." While we often feel pressured to talk till the bell—to pack as much content as we can into a class period—we also know that kids don't remember as much when they are overwhelmed. As we said in Chapter 1, less content can be more, if more is actually *retained*.

We already previewed this simplest of all writing-to-learns a couple of pages back. And the title says it all. At specific points during class, students stop and reflect in writing on the activities happening or information being presented. Some quick sharing either with partners or the whole class usually follows this writing.

When to Use It and Why

Remember that kids recall between 10 and 30 percent of what they read, hear, and see? Now think of our most common classroom activities: in-class reading, large-group discussion, teacher lecture, film or picture viewing. All of these certainly focus on covering content, yet alone they often leave students remembering far less than we would like. By incorporating *writing breaks* at regular intervals, about every ten to twenty minutes, you can really kick retention up a notch because writing and then talking about it moves the sticking rate into the 70 to 90 percent range.

Play by Play

Getting Started

Before starting your presentation, film, activity, or in-class reading, decide when students are going to stop and write. For a lecture or large-group discussion, you'll probably want to stop about every ten to twelve minutes since that is the maximum attention span adults have for focused listening (and perhaps optimistic for teenagers). For a film, it might be every fifteen or twenty minutes or after a key scene you want the students to zoom in on for further thinking. For examining a textbook illustration, slide, or transparency, students should study the graphic for a minute or two and write about what they see. For in-class reading, students might respond in writing at the bottom of each page or at a designated heading.

Once you've determined the breaks, decide what topics you'd like the students to explore in their writing. Your prompts might be general:

- What piece of information stands out and seems really important? Why?
- What are you thinking about right now?
- What does this remind you of?
- What questions do you still have?
- Rate your understanding of the material on a scale of 1 to 5 (1 low, 5 high). What makes sense? What's confusing you?

Or your prompts might be specific to the content:

- Which character's actions surprised you the most?
- What would you do if you faced this problem?
- What might have happened if Theodore Roosevelt had not overtaken construction of the Panama Canal from France?
- How would you describe the relationship between TRNA and RNA?

Just before you launch into the lesson, form students into pairs for today's writing breaks. They need to be sitting near their partner, each should have a blank piece of paper ready, and they should understand that this exercise depends upon clear, legible handwriting.

Working the Room

When you pause and students write, cruise the room and read over their shoulders. Besides offering the kids a moment to process the information before moving on, this writing time gives you a chance to see if students are stuck or confused anywhere. Even if they are not writing about their confusion, a struggle to write anything is a tip-off as well, indicating an unclear grasp or a possible lack of engagement. Either way, wouldn't it be great to recognize a learning gap ten minutes into the lesson rather than two weeks later, on the unit test?

Putting the Writing to Work

The best way to get students to use this informal writing is to follow with some pair sharing. Once the writing time is up, have students trade papers with their partner and read silently. Next, invite them to continue the conversation out loud, commenting on each other's ideas. After the partner talk, call on two or three pairs for a quick summary of their comments. This large-group part is *very* important because it creates accountability. If students know they might be asked to share, they will talk about their writing versus what happened at last weekend's party. Quickly clarify any questions that arise and then move on to the next segment.

Textbook Connections

Almost all modern textbooks have some questions that go beyond the standard factual-recall, skim-the-text-for-the-answers questions. Why not use some of those high-order-thinking questions for some of your writing break prompts? Modify them so that students respond in writing to these big ideas as they read. And, as mentioned earlier, have the kids look more closely at the charts, drawings, and pictures, the text features that students typically ignore as they read. After all, if they're going to carry around a fifteen-pound textbook for each class, they might as well start making use of those extras that are contributing to the added bulk!

What Can Go Wrong?

Any new strategy takes practice. Writing breaks require students to put thoughts down on paper quickly and clearly. In the beginning, make your prompts specific. That way the kids will be able to narrow their thinking and get something down instead of sitting and staring at the blank page. Also, after you've done writing breaks a few times, have students evaluate their writing with just a few criteria:

- Did I write for the entire time?
- How well did I support my ideas with specific details?
- How well did my writing create some interesting discussion with my partner?

At certain points, collect the writing breaks and give them a stamp, a check, a few points, a comment, something that shows this writing is important to the class. Also, collecting them from time to time will give you useful instructional feedback, plus some samples you can use as models with next year's class.

Example

In a history class, students were asked to examine a rather propagandistic 1860 newspaper drawing depicting Native Americans attacking homesteaders. In her writing break, Christina wrote about what she saw, based on three cues built into the teacher's prompt:

HISTORY

Clothing: The woman is wearing a long blue old-fashion style dress. The Native Americans are wearing loincloths and headdresses. The guy on the ground has his sleeves like he was working.

Things: Hills, a cabin, tree stumps, a river, a shovel, knife. These things say that the settlers live and work a lot outdoors. The Native American holding the knife is attacking the man on the ground.

Feelings: The settlers are scared for their lives because the Native Americans are trying to kill them. The Native Americans are mad because the settlers have moved onto their property. The woman in the back is on the ground begging for her life.

After students wrote for a minute or two, they shared with a partner and then compared their observations with the rest of the class. The kids found that different people noticed different things. No two people interpreted the illustration, something that students viewed as a pretty straightforward exercise, exactly the same.

Variation

A longer-range use for this kind of WTL is to help kids prepare for a test. After having students reread their writing breaks from the unit, ask them to discuss and list what else they remember. Once again, if you notice a certain topic seldom gets mentioned, that's the information to hone in on in your review, giving it the time it needs and not wasting valuable moments on concepts the students clearly control.

Exit Slip

What It Is

One of the simplest ways of dipping your toe into the waters of writing to learn is to save the last one to five minutes of class time and ask kids to quickly jot a response to the day's lesson on an index card. Then you read these notes later on and use them to help plan the next class session. Sound simple? It is.

LANGUAGE
ARTS

SOCIAL
STUDIES

In her American Studies class, Nancy's students are just finishing some small-group discussions about the first chapter of *Bury My Heart at Wounded Knee*. Now, just before the period ends, Nancy gathers everyone back together. She asks kids to write for just one minute: "What was the best discussion question you brought to your group?" The kids' exit slips cover a range of topics:

How do you think the Indians felt when they saw all these white people coming over and taking their land?

Why was Andrew Jackson called Sharp Knife?

Why do you think it turned out that the whites did not obey the Indian territory law?

Why would the Spaniards teach each other how to torture people if they always spoke of peace?

Why would Samoset give up the land that came from the Great Spirit?

As the bell rings, kids file out, handing their exit tickets to Nancy. The next day, she will begin the class by reading some of these aloud, initiating further discussion, and making distinctions between "skinny" factual recall and fat, inferential questions.

Play by Play

Getting Started

To implement exit slips, all you have to do is remember to stop whatever else you are doing toward the end of the period, before kids start stacking their books on the desk and eyeing the clock. Make sure they have paper and a pencil available, and then offer a simple, open-ended prompt like the ones in Figure 3–1.

You can offer students just one prompt or let them pick from several options. We prefer to keep exit slip topics very open and simple. With more choices, there's a better chance of tapping more kids' burning issues. OK, maybe smoldering.

- What did you learn today?

- How is this unit going for you?

- What was the most difficult or confusing idea we learned today—and why?

- What were the three most important ideas we learned today—and why?

- Pick one quote from today's class discussion or readings and comment on it.

- What are some questions you have about today's lesson? Where do you think you can get the answers to those questions?

- Predict what we will need to learn next in this unit and why. (Not just from the textbook contents page, please.)

- What would you like me to review in class tomorrow and why?

- If you were going to teach this to someone else, what would be in your notes? Show me!

- If you were going to make up an essay test question based on today's class, what would it be (and what would a good answer look like)?

- What do you need to concentrate on to finish this unit successfully? What goals can you set for yourself?

- What would be some good review questions about this material?

- What can I do to help you learn better in the class? Please be specific.

- Summarize today's lesson in twenty-five carefully chosen words. Try to get everything in.

Figure 3–1 *Exit slip topics*

Working the Room

When you first start doing exit slips, you'll need to tell kids to *use the whole time* for writing—no fair dashing down a quick "It was boring" and putting the pen down. With exit slips, like all writing-to-learn activities, we write informally but steadily, pushing ourselves to come up with more reactions, comments, and questions. Most teachers have kids put their names on the cards for accountability's sake (ten points per card is OK with us), though this isn't actually necessary to get good value out of the activity, as you'll see.

Putting the Writing to Work

So now the bell rings, you are standing there with a stack of twenty-five note cards in your hand, and the kids have scattered off to gym, science, or home. What do you do with these things? The ultimate goal is to use them to help teach the next class with these students. But now, all you have to do is read them. No matter what your prompt was, you are about to get some very interesting feedback on your curriculum and your instruction. Maybe you'll get some cards like this:

> Class today was really great. I'd been having trouble with this stuff. But I really get the algorithm now—I think it was that example with the chocolate bars that made it work for me. Thanks, see you tomorrow!

Notes like that will make you feel happy and accomplished. But you may also see six exit slips like this:

> Man this part B stuff is really hard. I don't get it and I don't think anyone else does either. Can you please go over it again.

As you can see, exit slips are highly *diagnostic*—they can tell you a lot about what students are understanding, what their misconceptions might be, and what their attitude is toward the subject. Many times the feedback from exit slips is much more honest and complete than what we get when we gaze around the class and ask, "Does everybody understand this?" Really, what kid is going to open his mouth and say: "Not me!" under that kind of public pressure?

So you read the exit slips and start figuring out how they'll help you teach the next lesson. The good news is you don't have to grade them—indeed, you must not! If you get tangled up in trying to differentiate a B+ exit slip from an A– specimen, you're sunk timewise; you're never going to use this activity very often if it saddles you with tons of homework. No, what you do is scan them for content, for themes, and for unique comments or questions. If seven kids didn't understand the last two problems, you're going to want to go back and review those. Deal the cards out in stacks. If three kids have raised interesting questions that could feed five or ten minutes of whole-class discussion, place those together. And if one student has written a funny or insightful remark, flag it, too. Then gather together the ones that point toward a needed reteaching.

The payoff comes next class period. At the very beginning of class, pull out the cards and read aloud just one or two from each topic you want to raise (with or without announcing the authors' names). You might say:

> Last night when I was reading all your exit slips, I noticed that about a third of you wrote about having trouble with problem 13. One student wrote . . . [*and here you read the card aloud*]. Another put it this way . . . [*read aloud*]. So I'm thinking we'd better loop back and work on that operation one more time today. But before we do, a couple of students raised really interesting and bigger questions about this

unit that I think we should talk about. One student wondered . . . [*read card aloud*]. What do you think about that? Who agrees or disagrees?

And your class is off and running. Some kids hear their cards read aloud, so everyone knows you are taking this seriously. If you are shrewd enough to read aloud a couple of funny or unique ones, kids will start competing to get their exit slips aired. And you've just hooked them on participating.

What Can Go Wrong?

Other than outright defiance, it's hard to see what could go wrong with exit slips. Hmm . . . go wrong . . . go wrong. It's just three minutes. Most of the kids will probably comply right away, and the ones who don't will join in the second or third time, when they have seen that you really honor the writing by using, not grading, it.

Variations

Some teachers make a point of having exit slips be submitted anonymously, to encourage really honest feedback about the content and the class. We don't know about you, but we usually recognize kids' handwriting pretty well by the third week of school (lots of writing, y'know), so that secrecy thing is a little dubious. And we've found that anonymity will invite the couple of truly grumpy kids in your class to give you a cheap shot. If you've got thick skin, go for it. We prefer keeping the names with the ideas and encouraging intellectual courage all around.

You can use exit slips to address class *processes* as well as subject-matter content. After Nancy's students first joined in small-group discussions (on articles about the war on terrorism), Nancy prompted: "What did you notice about how your discussions went?" The kids' exit slips gave plenty of diagnostic information:

SOCIAL STUDIES

- Once somebody started a topic in our group, everybody jumped in on it and said what they thought.
- We need to talk and bring more information to our group instead of just sitting there listening to one person speak!
- None of us are interested in this topic. If it related more to our sixteen-year-old lives, we could get into it more.
- For the most part, my group had a good discussion. We talked a lot about what's going on in Iraq. But it would probably help if we all had better posture and eye contact.
- Not all the members of our group participated. Most are preoccupied. Not enough questions asked to keep the conversation going.

The next day, Nancy used the kids' own positive and negative responses to further refine the small-group discussions.

You can also use exit slips for class management and discipline issues. During the first week of school last fall, Nancy's second-period class was setting a new world standard for off the wall. So, as part of the taming process, she assigned an exit slip asking, "What kind of teacher do you think Mrs. Steineke will be if the class acts respectfully?" The kids mostly got the drift:

☞ Nice. We will do fun group-oriented activities.

☞ You'll trust us; we might go on a field trip.

☞ Laid back class, do more group activities, teacher will be happy.

Want more variations and wrinkles on exit slips? More are coming right up in the next section, which is about *admit slips*. What a lovely couple exits and admits make! Read on.

Admit Slip

What It Is

Admit slips, though seemingly a bookend activity to exit slips, are actually a little more complicated. Here's the deal. Admit slips ask students to bring a short piece of writing to class *the next day.* It can be written on a note card, in a learning log (see page 65), or on a handout that actually looks like an admission ticket to great event. (Let a creative kid have fun designing this for you. For example, "One admission to Mr. Duffy's Third Period World History Class, Row 1, Seat 12" with a big blank center for writing.) Some teachers call these special ducats *entry tickets* or *startup writes,* and we'll comment on some variations later.

So what's the assignment? Typically we have students reflect upon the previous evening's reading assignment or something that happened during the last class meeting. (Most of the examples in Figure 3–1 work well for admit slips as well as exits.) When the kids arrive with their admit slips, we use them to start the next class period, much the way we do with exit slips. The major difference is that we haven't yet had a chance to read them. That's no problem, though, as you'll see.

MATH

Play by Play

Getting Started

First of all, you are going to need a just-right prompt or topic for your admit tickets. You can use open-ended ones like those in Figure 3–1 or you can design subject-specific ones along the lines of our suggestions in Figure 3–2.

You'll quickly learn how to cook up your own admit slip topics, based on what's happening in your class right now. For example, a Kentucky math teacher devised this prompt:

How can you tell whether two sets of data vary directly? How can you tell if a line is the graph of a direct variation?

At the next class session, students appeared with responses like these:

Two sets of data vary directly if the value of y divided by x is the same for all corresponding data. A graph of direct variation always goes through (0,0).

≈ Want to Jump Around?

Are you thinking, "I can't trust my kids to bring in thoughtful admit slips quite yet"? Then head straight to the "What Can Go Wrong?" section on page 43 and learn about a surefire alternative, *start-up writes.*

Social Studies

- How would the United States have been different if FDR lost the election in 1932?

- Of the three main causes of the Civil War, which do you think is most important and why?

- Do you think the use of atomic bombs in World War II was justified? Why or why not?

- Name three qualities of a good president and why they matter.

English

- What do you think this character would do if x happened? Why?

- If you could submit some questions to the author _____, what would you ask?

- After reading the poem _____ aloud a few times, comment on the poem's rhythm and rhyme patterns.

- After reading the scoring guide for informational speeches, what elements will you need to work on to perform well next week?

Math

- How could this formula be applied in a real-life situation?

- Find some examples of math or numerical evidence being used in the media and explain.

- Pick one problem on page x and write down in words the steps you'd take to solve it.

- Make up a problem like the ones we have been doing and bring it to class.

Science

- Make a drawing of a plant in or near your house and explain how its structures are similar to some in the textbook.

- Explain the advantages and disadvantages of indicators versus meters.

- On page x, the textbook says that global warming may be caused by human activity or may be part of a natural, random cycle of variations. Which theory do you believe and why?

- Some of the chemical reactions we have been studying also happen in your home every day. Name two and explain.

- Using the genetics we have learned, comment upon the patterns of eye color in your own family tree, as much as you can.

Figure 3–2 *Sample content topics for admit slips*

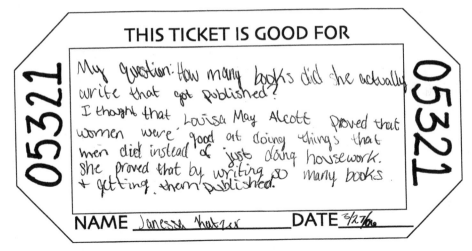

THIS TICKET IS GOOD FOR

05321

My question: How many books did she actually
write that got published?
I thought that Louisa May Alcott proved that
women were good at doing things that
men did instead of just doing housework.
She proved that by writing so many books
+ getting them published.

05321

NAME Janessa Hutzer   DATE 3/27/00

Figure 3–3 *Sample admit ticket*

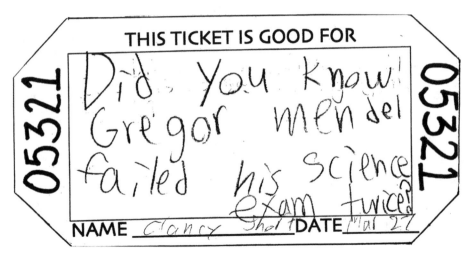

THIS TICKET IS GOOD FOR

05321

Did you know!
Gregor mendel
failed his science
exam twice?

05321

NAME Clancy Shol   DATE Mar 22

Figure 3–4 *Sample admit ticket*

If the ratio of each value in one set to its matching value in the other set is the same then the data vary directly. A line is the graph of a direct variation if the ratios of x and y are equal. (from www.wku.edu/3kinds/dmaesexam5.html)

So now what? What do you do with admit slips like these? As the kids enter the room, you collect the admit slips and use them to get the class session rolling. The options are very similar to those for exit slips.

Putting the Writing to Work

So many choices! So many ways to use admit slips, and many of these are analogues of the exit slip activities described just a few pages back. Here are just a few.

- The teacher collects all the admits, quickly scans through them and reads one to three promising discussion starters aloud, inviting class members to then chime in.

- The teacher finds two opposing or different takes on the topic, reads each aloud, and elicits discussion.

- The teacher does not collect the admits but simply asks volunteers (or calls on students) to read their card aloud.

- The teacher shuffles the cards and passes them out randomly; students anonymously read them aloud to spur discussion.

- The teacher has students pass their admit slips to the third (or fifth) student (down the row, around the circle). Then, the receiving student writes a comment on the card and passes it three more students along, for another round of comment. Then discussion starts when volunteer students read the three entries on their card.

- Students pass their cards as in the previous example, but each card returns to the student who made the initial entry.

What Can Go Wrong?

We said at the outset that admits were a little more complicated than exits. With admit slips, kids are doing their writing to learn as homework—and that means they must get it done and remember to bring it to class. That's a taller task than when you have them do exit slips right in the room, during the last three minutes of the period. In that situation, you may enjoy nearly total compliance. With at-home work, not so much. There are two ways to address this, frontally and sideways.

Our friend Wayne Mraz is fully frontal. He assigns admit slips almost every day to all his social studies classes, from basic level to Advanced Placement. And if someone arrives without her admit ticket, she isn't admitted to Wayne's classroom. She has to stand or sit outside in the hall and do her admit slip before she can get in the door. When they hear this story, some hard-bitten teacher friends of ours say: "Yeah, and I bet the kids *love* to be in the hall, making trouble." But they *don't* love it, especially with Wayne peeking out the door and telling them to hurry up. His students see no incentive to not coming prepared, and they forget only rarely.

The gentler, sideways approach works too. We suggested in the Jump Around box on page 40 that there's an alternative form of admit slips called start-up writes. Instead of requiring students to bring an admit ticket with them to class, simply set aside the first five minutes for them to write one while sitting in their seats. Here, you basically have the bookend of exit slips—the kids are all in class, there's no forgetting to bring something, and you can guide and monitor their creation of a worthwhile observation. Otherwise, the types of prompts and the uses in class discussion are just the same as for homework admit slips.

While many teachers begin using start-up writes instead of admit slips for these management reasons, there's no need to see this variation as a step down. In fact, some thoughtful teachers prefer the in-class version. They use the start-up write as a "sponge" activity that puts kids immediately to work when they step into the classroom. They put the day's admit slip question in a special spot on the blackboard and train kids to look for it upon entering the room and start jotting their responses right away.

Variation

Because exit and admit slips so effectively structure both class time and kids' thinking, many teachers use both of them daily. Steven Gabbard, a math teacher at Jackson County High School in McKee, Kentucky, says, "A good lesson is sort of like a story. It needs an opener, a plot, and a closing element. One way to accomplish this is through the use of admit and exit slips."

An article about Gabbard's classroom on the Education World website parallels the regular uses of admit and exit slips that we see in many content-area classrooms around the country:

> Gabbard uses [admit] slips as a class opener to focus the students on the topic of study, to provide direction for the period, and to review important skills needed for the lesson. His "openers" set the tone and offer background information for the "plot," or lesson, to come. "Class openers provide immediate feedback as to the readiness of the class as a whole for the lesson or skills needed for the lesson," Gabbard said. "These are usually problems that are representative of the previous day's lesson that provide a tie-in to the lesson being taught that day. Particular problems that I like to use include 'find the error in the work,' puzzles, riddles, or a real-world problem." At the other end of the period, Gabbard assigns exit slips. He says that they "make evident if a student has *got it,* or grasped the concepts of a lesson that has been taught." (Bafile 2004)

Admits and exits are among the rare strategies teachers say they'll never give up once they start using them. The diagnostic value and the class activities they spark are too great to ignore.

Brainstorming

What It Is

Did you ever wonder how the Shoebox division of Hallmark comes up with its snappy greetings? The writers brainstorm incessantly. *Brainstorming* is the fancy word for coming up with lots of ideas in a short amount of time. When you ask students to brainstorm, you are really asking them to take a quick inventory of what they know or think they know about something, writing down everything that comes to mind, even if they're not sure it's correct. The goal of brainstorming is quantity over quality. Students often stop after they've listed the most obvious ideas, but the harder they keep digging without judging, the more likely something interesting will surface. A big list needs to be created first before the revisions and corrections can take place. And if you were wondering, one Shoebox writer estimates that in eighteen years he's brainstormed about eighty thousand ideas; seven thousand of them eventually became cards.

When to Use It and Why

Written brainstorming is a quick and useful tool that can be applied at almost any point in a lesson or reading assignment. It's an excellent way to get kids started on a new topic by tapping into their prior knowledge. In the middle of a lesson, it can be used much like a writing break: take one minute and list every important idea, concept, or detail that you can remember. As a concluding activity, students can return to an earlier list, revising incorrect items and adding new pieces of information. Also, besides dealing directly with content, brainstorming is an excellent tool for examining the multiple solutions for any problem—real or fictional.

Play by Play

Getting Started

Beforehand, determine the topic to be brainstormed, when this activity will occur in the lesson, and what the brainstorming goal is. For example, it might be to inventory prior knowledge, review material, connect content to events outside the classroom, or correct previous misconceptions.

Then give students the topic and a minute or two to brainstorm individually. Next, have them share with a partner, extending their list by writing down items they hadn't already thought of.

⇒ Want to Jump Around?

For a more complex and extensive brainstorming activity, see the section on KWLs on pages 101–105.

Finally, create a class master list on chart paper or transparency. Go around the room and have one pair at a time share something off their list. While you (or the designated note taker) jot down the comments on the master list, the students should follow along, checking off items they already have and jotting down new items. Writing together as a class, after all, is still writing, and as long as it's helping students learn your subject material, it's serving the purpose, whether the effort is individual or collective.

Working the Room

As always, roaming the room during the process will help keep the kids on task. Also, pay close attention to the partner sharing. Make sure the kids actually talk about and clarify their ideas rather than just silently copy off each other's paper. Remind students that both partners will be expected to be able to explain the thinking behind all items on their list, not just the ones they personally thought of.

Putting the Writing to Work

Brainstorming before reading gives students a specific purpose as they head into the text: affirming previously learned information, surfacing misconceptions, and watching for new ideas. As the kids move into their reading, they should have their lists right at hand. It is also important for them to return to the lists later in the unit for reflection or further brainstorming. Just have the kids reread their previous lists and discuss a couple of questions, first with their partners and then with the large group:

- What inaccuracies do you notice in your original lists?
- On a scale of 1 to 10, how much more do you know about this subject now than when you began?
- What's one important item you would add to the list now that was completely overlooked earlier?
- Of all the items listed, which three are the most important based on what you know now?

Textbook Connections

One challenge in all content areas is the voluminous specialized vocabulary. Rather than having kids look up thirty words in the glossary, pick out a few of the key words, those absolutely essential to understanding the reading. Give students the definitions and then have them brainstorm scenarios from their own lives where these word might apply. For example, in British literature, a reader is never going to follow Sir Arthur Conan Doyle's *Hound of the Baskervilles* unless she has a clear mental picture of a moor. The definition of a moor is a swampy area that can look deceivingly firm. The brainstorm question: What places have you been that fit this description? Kids might brainstorm places such as the following:

- ☞ the swamp at LaGrange Road and 95th Street
- ☞ wetland behind my subdivision
- ☞ the peat bog at summer camp

What Can Go Wrong?

First, in order to brainstorm, students need to have some prior knowledge on the topic, so it stands to reason that this won't work very well if the topic is completely unfamiliar to students. In that case, you'll need to provide the background information and save the brainstorming for later in the unit when students have more to work with. Second, when students are brainstorming background information, misconceptions and inaccuracies are bound to appear on their initial lists, so it is *very* important for students to return to those lists and make corrections later on. However, correcting at the time of initial brainstorming can backfire because it will make students second-guess everything they write down, resulting in very short, predictable lists.

Example

Before reading an excerpt of Columbus' diary as well as accounts of how Columbus' colonization of the West Indies affected the indigenous people, one American history class brainstormed a list of ideas about Columbus. Though mostly accurate, the list revealed a superficial knowledge and showed that the upcoming readings would offer plenty of new information for these students.

HISTORY

discovered America 1492
three ships: *Nina, Pinta, Santa Maria*
explorer
thought he was landing in India
Chicago World's Fair in 1892 called the Columbian Exposition
king and queen of Spain paid for Columbus' travel
he was the one that coined the name *Indians*
brought foreign foods to Spain
brought European diseases to Americas

Drawing and Illustrating

What It Is

Students make quick drawings, sketches, or diagrams to illustrate ideas, events, science experiments, real-world situations involving math problems, and so on, in order to help themselves and others understand something they are trying to learn. These illustrations usually include words in the form of explanations, labels, or arranged lists of terms and ideas. And they needn't be highly artistic renderings; in fact, it is important to steer students away from such expectations, so those who feel they are all thumbs understand that their sketches are simply tools for thought and communication, and not entries in an art competition. Drawings can be of many types—stick figures or abstract representations of ideas, as well as illustrations of actual scenes or objects.

When to Use It and Why

SCIENCE

Drawings help most students, especially the more visually oriented, to understand complex ideas. When any of us reexpress an idea in a different mode than we first encountered it, we notice different aspects and are led to self-monitor, to notice the parts we do or don't understand. More basically, though, taking the time and effort—even if it's just a brief couple of minutes—to make a sketch or complete a diagram often leads students to digest and remember a concept, when a passive hearing or reading didn't sink in. Science teacher Jeff Janes, at Andrew High School in Tinley Park, Illinois, has found that drawings make a distinct difference in students' learning. After students were required to include drawings in a longer assignment—student-made booklets tracing the history of theories about the atom—Jeff polled three of his classes and found that 93 percent of the students asserted that the drawings helped them learn things they hadn't previously understood. Eighty percent felt certain that creating the booklets and drawings resulted in higher scores on their unit tests. Here's how various students put it:

- ☞ I got a better understanding of all of the models [of the atom] because I recreated them myself.
- ☞ Being able to visualize what happened made me understand it even more.
- ☞ It gave me a better idea of the models than just from reading about them.
- ☞ Drawing Thompson's and Rutherford's experiments, along with Einstein's Brownian motion, really helped me understand the concepts.

☞ Since we had to draw the pictures, I studied the experiments, and it helped me understand them better.

Play by Play

Getting Started

Rather than use drawings and diagrams as tests of students' learning, Jeff integrates them into his everyday teaching and learning. Often he'll have students complete quick sketches at the start of class, focused on topics he plans to teach or review immediately. Kids use their diagrams to contribute to a whole-class version on the overhead, which allows Jeff to correct misconceptions or add further ideas the students may have missed.

☞ Want to Jump Around?

Turn directly to "Mapping" on page 60 in this chapter, to compare drawings with more conceptual illustrations.

Working the Room

While students are completing their own quick drawings or diagrams, Jeff moves steadily around the room, just to get quick glimpses of their work, to see if they are getting it. This allows him to plan his next steps, depending upon whether the kids appear to be on the right track or to need more help.

If students do not correctly understand a concept, particularly in science or math, completing a drawing might further engrain their misconception. This is one reason Jeff skims around the room, looking over shoulders while the kids are working. For Jeff this is where the whole-class drawing is especially useful. Often, if he has spotted a misconception, he'll later ask the student to contribute to the drawing, after which another is likely to comment, "Well I have that on the other side of my chart" (Jeff takes time to instruct his students on respectful ways of disagreeing or correcting one another). This gives Jeff the opportunity to very naturally and supportively explain the concept correctly. When he sees that a misconception is more widespread, Jeff will have small groups compare their drawings and resolve their differences before contributing to a whole-class version, so that the students who get it are able to help those that don't.

Putting the Writing to Work

Jeff also helps his students think more broadly about learning and how such techniques can strengthen it. After the students completed and shared their booklets on the atom and discussed how drawings helped them learn, he pointed out the general value of the strategy. "If they worked well for you this time, they will also help you learn more and get better grades next year in biology, whether your teacher assigns

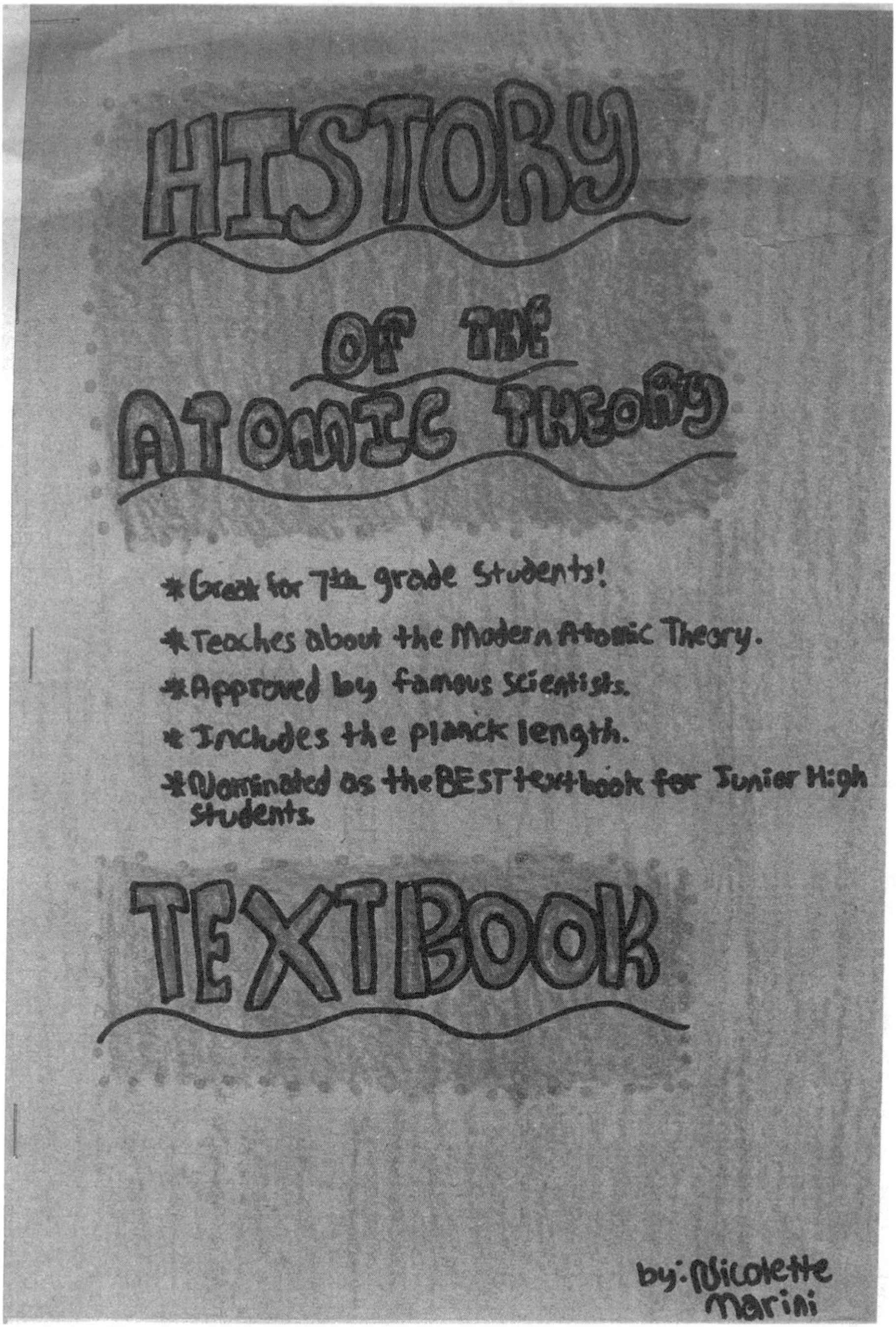

HISTORY

OF THE

ATOMIC THEORY

* Great for 7th grade students!

* Teaches about the Modern Atomic Theory.

* Approved by famous scientists.

* Includes the planck length.

* Nominated as the BEST textbook for Junior High students.

TEXTBOOK

by: Nicolette Marini

Figure 3–5 *Student booklet on the history of the atom and drawings of a famous experiment*

continues

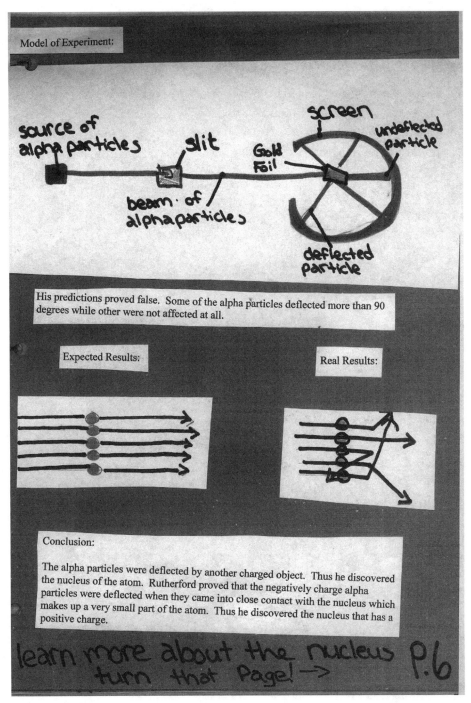

Model of Experiment:

source of alpha particles

slit

beam of alpha particles

Gold Foil

screen

undeflected particle

deflected particle

His predictions proved false. Some of the alpha particles deflected more than 90 degrees while other were not affected at all.

Expected Results:

Real Results:

Conclusion:

The alpha particles were deflected by another charged object. Thus he discovered the nucleus of the atom. Rutherford proved that the negatively charge alpha particles were deflected when they came into close contact with the nucleus which makes up a very small part of the atom. Thus he discovered the nucleus that has a positive charge.

learn more about the nucleus P.6 turn that page! →

Figure 3–5, *continued*

them or not," he explained to these freshmen who were still in the process of getting the hang of high school.

Textbook Connections

Jeff uses drawings to help kids with many topics in his physical science textbook. These are often assigned in place of or in addition to the questions at end of a chapter. But he frequently adds them in, as well, because he finds that this visual thinking is especially effective for improving kids' understanding of science.

ONE WORLD

Premier Issue, 1999

● **Impact of History and Tradition** ● Japan & America ●
Editorial

SYMBOLS OF JAPAN AND AMERICA:
Comparison and Contrast

APPLE PIE
What most Americans consider the ultimate representation of their culture. Its simplicity says so much for this complicated and structured culture; that and the fact that American's love food!

COCA-COLA
How unfortunate it is that commercial symbols have come to represent America, but they do accurately portray the powerful and prosperous commercial American businesses.

GRANDMOTHER
Americans have come to appreciate the friendly warm grandmother figure who provides affection and compassion that pleasently contrasts the "harsh adult world."

We all know the typical symbols that are used to portray both America and Japan, but what exactly do they *represent*?

American beliefs are ever changing. They do hold fast onto many traditional attitudes and assumptions, but they are often over-powered by their conflicting views. America's quest for knowledge affects their symbols greatly. What they hold important as representative of their country's beliefs, values, attitudes, and assumptions now, may be considered passe or even offensive in the near future. Japan on the other hand, keeps their heritage and traditional ever-present. They represent their country through age old symbols that America is familiar with, which helps us to understand their culture. Commerce, politics, and other interactions may be made more complicated, because the understanding of America's culture (for Japan) is very difficult and indefinite.

CHERRY BLOSSOM
Japanese have always had great respect for nature. culture. Although they struggle to maintain their effectiveness to protect nature, their devotion still remains.

CHOP-STICKS
The immediate image conjured by Westerner's when the Orient is mentioned most likely because Japan is one of the few places in the world that hasn't adapted the Eurocentric silverware.

KIMONO
This distinctive traditional robe plays a major role in Japan's history. Although they are used less in Japanese everyday life, they are still considered sacred.

Figure 3–6 *Marny's fusion article*

What Can Go Wrong?

When drawings are included within a project like Jeff Janes' booklets on atomic theories, it's no surprise that the Internet makes it easy for students to simply download illustrations. Jeff requires that the kids draw their own, but even when the diagrams are obviously very close to a published version, the students still testify that they learn from them. Of course for in-class activities, this is not a problem.

It often takes repeated reminders to help the nonartists in the room relax and understand that this strategy is not about displaying talent, but simply about thinking and learning. Even then, a few kids who are not visual learners will find the act of drawing unhelpful. Jeff openly discusses this and in fact maintains a set of posters around the room explaining the various modes of learning—visual, kinesthetic, and so forth.

Variations

There are many ways for students to reexpress an idea in two dimensions instead of the single in-line form of reading or writing. Kids enjoy making cartoons to represent a historical situation or event, a conflict, or a controversy. Cartoons can enable math students to write out explanations of the steps in solving problems (called for in many

Figure 3–7 *Lauren's graphic depiction of the Native American legend "Earth on Turtle's Back"*

standardized math tests these days). And they permit students to inject a sense of play or personal ownership into an idea that is otherwise pretty dry in the textbook.

Time lines help students visualize the flow of events in history. While they can be very simple, with dates and labels for events, students can further elaborate with added drawings of key turning points so they dig more deeply and place events in perspective.

More abstract sketches can especially help students explore concepts by inviting verbal explanation, whether written or oral. Once in a workshop for teachers on writing, we asked participants to draw their own writing process. One teacher explained the large red dots she had sprinkled across a piece of construction paper, saying, "That's my blood. That's how I feel when I'm asked to write something!" Everyone murmured agreement to this vivid confession—and we were then able to begin talking honestly about it.

Even traditional school assignments can take on a new life and evoke kids' craftsmanship with the addition of an illustration component. One social studies teacher simply asked students to "compare and contrast" stereotypical images that people have of Japan and the United States. Motivated by the chance to do some desktop publishing, Marny took an initial quick-write assignment and ramped it up (see Figure 3–6).

Clustering

What It Is

Clustering was first made popular with educators by Gabriele Rico, whose book *Writing the Natural Way,* first published in 1983, still gets glowing reviews on Amazon.com. On her own website, Rico describes the strategy thus: "a non-linear brainstorming process, clustering makes the Design mind's interior, invisible associations visible on a page. Clustering becomes a self-organizing process as words and phrases are spilled onto the page around a center" (from www.gabrielerico.com/Main/ClusteringSampleVignettes.htm). To put it simply, the writer jots a key word in the center of a page, draws spokes outward, and in associative fashion writes words connected with the key word in circles or balloons at the end of the spokes. Clustering is a way to surface ideas students may need for thinking or writing about a topic they are exploring, or to connect and review ideas they have learned as they study a particular chunk of content. It allows students to uncover possibilities they may not have considered if they were simply writing out linearly what they thought they knew. It is not usually a product, but simply a tool to help students get thinking started. While many people use pure clustering, with simply a word in the center and the bubbles around it, you may well prefer a version that includes phrases or statements written along the

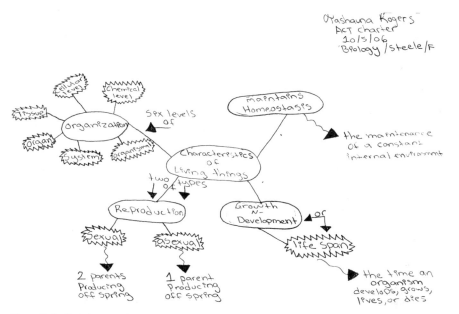

Figure 3–8 *Clustering example*

spokes to indicate how the ideas are connected, to lead students to think more deeply as they work (see Figure 3–8).

When to Use It and Why

While most descriptions of clustering found on the Web or in Rico's book focus on its use in creative writing, it's just as powerful for helping students deepen their thinking about nonfiction subject material. We often tend, as we teach our subjects, to focus in on very specific topics—oxidation numbers in chemistry, state powers and limits on them in Article Four of the U.S. Constitution, the definition of a formal Euclidean proof in geometry. But clustering helps students at various stages of their learning to realize what they already know about a subject at the start, or to organize their understanding of its various parts, to make connections with other topics within the subject or outside of it in their present-day world, or to help themselves get started writing about it. It's a tool students can use to get beyond the most obvious ideas that first occur to them—or to conquer the feeling that they really have no ideas at all—and to draw on more of what they know.

Kids are often hesitant to make a guess about a question the teacher has posed for fear of being wrong. By using a two-dimensional, associative strategy like clustering before answering, students can try out their ideas on paper and think more creatively and visually. It's easy to use as a quick classroom activity like this to get students' thinking recorded before you begin discussion on a topic. Three minutes of clustering first helps make sure that many of your quieter kids have answers ready and the courage to propose them, so you aren't always depending on the usual eager hand wavers.

Play by Play

Getting Started

The first few times you ask students to try clustering at the beginning of the year, be sure to model it for them on your projection equipment. Use a nontechnical topic, something related to the school or the neighborhood, so the students can see how the process works without worrying about new course content. Next time around, choose a concept close to, but not exactly the same as, the one you will be asking them about, and as you construct your clustering, share your thinking aloud, so the kids can see not only the product but how it gets created. A third try can involve students working in groups.

Working the Room

Once kids are accustomed to it, using clustering as a frequent tool for jump-starting their thinking is simple. Picture yourself in your classroom about to launch a discussion. Tina Steele at Chicago's Academy of Communications and Technology has her ninth-grade biology students start, for example, with a key word like *organization* to help them think about the various levels at which an organism is structured. Tina especially values having students write statements on the spokes to explain the connections they see between their central word and its satellites. She finds that when the students create their own explanations for how ideas are related, they remember them much more firmly. And she wants the kids to develop a larger conceptual view of the material, as well. "Then it's much easier for them to fill in the specifics," she explains.

Putting the Writing to Work

How do the students share their clustering? How do the results get used, in other words, in teaching and learning? Tina says that sometimes a quick clustering activity meant as a "bell ringer" can turn out to fuel instruction and discussion for the entire period. As the students share their clusters and the teacher comments on the ideas and helps kids elaborate on them or clarify confusions, the content that Tina needs to teach gradually unfolds. In the process, of course, Tina can observe the extent to which kids understand the ideas they've just studied. This informs her about what is getting through and what needs reteaching. It gives her just as much information just as quickly as a quiz, but without any punitive quality to the experience (though the students can of course tell, themselves, when they've got it and when they are confused).

Tina is happiest when she discovers that the students are using clustering as a study and review tool on their own. Many of the kids do this not only for her class but for others in their day as well.

Textbook Connections

Clustering is a great way to help students get a better handle on the material being presented in their textbooks. All too often, these heavy tomes lay out endless bits and bytes of material without helping students make connections, organize the material in their heads, or maintain a larger view of the big ideas along the way. Studying becomes simply memorizing one disconnected fact or definition or equation after another. So ask kids to pause in their reading to cluster on paper about it, or to create clusters when they arrive in class after having read the assignment the day or the night before, and then have them share the clusters in pairs or use them to contribute to a whole-class cluster. This can help ensure that students do more conceptual thinking and get the most from the textbook by actively reconstructing the ideas in their own way.

What About Kids Who Seem to Just Have Nothing to Write?

Even on a task as easy and open-ended as clustering, some kids will say they can't think of anything to write down. What if they haven't completed the assigned reading or are simply (well, it's never *simply*) unengaged? First you need to check on whether the student has special needs of some kind and should receive extra support—more time or a chance to talk with a fellow student first, for example. Then it's important to remember that a strategy like clustering is just one tool, a small part of a wider world of school and the lives of adolescents. Clustering may indeed be a motivator itself, helping some students feel like their ideas are welcomed. But for others, the issue may be larger, due to any one of a number of causes—lack of commitment to school, past experience with failure, a lack of skills, a lack of belief that hard work now might actually lead to a hopeful future, issues at home, or the much-debated peer pressure that seems to hold some students back. We cannot tackle these large issues in this book, though we've seen classrooms where the strategies we offer do help students achieve the kind of everyday success that can turn negative self-perceptions around. But we need to acknowledge that as teachers we face such challenges every day, and if a strategy fails to work when we try it, we must examine both our immediate technique and the larger context in our schools and neighborhoods—do not just conclude, "See, I knew that could never work with *my* kids."

What Can Go Wrong?

If students are not accustomed to associative thinking, they may hesitate, feeling like they need to have all the right words before they begin to write. They'll need reassurance that the object is not to get the right answer, but to get thoughts flowing. Point out that it's better to just get words down quickly, like brainstorming, and not eliminate anything until later.

Another challenge involves the teacher. Tina explains that if you have students write statements on the spokes in their clustering, it's all too easy to start judging the quality of their thinking by the length and complexity of the sentences. She says she has to remind herself that the statements are about helping the students develop and remember their own thinking, and if they do that job, then the quality or length of the sentences isn't really the important factor.

Variation

If the topic is unfamiliar to the students and they are just getting started on it, you may find it makes sense to provide the words and the cluster yourself, projected for the class. This is, however, a different kind of activity. It is often called *word splash* on the Web, and it involves having students write sentences using the words provided. Tina

Steele does on occasion use this variation, with the students writing out sentences to explain relationships between the various terms. While it's a useful activity for getting students started thinking about the topic and focusing them on concepts to watch for as they read and study, or for reviewing material before a test, it's quite a different process than the associative, generative thinking that true clustering invites.

Mapping

What It Is

Mapping asks students to arrange groups of ideas visually and to show relationships among them. The simpler maps are the various graphic organizers commonly found in our schools. We all know about Venn diagrams, flowcharts, concept wheels, and the like. We provide suggestions for making these effective teaching tools, rather than just cursory exercises. But there are also more colorful and decorative mind maps to try, activities that give students the opportunity to make ideas memorable and route them through another part of the brain by using vivid images.

Mind mapping is a specific version of this activity explored in a number of books, many of them by Tony Buzan. *The Mind Map Book: How to Use Radiant Thinking to Maximize Your Brain's Potential* (1996), is the most widely known, but another valuable resource is Michael Gelb's *How to Think Like Leonardo da Vinci* (2000). Gelb and Lana Israel have both produced videos on the strategy as well. These materials are geared toward businesspeople rather than educators, and—surprise!—a whole industry of high-priced corporate training, materials, and mapping software has grown up around the strategy.

As Buzan explains, "If you want to remember a page of notes, for example, words will help to some extent, of course, but more important for fixing them in your memory will be images, pictures, symbols, codes, colors, associations and connections" (*Management Consulting News,* 2006). The mind, Buzan argues, works by associating words with images. He views maps as colorful radiating figures, with branches and branches on the branches, though many other shapes are possible.

When to Use It and Why

Maps allow students to represent thinking that involves multiple, simultaneous associations, rather than just linear steps. Maps help us organize, consolidate, and digest knowledge. They can enable kids to recall multiple steps in a process for solving complex math or science problems. And of course as students create the maps, they review the material covered and in many cases go back to fill in blanks in their knowledge—so mapping deepens learning in several ways. More vivid mind mapping may be most useful toward the end of a unit or project, because it relates various ideas together and forms a conceptual whole. As one Amazon.com reviewer of Buzan's book explains,

I've used mind maps for about twenty years to organize engineering projects at work, remember books I've read, identify daily goals, learn chess opening ideas, outline papers I'm writing, and identify the important from the trivial. . . . You won't become a genius, you will still have to work at thinking, you'll just have an additional tool to help you. Mind maps are fun, easy-to-use, useful ways to organize and retain information and generate ideas. Linear notes just don't jog the memory. It's still amazing to me how a hastily drawn mind map on an article, book, movie, lecture—a map I'll scribble with stupid little drawings and doodles and throw away days later—can help me remember so much years later!! It works. I use it. It helps.

We don't necessarily agree with Tony Buzan that mind maps will revolutionize human intelligence, but they clearly support student learning and deepen kids' understanding of topics that we teach. And this more creative version of mapping is also a great strategy for differentiated instruction. Students can work at various levels of achievement and all produce results that both help themselves learn and illustrate ideas for their classmates.

Play by Play

Getting Started

Let's begin by looking at the process of using a simple graphic organizer and then we'll go on to the more complex mind mapping strategy.

Jeff Janes, at Andrew High School, especially likes to use Venn diagrams to help students think about topics quickly and immediately. At the beginning of the year, Jeff models the creation of several Venn diagrams for the kids, one comparing boys and girls (with accompanying wisecracks and giggles), and then one on a simple science topic. The students then practice together, on a topic like comparing mammals and reptiles.

SCIENCE

Working the Room

Often, as the kids walk into class, Jeff has them pick up sheets with blank linked circles and take a couple of minutes to contrast two related concepts studied the day before (see his completed diagram comparing ionic and covalent bonds in chemistry in Figure 3–9). As students call out items and explain where they go on the diagram, the concepts that Jeff wants them to learn gradually emerge. If students are confused, Jeff uses the occasion to clarify things. The length of time he takes for such discussion varies from a couple of minutes to fifteen or more, depending on the importance of the concept.

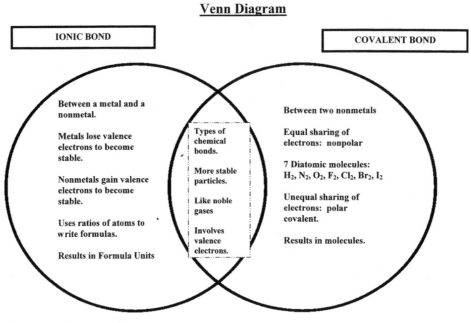

Venn Diagram

IONIC BOND

COVALENT BOND

Between a metal and a nonmetal.

Metals lose valence electrons to become stable.

Nonmetals gain valence electrons to become stable.

Uses ratios of atoms to write formulas.

Results in Formula Units

Types of chemical bonds.

More stable particles.

Like noble gases

Involves valence electrons.

Between two nonmetals

Equal sharing of electrons: nonpolar

7 Diatomic molecules: H_2, N_2, O_2, F_2, Cl_2, Br_2, I_2

Unequal sharing of electrons: polar covalent.

Results in molecules.

Figure 3–9 *Jeff Janes' Venn diagram*

Jeff always keeps his overhead projector ready to go in case he wants to stop and construct a diagram as a class, together, as the kids are hearing about or reviewing material. For example, as he explored the periodic table, he stopped to have students complete a Venn diagram to compare the properties of metals and nonmetals.

Getting Started with More Complex Mind Maps

When kids are first learning to create mind maps, it's a good idea to show them student-created examples. If you haven't used this strategy before, you can troll for samples that fellow teachers have lovingly saved or check the Internet. (The Wikipedia encyclopedia entry on "mind mapping" provides a quick overview with several examples and links to other sites on the topic.) And of course numerous companies on the Web are more than happy to sell you their mapping software. At Saline Middle School, in Saline, Michigan, math teacher Nancy Rodgers displays examples of her own maps. And she also shows kids a short video on the strategy, made as a class project by students of fellow Saline teacher Suzanne Brion.

When you show kids sample mind maps, don't flaunt any highly developed works of art—you'll just discourage the all-thumbs kids in the classroom. Before they get started, it's also good to have the students review the big ideas, concepts, and vocabulary terms they'll be mapping, to help make their maps more accurate and complete.

Figure 3–10 *Chelsea Harding's mind map*

Working the Room

Nancy Rodgers uses mind maps to help her eighth-grade students with math topics she finds they have the most trouble understanding. They get one class period to start on their maps, after which they finish them up at home. This is active learning time, not just entertainment. And it gives Nancy a valuable opportunity to observe how students are thinking and to teach brief individual or whole-class lessons if she sees students missing important ideas or depicting misconceptions. (See Figure 3–10.)

MATH

Putting the Writing to Work

Maps are great for reviewing material at the end of a unit, helping students to recall the various steps, concepts, historical events, and so on, as well as the larger perspective that relates all those parts together. Nancy Rodgers even allows maps for answers to questions on tests.

You can use the maps for deeper reflection by having kids look over each other's maps in small groups or posted on the walls. To ensure that students really process the information, rather than just stand and gossip about the weekend, you can easily convert this into a thinking-and-responding activity. Tape sheets of paper below the displayed maps. Have students rotate from map to map in small groups, reading the map and then writing a comment on the sheet below to add a further detail, idea, or connection (while you circulate to make sure the comments are on topic, civil, and not crude or rude). If wall space is tight, put up just five or six representative maps for the class to review.

⌇Want to Jump Around?

Go to "Carousel Brainstorming" in Chapter 4 (page 81) to see another way students can move around the room to write at multiple stations.

Textbook Connections

The bold headings, lists of major points, and italicized pointers in textbooks are usually intended to make the main ideas stand out. But these don't always help students grasp the larger picture. And they don't usually address issues or controversies or connections with other subjects or real-world applications. Maps provide students with the opportunity not only to review material in their textbooks but to reprocess it through a fresh set of neurons, and to add additional perspectives that go beyond the textbook. The more colorful mind maps can turn review of a chapter from a dull, plodding process with kids nodding off (and how many of us struggled with that as students, ourselves?) into an engaging act of self-expression. You should hang on to some of the kid-created maps as study or review guides for future classes—and to let your present students know that this is one of the more useful purposes for their hard work.

What Can Go Wrong?

One big challenge is likely to be the students who consider themselves completely hopeless artistically. Either in a talk with the whole class or in individual conferences, you'll need to help these students realize that great art is not what this is about, and there is no need for the map to realistically represent or even depict physical objects at all. Nancy Rodgers finds that her students who aren't budding artists tend to imitate her examples rather than branch out on their own—and that's fine.

Another difficulty may occur for students who have learning disabilities—or even just natural learning patterns—that make very complex, two-dimensional masses of material difficult to decipher. In fact, we find some of the maps in Tony Buzan's book dizzying and confusing rather than helpful. Brief individual conferences, as you circulate the room, can help such students to use accessible shapes or to divide the task and create several submaps instead of one big one that jams everything together in one overwhelming, crazy-quilt diagram.

Learning Logs, Notebooks, Sketchbooks, and Buttpads

How's it going? We hope that as you've sampled the first seven writing-to-learn activities, you've started trying them out with your students, and that they're adding value to your teaching.

If so, you're probably already wondering: "What am I going to do with all this paper?" You need a place for kids to *collect* all these pieces of their thinking. In fact, you may already be doing quick daily activities, like start-up writes, and you don't want to be handing out blank paper, making up handouts, or even waiting for kids to drag a piece of paper out of their backpacks every time.

That's where learning logs come in: they are a tangible, long-term commitment to the idea of writing to learn, and a way to keep it all organized. These handy little tools are called by various names in different subject fields and different grade levels: notebooks, lab notes, sketchbooks, or buttpads (the smaller back-pocket type). The main idea is for learners to have a place to *do thinking* and to *save thinking* for later use—and perhaps, for assessment by their teacher. In fact, we find that a well-kept learning log is a far better and more usable record of student learning than any series of classroom tests we could ever devise.

We've tinkered with learning logs for years, and they need to be carefully tailored to your class and the subject. Here are some of the things we think about when trying to create the just-right format for a given class. To begin, you need a bound, continuous section of paper (like a spiral notebook). You might automatically think of lined paper, but don't be too quick. Many teachers think the freedom signaled by blank sheets communicates to students that writing to learn is different from other school writing and that graphic responses are just as valuable as words and sentences. Your pick.

Then you need a container, pocket folder, or envelope to keep loose pieces in. Now it would seem more logical to just have kids do *all* their writing-to-learn activities in one place, like a designated spiral notebook, but that doesn't suit the way we often use WTLs in class. We often have kids write, for example, exit slips or admit slips on variously sized index cards, ready to immediately pass around or carry to a group meeting. Doing this with spirals gets cumbersome. Sometimes we do writing breaks on sticky notes so kids can stick them on a poster, around which we gather to talk. Additionally, using small pieces of paper dials down kids' blank-page fever, their fear of getting started with writing because the task seems so big. Another drawback with spirals: if you get too religious about writing only in one place, then every kid has to *remember* to bring her learning log, which will never happen in this millennium. We don't ever want a WTL activity to be delayed because seven kids must first go search their lockers. Responding to this management issue, some teachers keep learning logs right in the classroom, no circulation allowed. But learning logs make a perfect companion for at-home reading assignments—a tough choice!

Do you love to prowl the aisles of the local Staples/OfficeMax/Office Depot? If so, you're in for a good time. A spiral with an attached folder or pockets at the

continues

continued

ends can work, though loose stuff, especially note cards or small slips of paper, can fall out. Though it is heavier, a small (one-inch) three-ring binder covers all the bases; you put a hunk of blank or notebook paper in the front and then select from all kinds of fun prepunched pockets, folders, and containers for the rest.

Whatever storage system you design, make sure that kids stick, tape, or glue all small writings (originally done on sticky notes or index cards) onto full-size paper, three-hole punch them, and stick them into the binder. This is much safer than keeping papers in pockets, and it invites students to organize their entries by chronology or topic.

While we usually think that teacher-made tools are better than commercial ones, for math teachers we highly recommend the learning logs available from Universal Learning. These preprinted journals have three kinds of space: one for symbolic computation; another lightly graphed area for drawing and representations; and a lined section for explaining mathematical thinking in prose. A person could also copy this format quite easily, but that would be wrong.

Are we sounding a little too concrete here? Can't help it, we love school supplies!

Now enjoy the next set of WTLs, coming right up.

Variations

"Where is the line between drawing and mapping?" you might ask. And are Venn diagrams really a kind of clustering or mapping? Should mapping be used only at the end of a unit, or can it help students develop ideas in the middle, or as they begin a project? Are radial diagrams the only ones that are truly mind maps? Must they be formal and fancy or can they be just quick sketches? Truth is, we don't really worry about the labels. If you find, as you teach, that combining words with two-dimensional figures helps students better understand and remember what they are studying, at whatever point works for them, and in whatever level of refinement helps and fits in your schedule, then you are doing the kids a service. With so many different kinds of thinking and relating of ideas in our fields (think of how different algebra and geometry are, for example), we need to try out this larger strategy at various points and see what works and when.

Works Cited

Bafile, Carla. 2004. "'Let It Slip!': Daily Exit Slips Help Teachers Know What Students *Really* Learned." Education World, March 8. Accessed September 2, 2006, at www.education-world.com/a_curr/profdev/profdev091.shtml.

Buzan, Tony. 1996. *The Mind Map Book: How to Use Radiant Thinking to Maximize Your Brain's Potential.* New York: Plume.

Gelb, Michael. 2000. *How to Think Like Leonardo da Vinci: Seven Steps to Genius Every Day.* Revised ed. New York: Dell.

Management Consulting News. 2006. "Meet the MasterMinds: An Exclusive Interview with Tony Buzan." www.managementconsultingnews.com/interviews/buzan_interview.php.

Rico, Gabriele. 2000. *Writing the Natural Way.* Revised ed. New York: Tarcher.

chapter four

Going Deeper with Writing to Learn

In This Chapter

Dear Reader,

How'd it go with the quick writes? Get some good ideas there? We hope so, and now here are eight more strategies for learning with short, informal writing. These are a little more involved and take a bit more time, but they offer even more applications.

Did you notice that we are writing you a little letter here? That's because many of the strategies in this section use written correspondence to deepen kids' understanding of subject matter. Enjoy!

Smokey, Steve, and Nancy

Written Conversation

What It Is

Do your students love to write notes to each other, sometimes during the middle of your fascinating lecture? Ours do. We've also observed the vast adolescent postal system through which kids distribute those notes around the school. (Guess that's why they call it a "passing period"when the bell rings, because that's when they pass out all those notes to each other.) You've probably captured plenty of samples of these missives or found them discarded on your classroom floor. Most specimens of this genre are not very, uh, curriculum centered.

But they *could* be—and that's what written conversations, sometimes called dialogue journals, are all about. By legalizing letter writing and dragging it out of the gossip world and into our subject matter, we can capitalize on the kids' love of one-to-one correspondence to spark discussion of the curriculum. At Woonsocket Middle School in Rhode Island, Tonya Curt and Kara Alling have their students work in pairs, writing letters to each other as they read a book they have picked together. Today Jintana Souvannavongsa and Daniel Thipphavong are discussing pages 91–111 of Roland Smith's young adult novel *Zack's Lie* (2002).

LANGUAGE ARTS

Dear Daniel,
Zack sure had a rough day at school. I can't believe Zack said Commander I. F. wasn't his, when Caitlin picked it up for him. I think Caitlin and Zack are gonna hook up. What do you think's gonna happen next? Zack is lucky he didn't get suspended.
I'm happy that Zack met a new friend, Darrell. Speaking of Darrell, I don't think his Dad really likes Peter. Do you think Zack's friendship with Darrell is gonna last? I think that Zack's going to tell Darrell about his father.
The author, Roland Smith, is a really talented writer. What do you think?
Do you think everybody in Elko really knows everything about everybody? That's creepy. Well, at least they don't know about Zack's "history."
I think Sam is with the witness protection program. He's like a stalker or something. He seems like an interesting person, though.
Have fun reading.
Your best buddie,
Jintanzi

Dear Jintana,
Haha, you're smart. I never thought that Sam could be a spy to check up on him. Maybe Caitlin and Zack is going to get together. Yeah, you're also right about Commander I. F. since it was from his Dad. I thought he would said it was his. Ha. I guess you can tell

Darrell's Dad hates Peter. For example Darrell's Dad: "I heard that you hit Peter. Is that true?" Zack: "I guess so." Darrell's Dad: "Good." Ha ha. I thought that was funny. Yeah.

After this book I know I'm going to the library to look for more of his books. Well I am almost out of time. Write to you later—bye.
Your friend,
Thipphavong

Many versions of written conversation have been cooked up by clever teachers all around the country, and the next strategy in the book is yet another powerful letter-based activity called the write-around. All of these epistolary WTLs have a common purpose. They are tools for engaging and discussing ideas. They replace or supplement the weaker kinds of discussion in the classroom—especially whole-class discussions, during which one person at a time gets called on and everyone else tries to avoid getting a turn. And interestingly, when we have written conversations, sitting side by side with our partners, we can all "talk" at once and it's still *quiet* in the room. A final bonus of written conversations is that, unlike out-loud discussions that vanish into the air, letters leave artifacts behind that can be used or assessed later.

Play by Play

Getting Started

SOCIAL STUDIES

In Steve Keck's class in central Indiana, the middle schoolers study ancient Roman life each year. In class today, they have read a meaty one-page article with lots of information about different levels, ranks, and occupations in Roman society. Instead of calling for a whole-class discussion, Steve asks kids to correspond with their dialogue journal partners about which role in Roman society they would most like to have and why. Trey and Brittany get into a lively written conversation about the merits of that occupation:

I'd like to be a gladiator because you get to kill people and animals. You also get a nickname and you'd be wildly popular.—Trey

Trey, why would you do that? You would have at least a 50% chance of getting killed. —Brittany

No, no, I do not. I have a 0% chance of getting killed. Before they could kill me I'd stab them 5 times in the heart. I would because I'm better than all the others.—Trey

Trey, how would you be able to do that? You're not Achilles. So I highly doubt that you'd be able to stab them in the heart 5 times. My point is you're too skinny. A gladiator would break you like a twig.—Brittany

While this exchange is funny, we can see how Brittany is drawing on facts from the article to counsel her impetuous classmate away from a brief career.

Managing Written Conversations

There are two basic kinds of written conversations: the "live" here-and-now type, where two people sit together and pass notes back and forth, and the take-away kind, which works more like a letter—one partner sends a note that waits somewhere (in a folder, journal, or classroom mailbox) until the receiver has the time to open it, read it, and write a response. Both are highly useful in the content-area classroom.

In the live version—like Trey and Brittany's gladiator exchange—we tend to set kids up for short interchanges that eventually shift into a whole-class activity. Pairs of students sit face-to-face, writing and exchanging notes here and now. In early trials, the teacher usually structures things carefully, first by providing a common experience for everyone to react to (e.g., reading aloud a rich selection of literature, conducting a science experiment) and then by setting the pace of exchange, watching the clock and calling for note swapping at one- to three-minute intervals. This live version is especially good for training inexperienced student journalers to dialogue effectively.

In the take-away version, partners send each other notes that will be read and responded to over intervening hours or days, following an agreed-upon schedule. That's how Jintana and Daniel's conversation happened, as part of an ongoing reading workshop structure where students typically have a regular dialogue journal buddy and write to each other once a week. These take-away conversations offer the chance for writers to take a little longer and be more reflective, and they often lead to deeper sharing between kids. Nancie Atwell has pioneered this model, using what she calls *literature letters,* in her wonderful book *In the Middle* (1998).

Written conversation can be adapted to any subject, and it provides a quiet but energizing way to help students move into, through, and beyond any content, issue, text, or event. This is also a recurrent activity: once students have internalized a few simple rules and procedures, they can dialogue over and over—new content always makes the experience fresh.

What Can Go Wrong?

Written conversation, being a pretty natural human endeavor, tends to work pretty well. As in any pairs activity, you may find a few partners who don't get along and you'll have to make those routine interpersonal adjustments. And don't make trouble for yourself by trying to read all of the kids' conversations. You have to trust the writing-to-learn process; unguided practice works in all areas of life, including school.

Variations

The big variation in written conversation is joining in yourself. It is excellent modeling for you to take a student partner and join in on those short, live, in-class written conversations, just like everyone else. Then you can share your real, on-the-fly thinking and provide kids with yet another demonstration (they can never get too many) of how a proficient thinker operates. Bonus: as you work your way from kid to kid, over a period of weeks, you are also making a nice little personal connection with each one.

Then there's the idea of entering into long-term, take-away kinds of correspondence with students, either one kid at a time or with whole classes at once. Indeed, that's the very essence of Nancie Atwell's reading workshop model, alluded to earlier. "Whoa," we can hear you thinking, "there's a pretty big potential workload there." True dat, as the kids say. Later in this chapter (pp. 106–111) we talk at length about teacher-student correspondence, which we do strongly recommend, but with controls and cautions. But for now, let us just encourage you to join in on as many written conversations as you can without swamping yourself with too much incoming mail. You need to be able to respond with a free, generous, and open spirit, and no teacher with a stack of 150 dialogue journals to answer on a Sunday evening is likely to display this beneficent outlook.

In Houston, Texas, Sheila Newell's middle school kids have written conversations about poems, short stories, and brief news articles in a truly hands-on way. After picking a great short text, she blows it up to the maximum possible size that fits on an 8½-by-11-inch piece of paper (using bigger fonts on the computer or the "enlarge" feature on the school copier). Then she glues a copy in the center of a piece of chart paper, creating a piece of text with huge margins. She makes one for each group of four students, pushes four desks together into a "table," and lays one big text on top of each.

Then the kids sit down and start reading the text, usually picking one student to read it aloud. Next, each using a different-color pen, the kids begin a ten-minute written conversation directly in the margins of that great big page. (See Figure 4–1.) They can make comments, connect to particular phrases, draw arrows, speculate. As more entries go down on the page, students may start reading each other's comments and then agreeing, disagreeing, clarifying, and answering each other's written thoughts. When the teacher comes by, she hovers over the text, reading all the comments and uses her own different-color marker (purple, in Sheila's room) to write down a question that will spur kids to further discussion. Then she leaves to visit another group.

Sheila and her kids call this activity *collaborative annotation;* across the country others call it *text on text*. Whatever the name, we love the idea of kids diving right into the surface of some vital words, digging out meaning, making connections, and talking with each other (in writing) along the journey. The text, of course, is key to the success

Figure 4–1 *Students join in collaborative annotation in Sheila Newell's class.*

of this activity. You need something short, complex, and central to the subject field. In a California social studies class, we saw a smashing version of collaborative annotation done with the Pledge of Allegiance. Students were stunned to see what they had actually been mouthing for a decade, and within minutes they were debating the meanings of *liberty, allegiance,* and *republic.*

Write-Around

What It Is

The write-around is one of the most powerful of all writing-to-learn activities, and it has an equally lively cousin called *silent discussion* that we'll introduce in the "Variations" section. Once you try them, these structures will probably replace some of the whole-class discussions now happening in your classroom, because they are more efficient and powerful.

In a write-around, a group of three to five students (four works especially well) write short notes to each other about a rich, complex topic assigned by the teacher. They jot comments, pass their papers, read what the previous student(s) have written, and add their own remarks, basically creating a string of conversation as the pages circulate around the table. Each student starts a letter, so at all times everyone is writing; there is no off-task time in a write-around.

Examples

SOCIAL
STUDIES

LANGUAGE
ARTS

In Nancy's American Studies class, the kids are studying the McCarthy era, the communist scare, and blacklisting. As part of the unit, she and team partner Kate Schwartz have shown the 1999 Woody Allen film *The Front,* which inserts a fictional character into a re-creation of the blacklisting hearings. Now it is time for a discussion of the movie and its big historical themes. Nancy and Joe want high engagement and accountability, so instead of a whole-class out-loud discussion of predictably mild impact, they elect to put kids into write-around groups.

After about about ten minutes of quiet writing, the kids have created papers like this:

FW: I never knew what blacklisting was until now and I think it's terrible. I also don't see how the jury can ask Woody Allen questions like that and expect to get a straight answer. He can't and I know I would never rat out my friends and neither would he. Also why would it matter if he knew Hecky Brown? He's already dead so what good would it be to them to know? I thought it was interesting that Woody Allen just went off at the jury at the end. It was very brave of him!

BC: Seeing he was being questioned by the jury when he didn't even do anything wrong, then I don't think he should have to answer the questions. I think he did the right thing in the end. This whole thing reminds me of when a number of baseball players were chosen to speak to congress about steroids. It is basically the same thing. They were asked to give up names of their friends.

DW: Hecky was just another communist and they wanted to see if Woody knew him. I think that he just should have pled the 5th then he wouldn't have gotten into trouble. I remember the steroid case, and Mark McGuire answered just like Woody, saying "The past is the past and I'm here for the future." Not lying, but not denying either.

BC: Yes, but like Woody Allen, McGuire was accused of everything just by saying "The past is the past." And not giving straight answers to the jury. But going back to the Hecky topic, even though he is dead, if Woody was friends with him that means that he associated with communists. Now, in turn, he is labeled a communist.

FW: It makes me mad people would think this way. Just because you talk to someone doesn't mean you believe the same thing. If I talk to someone who is atheist doesn't mean I don't believe in God! See how ridiculous this all is! Why don't people realize this?

Keep in mind, in this three-member group there are two more papers like this one, each with different conversations about the topic.

This interchange shows just what we are looking for in any thoughtful discussion, oral or written. The kids are listening to each other, commenting and building upon each other's ideas. The conversation both deepens and widens as it goes on, making good connections to other times and places. Kids police the loose ends, going back to finish unanswered questions. And there's energy here, plenty of it. So when Nancy later calls the write-around groups back together, she isn't too surprised to find that people have tons to talk about. The ensuing discussion is half as long and ten times as valuable as the usual version.

Getting Started

The format is pretty evident: the kids sign in at the left margin with their name or initials, and each one starts writing an initial comment on the chosen topic until the teacher says "Pass!" Then papers rotate (in the same direction each time), kids read the entries on the page, and then write comments until the teacher calls "Pass!" again. And so on. In this particular class session, Nancy allowed lots of time for silent discussion—going from two to four minutes per turn, as the texts got longer and kids had more to read before writing their next comment.

But silent discussions can also be very short. Deb Evans' math class in Wolcottville, Indiana, reviews what has been taught in class using write-arounds with a half

MATH

minute per turn, just enough time for jotting a sentence or two before passing. In the following exchange, a little dispute arose between Christine and Mike about the definition of an *open figure.*

Christine: I learned that if it is open, then it is not regular.

Blaike: I learned that too and if it has sides that are not equal then it is irregular.

Mike: I don't remember learning that, Christine. I remember learning that if a side is open, it's an open figure. Remember? The dog could get out.

Christine: Well you must of herd rong Mike.

This slightly contentious exchange actually shows one of the useful features of write-arounds: kids can challenge and correct each other's misconceptions. Deb reports that Mike stood his ground on the definition of open figures and that group morale was quickly restored.

In both examples, we hope it's clear how much these students will have to discuss when they shift from writing to an out-loud discussion in their groups. And then everyone can join in a productive whole-class discussion, because every single student in the room has already been writing and talking about the topic for five or fifteen minutes. Talk about time well invested.

Play by Play

We've made these instructions very schematic because there are a lot of steps (though each one is simple) to follow. You will have to identify the topic that the write-around will address. Just make sure it is something complex, where interpretation is needed, where plenty of questions will pop up, and where reasonable people can disagree. You might choose to make the actual student instructions in the following plan into transparencies to use with the activity the first few times.

Instructions for a Write-Around

➣ Form a group of four, pull your seats together, and introduce yourselves or discuss the assigned warm-up question. *Threes or fives are OK, but push for as many groups of four as you can get. Yes, your kids already know each other, but we always believe in quick warm-ups, even with groups that have been together for a while. Learn more about this in Nancy's book* Reading & Writing Together *(2002).*

➣ Each person please get a large blank piece of paper ready to use. Put your initials in the upper left-hand margin.

☞ As we work, please follow these two rules:

1. Use all the time for writing.

2. Don't talk when passing.
   You will probably need to reiterate these rules as you go along, especially with students who are new to write arounds.

☞ Ready? OK. Write for one minute. Write your thoughts, reactions, questions, or feelings about our topic, _____. *Fill in the blank. Keep time not by exact minutes and seconds, but by walking around and watching kids write. When most students have filled a quarter of a page, it is time to pass.*

☞ Pass your papers. Decide which way the papers are going to go and stick to it. *Here you should provide the instructions by saying:* Now read the entry on the page, and just beneath it, write for one minute. You can tell your reaction, make a comment, ask questions, share a connection you've made, agree or disagree, or raise a whole new idea. Just keep the conversation going! *Then walk the room, looking over shoulders to get the timing right.*

☞ Pass again, please. *Reiterate the instructions if needed, especially about no talking while passing:* Remember, we are having a **silent** discussion here!

Repeat and continue. Four writing times, total, if that's the number of kids in your groups. If there are mixed group sizes, no problem; the threes and the fives will still do four trades. Important: You need to allow a little more time with each entry because kids will have more to read with each successive exchange. Again, don't time this activity by actual minutes, but by watching how kids are coming and calling "Pass" only when most people have written at least a few lines.

☞ Now pass one last time, giving it back to the person who started the writing on this page. Read the whole thing over and see the conversation that **you** started. You won't write an answer this time.

☞ *As soon as kids are done reading and start talking—and they will—say:* OK. Please feel free to continue the conversation out loud for a few minutes. Use your writings however they help you.

☞ *Option: At this point, you can announce a more focused prompt ("Do you think that blacklisting could ever happen again in America? Why or why not?") and send kids back into their now warmed-up groups to discuss it. Or you can shift directly to whole-class discussion.*

☞ Let's gather as a whole class and see where this quiet conversation took us. Will each group please share one highlight, one thread of their discussion? Something you spent time on, something that sparked lively debate, maybe something you argued about or laughed about. Who'd like to share? *Now here comes the beauty part: there will be plenty of volunteers.*

Don't forget that you now have two things to discuss—the topic you've just dug into and the process the kids have just used. It is important to reflect upon the activity itself, because you want this write-around tool to enter your kids' thinking repertoires for repeated use.

☞ Let's discuss this process. What worked for you and what made it hard? How could we make it better next time?

What Can Go Wrong?

This is a pretty sturdy and fast-paced strategy. As long as every kid has shared the experience to be discussed (heard the lecture, read the article, watched the film), it tends to work very well. Obviously it is vital that the topic be interesting, multifaceted, and debatable—including something that reasonable people can disagree about, probe, and chew on. $E = mc^2$ doesn't make a good write-around topic, but the book of the same name by renowned science writer David Bodanis (2004) surely does.

If you apply write-arounds to work that has been done outside of class, then you'll probably have a few unprepared students, who can be handled in a couple of ways.

1. Hold them out of the write-around so they can catch up on the work and no group will be saddled with a blank writer taking turns at their table.

2. Let unprepared students participate in the write-around by sharing whatever they do know for their first entry and then writing insightful and intelligent questions about other students' entries as they receive them.

Worried about kids with heinous penmanship? This is a case where natural peer pressure may work better than any teacher exhortations. In one Ohio classroom we saw a write-around partner toss another kid's scribbled paper across the table, saying, "Brian, how are we supposed to read this crap?" Ouch! But of course, you should try to head off such exchanges by warning about legibility issues from the start, encouraging kids to print if that works better.

Write-arounds are timed and pressured, in a way that's usually pretty fun. However, if you are a student who writes (or thinks) a little slowly, and you're sitting between a bunch of voluble, fluent writers, it can make you feel like a doofus. Some teachers do a little subtle grouping for write-arounds, arranging kids by writing fluency so everyone's about on a par. Still, we often feel that heterogeneous groups are fine. So what if I write eleven lines and you write two? You may have a much more important and discussion-worthy topic than me, and we each worked for the full minute before the teacher hollered, "Pass!"

We glanced over the issue of group sizes earlier. We realize that by suggesting groups of four, we make it harder for you. Threes would be so much more convenient and maybe quicker. But that one extra viewpoint, that fourth voice, brings a richness that we have come to value. But your chances of getting classes that are groupable by four are only 25 percent (somebody check our math on that). Of course if you offer to put yourself in a group to make a fourth—something we highly recommend, especially for groups that need a little modeling or nudging—you can raise the odds to fifty-fifty (something really weird about that math). Just one warning: It is really hard to both participate in and conduct a write-around. You'll probably get sucked into the writing and lose track of time. So don't try that until you are a true silent-discussion veteran. Anyhow, threes work just fine and are easier to form. And we happily live with mixed-size groups.

Variations

You can have a silent discussion on just about anything that can be talked about out loud. Jan Booth's middle school students in Elgin, Illinois, receive copies of *Science World* magazine every month. Jan thought that adding an ongoing written conversation would enhance their enjoyment and understanding of the magazine's somewhat scattershot contents. Here is part of Katie Cai and Sara Kish's twenty-seven-entry conversation about one monthly issue.

SCIENCE

KC: Did you read the passage about the giant squid? I thought that it looked quite gross. Especially the tentacles.

SK: Which passage? The one with the tank on the floor or its tentacle?

KC: The passage when it was talking about its suckers. Eww.

SK: OMG! That was so gross and it looked so slimy. . . . I think that drug overdose article is kinda scary ☹

KC: Yeah, it sort of reminded me about D.A.R.E. Why would anyone want to take drugs that they know can hurt them?

SK: I think that's the problem. Teens don't know that it can hurt them. I thought it was interesting that Saturn's ring raps around it many times.

KC: What do you think will happen when it winds tighter and tighter around Saturn? I think that the rocks might settle on the planet or something.

SK: I agree with you. . .

KC: Well, I have enjoyed talking—whoops—writing to you Sarah. I think we should do it more often ☺

Our friend Jeff Wilhelm has a great variation on write-arounds called *silent discussion* (Wilhelm 2001) that does not require the small groups. After reading a piece of subject-matter text, or hearing a lecture, or sharing an experience, each student jots down two questions she has. These must be "big fat questions" that invite interpretation, discussion, and even argument, not closed-ended, factual recall items. Then students pass their papers in some direction—left, right, to the kid behind them. The receiving student must pick one question and write a comment or answer to it and then write down a third question, either a brand-new one on the topic or a follow-up to one of the two originals. Then kids pass papers again, in the same direction. The receivers read through all questions and answers so far and pick one unanswered question to respond to. Then they add yet another new question, and papers pass again. This can go on for three to five passes before the class shifts into an out-loud conversation that's bound to be lively—and informed.

Carousel Brainstorming

What It Is

While traditional brainstorming focuses on jotting responses on a single topic, carousel brainstorming enables students to simultaneously share ideas and respond in writing to three or four different prompts. Use separate sheets of chart paper for each prompt and give each group of three to five students a different-color marker. Groups visit a station, discuss the topic written at the top of the sheet of chart paper, and add their own contributions, which are identified by the color of their marker. Then they move on to the next station, focusing on a new topic.

When to Use It and Why

Carousel brainstorming works best for introducing a new topic or actively involving students in review. Because of its out-of-your-seat nature and dependence on good student collaboration, this activity may work better a bit later in the year, once the students have developed good working relationships with one another.

Play by Play

Getting Started

Depending on whether this is an introductory or review activity, design three or four questions, headings, or statements that have the potential for eliciting multiple responses. Write each topic on a separate sheet of chart paper. Then either tape each sheet to a different wall area of the room or spread them out on the desks or the floor. The idea is to get some work space between the groups. Next form groups of three to five, and give each group a different-color marker. Send the groups off to the various charts with these instructions: "When you get to the chart, you'll have a couple of minutes to discuss the topic and brainstorm ideas. Remember that brainstorming means thinking quickly and in quantity. Write down all of the group's responses on the chart with your marker. Do not move to a new chart until I tell you."

When the two minutes are up, call time. Tell the groups to move clockwise to the next chart but wait for instructions. Once everyone is situated, say, "As you progress to each chart, your group's job is going to become progressively harder. First you need to read all of the other groups' ideas, and then you have to brainstorm new ideas to add. Don't repeat what another group has already written. Be sure to really think and talk about the previous responses because that is what will jog your minds and help you add to the ever growing lists. Also, make sure that you use a new recorder for each station. Though your marker color identifies your group, I should see your color in a different handwriting on each chart."

Working the Room

As you already know, the potential for mischief increases when groups spread out and roam the room, so keeping an eye out is important. On the other hand, this is a fast-paced activity without much downtime. Plus, you'll be watching the clock so you can give more or less time as needed. Typically, by the time each group is on the very last chart, they're having a much harder time coming up with new additions since so much has already been written. At that point you'll either want to cut the time short or give the groups some hints that might send them down some different avenues of thinking.

Putting the Writing to Work

Once groups have returned to their original chart, there are several different ways to make use of all this writing.

- Have each group reread all of the comments from its "home" chart and then report out to the class. Their brief summary should include how the ideas evolved from their initial thoughts (remember they were the first ones to write on that topic) and which ideas they think are the most important or have the greatest potential.

- Engage in a "gallery walk," with each group moving through the stations a second time in order to read all of the responses to each prompt. During the walk, individuals can take notes on what they think are the three most important ideas listed on each chart. Afterward, have a short large-group discussion focusing on the selected highlights as well as what questions related to the topics have yet to be answered.

- Have a *silent* gallery walk. Groups move through the stations again, reading but not talking. Then they return to their seats, spend a few minutes on a nonstop write (see page 92) in response to what they've read, and finish up with a small-group or large-group share.

- After the gallery walk or group presentations, have groups choose one of the topics on which to become experts. The first list that follows shows what three groups in a sophomore world cultures class were able to brainstorm about Afghanistan, on one particular chart. The second list shows the final thinking by a second group after reading a collection of nonfiction articles as well as the books *The Breadwinner* and *Parvana's Journey,* both of which take place in

Afghanistan. Expert groups can present their information to the class as well as compare their information with the initial brainstorming.

Afghanistan (initial brainstorm of three groups)

- Osama bin Laden
- sandy
- at war with United States
- lots of mountains
- hot weather
- camels
- had communism
- oil
- women wear cloth around their heads

Afghanistan (further brainstorming after completion of reading)

- Taliban took over country but doesn't run it anymore.
- Life is very hard for women. Must wear burqas. Cannot work. Women expected to get married at a young age. Cannot go out in public without a man.
- Lots of landmines. At least 250,000 are victims of landmines. Many disabilities/injuries/deaths related to the landmines.
- Landmine victims are not accepted in society and cannot find work.
- Poverty stricken country. High rate of unemployment.
- 40,000 children work on Kabul streets to help support their families.
- Nearly 80 % of the country's women and girls are still illiterate.
- Heroin production is booming.
- No plumbing. People have to fetch water and boil it before drinking.
- Under the Taliban men were required to grow beards.
- A lot of refugee camps.

Though the latter was just a quick ten-minute summary brainstorm after the group had done its research, the differences in the two charts are striking. Whereas in the first chart students were guessing somewhat blindly, the second chart shows some real authority and detail in the information. Plus, the second chart shows that students were starting to understand the daily hardships many people in Afghanistan face.

Textbook Connections

Carousel brainstorming offers tremendous textbook connections. The topics or questions on the charts can be taken from key headings in the text, important vocabulary words, or the better problem-solving or high-order thinking questions at the end of textbook sections or chapters.

What Can Go Wrong?

Except for the intoxication of freedom that might ensue once students are released from their seats, this is an activity that usually works pretty smoothly. As mentioned earlier, the biggest problem arises toward the end of the brainstorming when everything has already been said. In that case, just cut the time short and move on to the next step, or give students some extra prompts or information that will inspire fresh thinking. Clearly, from our example you can see that the extent of students' thinking depends on the amount of knowledge they have acquired.

Variations

This activity can be adjusted for class size. For example, if you have a class of thirty and decide to use six groups of five, you have two choices.

- You can have six different stations. The advantage is that with more stations there will be more reading and more writing, thanks to more prompts. The disadvantage is that it's going to take more time to move the groups through all six charts.

- If you are looking for a shorter activity, use only three prompts but put them on six charts. That way each group moves to only three stations. Initially keep the identical prompts far apart so that all groups have the chance for original thinking. However, move the charts closer together for easier comparison in the gallery walk phase.

Double-Entry Journal

What It Is

Have you ever faced a big life decision—whether to take a new job, move to another state, go back to graduate school—and used a plus-and-minus or pro-and-con list to help you decide? If so, you're already a veteran of double-entry journals. Hey, we even know a woman who uses these handy little tools to compare two guys she's dating.

When to Use It and Why

Any time you have kids divide a page in half hotdog style (vertically), you are setting up a potential double-entry journal. Often we use double-entry journals as a form of note taking; this version is sometimes called *Cornell notes*. This structure enables students to do two kinds of thinking by recording ideas side by side in two columns on their paper. In the left-hand column go notes that outline information as students read, listen to a lecture, or otherwise take in information. The right-hand column is used to respond to or reflect on the information in some way. Though the writing can be done in words, phrases, sentences, and paragraphs (what we think of when we hear the word *journal*), notes, drawings, and symbols are equally useful, depending on the goals of the assignment.

Double-entry journals are very flexible. Within a unit, double-entry journals can be used to deepen text understanding, show the thinking behind problem solving, or compare ideas, information, characters, and so on. Here are some examples of possible column headings, but once you work with this strategy, you will think of many others.

COLUMN 1	COLUMN 2
Computations	Explanation of Thinking for Each Step
Problem	Solution
Reasons For	Reasons Against
Opinion	Proof
Quote from Text	Explanation of Importance
Quote from Text	Personal Connections
Quote from Text	Relations to Previous Unit
Quote from Text	Discussion Questions
Agreements	Disagreements
Notes	Interpretations
Observations	Inferences
Advantages	Disadvantages
Words	Images
Facts	Feelings

For example, before reading *The Great Gatsby* in American literature, students watched a film adaptation of an F. Scott Fitzgerald short story. Before viewing, students developed a list of what they thought they knew about the 1920s. Afterward, they revised the list, adding new information, starring information that was confirmed, and crossing out items that were clearly erroneous. All of these notes stayed in the left-hand column. Several weeks later after finishing *Gatsby,* students revisited the early brainstorm, examining how those items reflected certain values of that era.

1920s—THE GREAT GATSBY

INFORMATION

Great Depression
Orphanages—people gave up kids they couldn't afford
Prohibition*
Organized crime
Charleston—popular dance*
Low wages
Fancy clothes—no casual ware*
Flappers—clothing style for women*
After World War I*
Women fighting for voting rights
Some people were very rich (new)
Transportation: cars and horses (new)
Local telephone service—no long distance (new)
Telegrams (new)
Spouses/partners deceived each other, cheating (new)

VALUES

Even though liquor was illegal, people broke the law and drank
Being up on popular culture and fashion was important
People were impressed by wealth
Women were trying to push the envelope—flapper fashions, voting rights
Most women did not work—expected to get married and be taken care of by husband
Cars were a status symbol
Wealth enabled some people to get away with more
Cheating on spouses was selfish

Play by Play

Getting Started

Decide on your headings, when students will complete this activity, and how you will follow up on the journaling. These notes can be homework, in-class work, part of a large-group discussion, or some other combination. Next, demonstrate the process. Have the students fold their papers in half (remember: hotdog) and label the columns. Model part of the note taking together so that students understand what kind of thinking goes in each column. Finally, tell students the ultimate purpose of this assignment. Will it be the basis for tomorrow's discussion, evidence of completing the reading, or something else? Once students understand the process and expectations, they can continue individually.

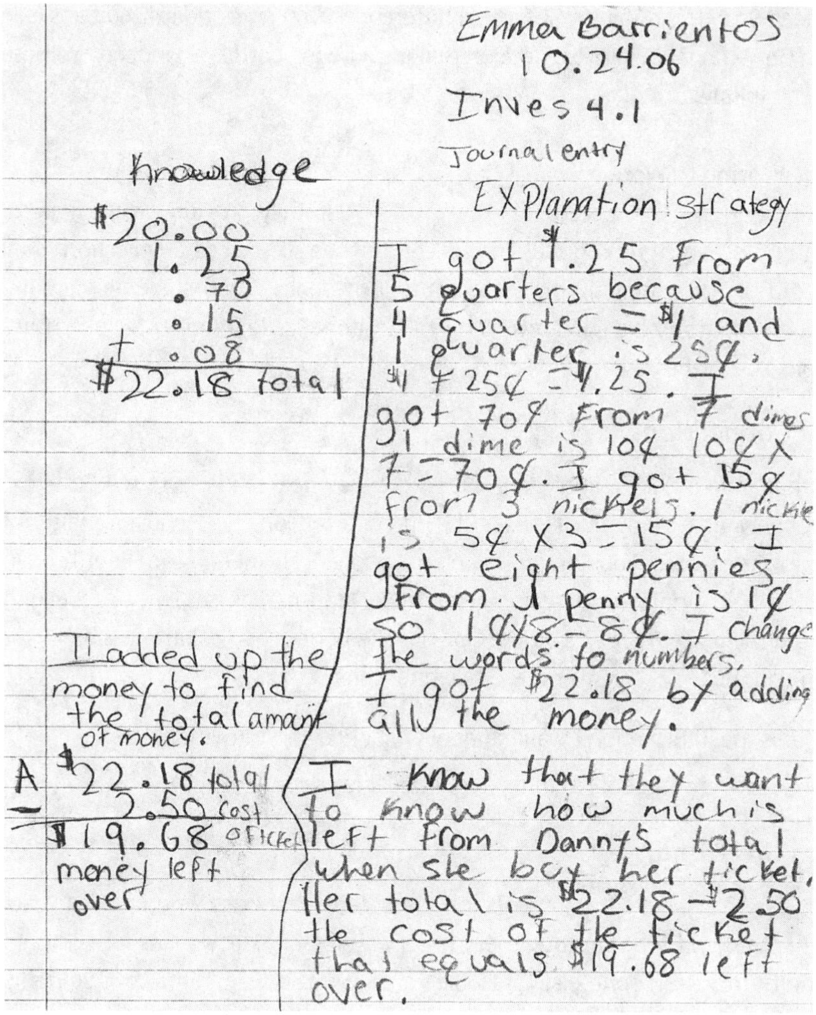

Emma Barrientos
10.24.06
Inves 4.1
Journal entry

Knowledge

$20.00
1.25
.70
.15
+ .08
$22.18 total

I added up the money to find the total amount of money.

A $22.18 total
− 2.50 cost
$19.68 of ticket money left over

EXPlanation strategy

I got $1.25 from 5 quarters because 4 quarter = $1 and 1 quarter is 25¢. $1 + 25¢ = $1.25. I got 70¢ from 7 dimes 1 dime is 10¢ 10¢ X 7 = 70¢. I got 15¢ from 3 nickels. 1 nickle is 5¢ X 3 = 15¢. I got eight pennies from. 1 penny is 1¢ so 1¢ X 8 = 8¢. I change the words to numbers. I got $22.18 by adding all the money.

I know that they want to know how much is left from Danny's total when she buy her ticket. Her total is $22.18 − $2.50 the cost of the ticket that equals $19.68 left over.

Figure 4–2 *One student's math journal*

Working the Room

Of course, if students are working in class, keep an eye out for confusion. The bigger part of monitoring, though, is when students begin to share their notes. Are their conversations quick and superficial, or are the kids moving beyond their initial notes, coming up with new ideas and returning to the text for clarification? If you aren't seeing enough of these deeper levels of thinking, then try doing a brief minilesson to model the kind of thinking you want to encourage. Worried about the time this will take? Remember, when you use this strategy, you are truly teaching your subject, and the kids' deeper understanding will make a difference, even on standardized tests (see "What Can Go Wrong?" below for more on making sure the entries do indeed promote higher-level thinking).

Putting the Writing to Work

Double-entry journals are most useful in two ways. First, they provide a starting point for small-group or large-group discussion. Second, when viewed as a collection, they offer a record of one's thinking throughout a unit or book. When students view the journals together, it can be a good review for the test or excellent fodder for determining the topic of a final essay.

Textbook Connections

The great thing about double-entry journals is that they help students to read the text more thoroughly. Answering questions at the end of a section is often just a matter of skimming for key words. Looking for important quotes can mean searching through headings and bold print, but explaining one's thinking makes students go beyond copying from the text. In order to come up with the perfect two-column headings for notes from your textbook, answer these two questions:

≈ What is the information I want students to notice and remember?

≈ How do I want students to think about this information?

What Can Go Wrong?

First, if you assign double-entry journals (or any other out-of-class writing-to-learn activity, for that matter) for homework, there will always be one or two kids who'll try to copy the notes from someone else. This illicit shortcut can be minimized if students are clear on how the notes will be used the following day. If you're just going to check that they've done the work, that makes cheating more likely. If they are going to have to discuss, explain, and do further writing on the information in their notes, it's far more likely they will take the time to really do the assignment.

Second, it will probably take repeated modeling and follow-up to get the kids to make their thoughts detailed and specific. Many students will have no trouble copying a quote from the text, but then in the "What You Thought" column they'll write a quick cryptic response like "Wow" or "That's surprising." Students need to learn to expand and explain the thinking behind the "Wow." The more opportunities the students get to talk in depth about their thinking, the faster this transition will happen.

Another way students will try to shorten their work time is by grouping all of their reading responses within the first few pages of the assignment. Not that clever, really.

So you may need to dictate that responses need to be drawn from throughout the reading. And then, to make expectations even clearer, give the kids a minimum number of entries needed—perhaps for the minimum possible grade? Your call!

Finally, the value of these notes is often cumulative, so be sure to devise a system for students to organize them. They might be contained in the learning log we describe at the end of Chapter 3 (pages 65–66).

Variations

If your students take notes on a regular basis, have them place their two columns of notes only on the right-hand pages of their spiral or composition book. Then, before a test, have students read through their notes, using the blank pages on the left-hand side as a third column to jot down questions, ideas for remembering the information, and other thoughts pertaining to the material.

Though quite useful when students are in the midst of content study, double-entry journals can also be combined with an initial brainstorming activity. For example, when students reached the point in *To Kill a Mockingbird* when Tom Robinson is killed trying to escape from prison, they could brainstorm all of the possible solutions Tom could have tried in addition to trying to escape. Later, after reading about Jim Crow laws and watching a film about the trial of the men who murdered Emmett Till, students could return to their lists and predict the likely outcomes of the solutions they proposed.

POSSIBLE SOLUTIONS	OUTCOMES
Wait for Atticus' appeal	Unlikely that appellate court will be any more sympathetic than Maycomb jury.
Get a new defense lawyer	Unlikely that any other lawyer would ever take this case since Tom is accused of raping a white woman. Plus, Tom has no money to pay for a lawyer.
Write letters to reporters about wrongful conviction	Letters will be ignored.
Write to governor for a pardon	It would be political suicide for the governor to pardon a black man accused of raping a white woman. Plus, blacks are treated as second-class citizens.
Complete sentence and return to family	Strong likelihood of being lynched if Tom returned to the community.

POSSIBLE SOLUTIONS, *cont.*	OUTCOMES , *cont.*
Escape from prison	Mistreatment in prison a strong possibility; Tom saw no other solutions than escape or death in trying.

Example

Tired of the kids trying to catch a quick forty winks when you roll the videotape or DVD? Two-column notes are an excellent way to keep them awake and focused while also providing nutrient-rich fodder for postfilm discussion. The two-column notes in Figure 4–3 were used in an American history class as students viewed the film *The Atomic Café,* part of a study of the cold war.

The Atomic Café   Name Nick Nevins   Date _____ Hour ____

DIRECTIONS: This movie is a collection of archived imagery compiled from film shorts, many originally produced by the United States either for military training or to inform the civilian population. Most of these films were made in the early to mid 1950's. This film has very little narration; therefore, you need to pay close attention to the visuals. *As you watch, take notes on what you see that stuns or surprises you. After viewing for the day is complete, go back and explain what you were thinking. Why did these visuals stand out to you? How does what you've seen connect with the Cold War information we've read and discussed?*

Stunning/Surprising Visuals Or Ideas	Response To Visual: 1 This makes me think about… 2 This stands out to me because… 3 This makes me wonder… 4 This connects with the Cold War…
"Beautiful" explosion	2. Its not beautiful, its a weapon of mass destruction
"Harmless" radiation	1. if the US would care about troops that were exposed to radiation
Bad Acting	3. if I could see that there is bad acting in this film how could others seeing this take it seriously
Duck & Cover	2. ~~because~~ it seems so cheezy
Fall out shelters	4. because many people were so frantic about it that they built Fall Out Shelt
Protection + Tranquilizers in shelter	1. this movie is, its so non-realistic

Figure 4–3 *Nick's two-column notes on The Atomic Café*

Nonstop Write

What It Is

A nonstop write is a timed writing, usually between three and five minutes, in which students are asked to respond to a prompt. This might be a specific content-related prompt: "Describe the cycle of photosynthesis as if you were a plant." Or the prompt might be something much more open-ended: "What were your reactions to the film? What did it make you think about?" In either case, students respond in sentences and paragraphs, writing quickly and continuously, focusing primarily on presenting ideas rather than stopping to ponder the spelling of a puzzling word. As with brainstorming, the goal of a nonstop write is to get lots of thoughts down in the given time. Spelling, punctuation, and other conventions are de-emphasized during nonstop writes.

When to Use It and Why

Nonstops are very versatile and can be used throughout the study of any content. Students can use their writing to explore ideas about a subject before studying it, or they can read some text and then respond to the information. In addition, students can use nonstop writes in order to trace changes in their thinking about a subject and recognize the depth of their learning.

Play by Play

Getting Started

In the beginning, students might have difficulty sustaining their writing over several minutes, so it's better to start with only one or two minutes and then work up to five to seven. Also, at first some students will have difficulty responding quickly in writing. They'll run up against the wall, not being able to think of anything to write about or running out of ideas before the time is up. After explaining the writing prompt and the need to keep writing until time is called, you can alleviate writer's block by giving partners a minute or two to talk and brainstorm about the topic. Follow this with a quick class brainstorming list written on a chart or overhead. Before having the kids write, let them know how their papers will be used. Will you be collecting them to read? Will they be reading them aloud to their partners? Will their small group be pooling the important points from their individual papers into a final share? Once students are clear on the concept, call for silent work time while students get down to business.

Working the Room

As students write, you need to watch for one main problem: students who write a couple of sentences and then shut down. This happens for three main reasons:

- ☞ Putting thoughts onto paper quickly is a skill that takes practice.
- ☞ The continuous writing of sentences and paragraphs takes more effort than brainstorming a quick list.
- ☞ Continuing to write for five minutes requires the writer to expand on details or move on to new topics when a previous one is exhausted.

The quickest response to a shutdown is to say, "You have two minutes left and some space left to fill. See if you can add some more examples to an idea you already wrote about or look up at the overhead and start writing on a second topic." As students become more practiced with this writing strategy, they will become more skilled at getting their thoughts down on the page and using the entire time for writing. So it's a good idea to use this strategy frequently for a while, to build up kids' perseverance. Keep in mind that this is good training to help students do well on timed essay tests, too. Consider perusing the language your state or district uses in its writing prompts. Though the retired topics may not fit your content, wording your own prompts similarly to those that students will encounter in high-stakes tests gives them a comfortable familiarity with a prompt's style and inherent requirement for a specific type of response.

☞ Want to Jump Around?

We've just suggested that nonstop writes can be great practice for high-stakes, on-demand writing situations that students now face on college entrance exams and state assessment tests. If you want to learn more about preparing kids for those challenging occasions, jump ahead to pages 253-268, where we devote a whole chapter to helping kids score well on such pressured and important writing.

Putting the Writing to Work

Students will take these timed writings more seriously when they know the task will be used for something other than just five minutes of writing. The next step depends on your goal. Many times we have students write to remember information but also to connect information and concepts to their own personal feelings, ideas, and responses. Therefore, sharing these writings with others is an excellent springboard for discussion. Reading aloud and discussing their writings in pairs is an easy way to share. Putting students into groups of three or four takes a bit more time, but sharing more viewpoints enables the kids to begin to trace common threads of thought within their individual writings as well as recognize divergent viewpoints. In either case, pairs or groups should be responsible for some final reporting out since a little bit of accountability will help keep the discussion content specific.

Like the double-entry journals, nonstop writes have a significant cumulative effect because they offer students the opportunity to examine their own writing and ideas over time (Graves and Kittle 2005). After students are finished writing, have them go back and reread their page, examining their text for specific attributes and marking accordingly:

- Which sentence in your writing really explains what you're writing about? Underline it.

- Which parts give specific examples or details related to the sentence that you underlined? Put brackets around these parts.

- Which sentences don't say much or get off the topic from the sentence that you underlined? Draw thin lines through these.

- Find the three words you like the best—words that sound great aloud or words that really create a picture in your head. Circle them.

Guided rereading helps kids improve their revision skills and recognize the good parts of their writing, attributes we want them to consciously consider when they are writing for audiences beyond themselves. As students expand their collection of nonstops, they will be able to trace specific improvements and mastery.

What Can Go Wrong?

As mentioned earlier, kids who shut down and those who just don't write enough are the two biggest problems with this strategy. Most kids will outgrow these roadblocks as they become more practiced. After two or three of these sustained writings, have the kids reread their entries and do a little self-evaluation. First have the kids complete the following three steps.

1. On a scale of 1 to 5, rate how quickly you get off the mark and start writing.

2. On a scale of 1 to 5, rate how well you keep writing for the entire time.

3. Count the number of words in each entry.

Then say, "From now on, full credit for a nonstop write means writing at least 150 words [this number has worked well for us, but the length of the writing is up to you]. Take a look at your word count. What do you need to start doing differently in order to meet this goal? What do you need help with? Take a minute to jot down your answers." After the writing, discuss solutions to the problems and then end with each student developing a one- or two-point action plan that will result in improved quantity and quality in future efforts.

Example

Before beginning a unit on westward expansion and how it impacted the lives of Native Americans, American history students spent five minutes writing about what came to mind on the topic of Native Americans. Later in the unit, students will return to their initial pieces, examining them for stereotypes and information gaps before writing again on the topic, highlighting their new knowledge. Here is what Christina wrote at the beginning of the unit.

> When I think of Native Americans, I think of tee-pees and headdresses. I think of tee-pees because in almost every movie Native Americans are in you see tee-pees around a fire. I also think of headdresses because again—the movies. Whenever I see a movie with Indians in it, they are wearing headdresses. Native Americans are usually associated with horses; they ride horses everywhere. Also, Native Americans are associated with Pilgrims. I think of the first Thanksgiving—hunting and fishing. If it wasn't for the Native Americans, the Pilgrims would have had a tough time surviving. They probably would have starved and froze. The Natives taught the Pilgrims that when they hunt to use not only the meat but the fur for clothes or housing. The Native Americans helped with many things. They discovered the land, helped the Pilgrims, and still lived in tee-pees around a fire. Native Americans are amazing. They are very resourceful in many ways.

You can easily envision how Christina's initial knowledge about native Americans will be challenged and revised as the unit unfolds.

Reflective Write

What It Is

Philosophers tell us that one of the things that most separates humans from the rest of the animal kingdom is our awareness of ourselves. As educators, a central part of our job is to help young people become more conscious—of what they are learning, how they go about learning it, and what the learning can mean to them. So once an assignment or project is completed, whether it involves writing or not, it's a good idea to ask students to reflect on their learning and on the task itself. The activity involved may be just about anything the teacher has arranged for kids to do: a single in-class discussion, a field trip, a small-group collaborative task, a lab experiment, a newly introduced algebra operation, a big monthlong project. The reflection may be informal, a brief in-class jotting on a note card so students can quickly record thoughts on what they've learned and how they went about learning it. Or it can be a full page that the kids write down as quickly as possible, like the nonstop write described previously.

When to Use It and Why

Obviously, reflection comes at the end of a task—or if it's for midcourse corrections, far enough along that the student can think about where she's headed and how she's doing. Reflective writes serve a number of purposes. While some students approach school as nothing more than a series of work tasks to be done as quickly and painlessly as possible, turned in, and forgotten, reflection invites them to pause and take note of what they've learned and how they went about it. It helps install learning more fully in students' minds, places it in a larger context, and asks them to value it more deeply. Students begin to recognize the strategies they use for learning—particularly if the teacher has talked about these—and to realize their strengths and plan ways to improve in the future.

Reflection in the middle of a longer project can help students self-correct their effort and encourage themselves onward. At midstage it can reveal which students are on track, which need a little help, and whether any are in deep difficulty. Reflective writes give the teacher a great deal of information that often cannot be seen in the final product itself. At the end of the work, a teacher can learn what came easy and what was hard for students, how deeply they understand the concepts that were taught, and how they have connected the learning to their lives.

Student Sample: Reflection on a Family History Project

In Saline, Michigan's middle school, Suzanne Brion's eighth graders engage in an interdisciplinary project connecting family history and twentieth-century formal history, through family interviews and research on "events and people who changed the course of history during the time of our ancestors." Students conclude by writing reflection pieces like this one:

> Throughout this project I have dug deeper into my family roots than ever before, for school and for amusement. I have interviewed family members thoroughly. My parents are sick of me. I've been all over them asking questions—lots of them. Anything I could think of I said; I reeled them off, one after another after another after another. Well, you get the point.
>
> I started with my ancestral interview where we had to interview a grandparent or elder relative and find out how he or she lived their life. I chose my Grandpa Nagle because he was born in a different country and I don't really mind talking extensively with him. So, I reluctantly called him in Florida, and prepared for a boring grandparent story: the ones with the stuff in them like, "When I was your age I *walked* to school . . ." Surprisingly, it wasn't that at all. It was enjoyable talking with him about his can-kicking days in Ireland and his cozy Cork (Ireland) home filled with family singing and bumbling all night. He even made me laugh (really)! All in all, I'm glad I had to, and I think I might do it just for "kicks" once in a while.
>
> The interview *paper* was a different story. No one likes to write papers, but this one didn't seem too bad. Mine was long enough to go into detail, but short enough to keep the interest of the reader.
>
> I have never had in-depth units on researching and writing for research papers, so this year has been an eye-opener with our I-search paper and now the public history paper. I have never been efficient when researching and this time was no different. It was very confusing and I didn't even understand what to research until well into the project. By then, classroom research was out of the question and the homework load grew. But I got my act together and decided on some major twentieth century events. Afterwards, I guess I mustered up a well done paper and hey, I learned some stuff too.
>
> I admit the public to family history connection was easier. A paragraph or two on four different events with some pictures here and there, voila! Plus, presenting has always been a strength of mine.
>
> My favorite part of the whole thing was the interview. It was fun, educational, and I spent some quality time with my Grandpa. I'm glad I did the project, and I can't wait to include it in my ongoing autobiography.

Play by Play

Getting Started

Students who are new to conscious, school-focused reflection are likely to need some direction from the teacher. They need to see what sorts of issues can be addressed. They may not realize that it's worthwhile to look at the steps they took as well as the understandings that emerged, or that by noticing both their strengths and weaknesses, they can figure out how to do better in the future. Looking at a mistake as an opportunity to learn and improve, rather than an embarrassment to be hidden, is something we could all learn to do more gracefully. So it's a good idea for the teacher to describe to students a learning task he has undertaken and then write a reflection spontaneously, projected for the kids to see. Alternatively, Suzanne Brion shows students a variety of reflections from previous years. She includes weak as well as strong ones and shows various formats that students use, as well as issues they cover. Students can then write a brief reflection, themselves, perhaps on a simple, physical task she has them do on the spot. Comparing these together can further help the kids see some of the different ways they can reflect.

Working the Room

It's a good idea to have kids write the reflections right in class—or if time is short, at least get started there. This not only helps make sure the work gets done but also allows you to circulate and take a quick snapshot of whether the students understand the task and are getting into it. If just a couple of kids are struggling, quick individual conferences may get them on track. If most appear confused, it's probably time to pause and review the task, ask students to discuss it as a whole class or in pairs, or do some more modeling.

Putting the Writing to Work

Sharing reflections is especially valuable for reinforcing learning. Insights from some students will help others realize they were thinking the same way—or that they can try something new in the future. After reading over the reflections, you can pick out key ideas that are important for all the kids to hear and copy excerpts for all to read. And when the students keep their work in a folder, they (and you) can periodically review it and write reflections to gain a longer-range view of their efforts. Often, kids don't realize that they really are learning a great deal, and reflecting over time can help them gain confidence and give direction to their school lives.

Textbook Connections

Most teachers would like to see their students make better use of the expensive and weighty tomes they must plow through. Whatever the limits on many textbooks, they are tools that most subject-area classrooms use extensively. So thoughtful teachers often provide guides and activities to help kids navigate them more successfully—showing how to spot key concepts, vocabulary words, definitions, headings that signal new or important shifts in focus, and so on. We can help students learn to use example problems, glossaries, and review questions. But it's not unusual for students (and most of the rest of us, as well) to sometimes tune out and read robotically, realizing at the end of a reading session that they recall nothing from the words they buzzed through. So we can help them to pause, review, question, and digest. Obviously, reflective writes, particularly brief ones after short stints of in-class reading, can make students more conscious of what they've understood or where they were confused, how a particular reading strategy helped, or whether they need to try something else. This is note taking not as a mechanical jotting of information but as a thinking response to ideas.

> ## Want to Jump Around?
>
> Double-entry journals are a great tool for housing the kind of reflection we describe here. Consult pp. 85–91 in this chapter to consider how that strategy and this one can be combined.

What Can Go Wrong?

Students need enough time to think and enough material to wrap their minds around if reflection is to be meaningful. Conversation among peers also helps. So even though time is always tight, be sure to leave enough for reflection to really develop. If you observe that many students are not thinking very deeply, you may need to provide more direction or more modeling, demonstrating the specific kinds of thinking you want kids to try. Scheduling class time to write reflections gives the teacher more opportunities to give guidance. It also helps ensure that parents don't do too much of the work for their kids.

Some students who are really struggling, or perhaps having a difficult time in their home lives, may find it hard to reflect on their work. This is where in-class writing workshop (see Chapter 8), with time for one-on-one conferences, is especially valuable. You may need to take a few minutes to walk a struggling student through some of the thinking about what he *can* do well, or help him focus on just one or two things he might try to do better next time and some specific steps that will help him achieve.

Variations

Short in-class reflections can be as useful as longer think pieces. In this sample from Saline Middle School, student Chandni Patel reflects on an activity in which her math teacher, Heather Meloche, had kids create their own quizzes:

I thought writing this quiz was interesting. After I wrote it, I felt how a teacher feels writing one.

The thing I would change about my quiz would be that I should have made the questions come out as an integer on the answer instead of a decimal. This way it'll be easier for students next time.

Writing this quiz was an awesome experience for me to try. I would like to do more projects like this, and I would also like to help sometime to make questions up for a quiz/test. I am glad I got an opportunity to make a quiz up which seems to me like a real one you would give students.

KWL

What It Is

This elegant and well-known strategy uses brainstorming and listing to drive kids' thinking all the way through a unit. The acronym stands for What do you **k**now? What do you **w**ant to know? and What have you **l**earned? KWL writing includes a series of lists made by individual students, small groups, and the whole class, with the teacher serving as the recorder for the latter. These jottings are used before, during, and after the unit is taught, and they help to surface, steer, and monitor students' learning.

We were actually tempted to leave KWL out of this book, because its use is already so widespread. But we changed our minds—and not just because the developer of KWL, Donna Ogle, is a friend and colleague. When we started asking middle and high school teachers about KWL, we encountered a lot of blank looks. We discovered that although elementary teachers across the country have really taken KWL to heart, its value has not yet been as widely recognized by secondary teachers. If you're among those new to KWL, you have a very practical addition to your teaching repertoire just ahead.

When to Use It and Why

KWL works best when students have a little prior knowledge about a topic. If you think about it, our curricula include many such subjects, like

asteroids	probability	Shakespeare
global warming	graphing	persuasive essays
waves	improvisation	right triangles
Impressionism	parts of a cell	manifest destiny
the Gettysburg Address		

KWL embodies the principle of cognitive science that learners can build new knowledge only upon what they already know, including misconceptions and fragmentary information (Hyde 2006). So, before you launch a unit, you intentionally activate students' prior knowledge, helping them to list and discuss it. Next, kids pose questions about what they want to (or expect to) learn during the unit. After a period of study that may last days or weeks, students use even more listing to review what they have learned. This multistep use of informal writing pulls kids into, through, and beyond the subject matter, as the teacher adds in information and arranges experiences.

Play by Play

Getting Started

Let's say you are about to begin a unit on photosynthesis. Before assigning any reading or presenting any information, you set up a KWL. Have students get out a blank piece of paper and say:

> *Write down whatever you know or think you know about photosynthesis. You've probably heard the word before, maybe even studied it when you were younger. Now just jot down anything that comes to mind—words, phrases, sentences, a list. Go.*

When students have jotted for about one minute, or long enough that each student has at least three entries on the page, call for a whole-group discussion. You serve as the scribe on a flip chart (preferable, for hanging up later) or overhead transparency divided in half vertically, with a big *K* over the left column and a *W* over the right.

Ask volunteers to call out facts or ideas about photosynthesis, and list them under "K" using the kids' own words if possible. It will look something like this.

What We KNOW About Photosynthesis

something to do with plants
green stuff
chlorophyll
makes oxygen
releases carbon dioxide
formula CH something
energy
it's how plants breathe
roots suck up water
how the sun feeds
it's a cycle
like plants eating

What if kids volunteer incorrect ideas? This is the hard part for a dutiful teacher. Right now, you are simply surfacing kids' conceptions and misconceptions; the content of the upcoming unit will remake and correct these. This part is just the warm-up, the activation. But if it feels too weird to put "involves some red stuff" on the "K" photosynthesis list, it's OK for you to put a ? beside the entry. Indeed, if kids dispute or correct each other, a question mark can go next to the contested ideas as well, as you say:

OK, you guys, we have some different ideas about this, and over the next couple of weeks we'll be finding out what the real deal is. So let's just put a question mark here and move on.

You'll see in a minute how quickly these question marks get put to use.

Only ten minutes gone in the period, and it's already time to get kids to turn their prior knowledge into questions about the upcoming photosynthesis unit. Here's what you say:

Now, working in groups of three or four, please make a list of questions you have about photosynthesis as a result of our work so far. Looking at the list we have made, you should be able to think of three or four. And remember, you can always pose questions about the topics we disagreed or wondered about. Go ahead.

Let kids work in their groups for two to four minutes—however long it seems productive.

Now, reconvene the whole group and solicit entries for the "W" column on the flip chart. We often instruct the group:

If somebody mentions a question you are wondering about too, nod your head so we can see that more than one person is interested.

We also try not to censor or edit too much; between the goofball questions there will be plenty of bread-and-butter topics that can frame the photosynthesis unit you're about to teach. The class might settle on something like this:

What We WANT to Know About Photosynthesis

Is photosynthesis a form of eating, for plants?
How does photosynthesis affect people and animals?
Can it happen in the dark?
Is chlorophyll the same stuff they put in gum and mints?
Does photosynthesis give off good or bad gasses?
Could we get electricity from plants?
Does photosynthesis stop in the winter?
Do plants have to be green?
How does water fit in?

See? Most of the questions these kids have raised are perfectly relevant, if not comprehensive—and you see that experiences you've got planned for the next few days will probably work just fine in answering their questions.

With KWL, this will happen most of the time. The structure usually engineers a situation where the kids are asking us questions that we were going to address anyway! But just because the outcome is predictable doesn't mean the process isn't sincere—and powerful. KWL puts kids' existing knowledge into the foreground, makes them active, and engages them in coplanning the unit. The dynamic of this fifteen minutes is *totally* different (and cognitively much more advantageous) than us saying: "Take out your notebook. I'm going to start lecturing about photosynthesis."

Putting the Writing to Work

Now the unit can proceed pretty much as usual—we hope with plenty of other practical writing activities (admit slips, double-entry journals, whatever fits the topic best). You just hang that KW chart on the wall, making a point to return and check off questions as they are answered.

As the unit comes to a close, it is time to make the L list—what we learned. This can be a nice, ceremonial wrap-up to an important unit—and once again, it gets kids thinking about their thinking and running their own brains. Get all the lists and charts up, and go back to the K's and W's, reviewing where you started and what questions were posed. Turn key learnings into statements in the "L" column; often these will derive directly from former W list entries that were crossed off somewhere along the line. Smart teachers finish off this review by making one more list: Now that we have studied photosynthesis, what *new questions* do we have about the process, about plants, or about life processes in general?

What Can Go Wrong?

Well, if you ask adolescents, "What do you want to learn about manifest destiny?" they're going to shout out in unison: "Nothing!" Or at least they'll think it. So if you anticipate that kind of resistance in your group, just swap the language around and say, "What do you predict we will learn in this unit?" This takes a bit of the volunteer spirit out of the transaction, but at least it's not throwing red meat directly to the class cynics.

KWL works well for a broad array of topics, but not every one. We do teach topics in school about which kids really have little prior knowledge, that hit them cold. Quadratic equations, vectors, and other math topics seem to come out of the blue, even though they are usually outgrowths of previous content. So appraise your kids before leaping into a KWL. For those tough topics, it is *our* job to fill in some information first, using the writing activities along the way rather than at the very outset.

Some teachers think KWL can be overdone, that kids get tired of the structure if you use it over and over again. We feel torn about that. Yes, kids (and adults) do crave novelty, and to some extent it is always OK to spice things up with new activities and tools. And yet KWL is so basic and pure we don't think it should ever be treated as a fad. All the structure does is externalize what goes on in the mind of a powerful learner who is encountering a new set of concepts: you connect, you question, you add information, you readjust your thinking, and you set goals for more inquiry. That's a universal process that never gets old!

Variations

At every step of the way, when kids are making a K, a W, or an L list, there are plenty of choices for how to work. In our earlier example, we had kids make K lists individually and then go straight into a whole-class listing. But it's often valuable to put kids into small groups (as we did in the W phase, later) as an intermediate step, telling them to compare their personal notes and come up with five things they agree upon about photosynthesis to be reported to the whole group in three minutes. This tends to root out some of the loonier (but sometimes more amusing) ideas, and it gives kids more active airtime and responsibility along the way. The tradeoff, as always, is that each extra step takes time—but remember our mantra, *going deeper into a smaller number of topics*. The kids will learn photosynthesis better!

There's a nice variation to add after making a W list, which Donna Ogle (Carr and Ogle1987) calls a KWL-plus. Once kids have compiled a list of questions about photosynthesis, they try to figure out where they could look for the answers to the questions they have posed. Of course, everyone will quickly blurt out, "The textbook," and that's an important source. But smart teachers remind kids: "OK, but there are other sources, too. Keep thinking." Here's what one group of Chicago kids came up with:

Where Could We Get Answers About Photosynthesis?

Ask Mr. Griffin.
Look in *Discover* magazine.
Do an experiment.
Ask somebody who has a garden.
Go to the arboretum.
Search the Internet for articles.
Google "photosynthesis."
Read a book about plants (botany).
Interview a farmer.

Teacher-Student Correspondence

What It Is

What would you say if we suggested that you develop an active correspondence with all your students, writing letters back and forth to them all year long? Probably you'd say, "I *knew* these guys were nuts!" Give us a minute.

Many elementary teachers regularly exchange personal notes with their students, sharing news about classroom and family events and chatting about books the children are reading. This simple adult-child correspondence allows the teacher to model good writing, to create a just-right text for each child to read, to see and assess each student's writing skills, and get to know the student personally—an elegantly productive use of a few minutes. And when you teach the same twenty-five little kids all day long, most of whom can write only a few lines, this is a manageable as well as powerful activity.

Very nice, but this doesn't sound possible with our big kids. After all, we see more than a hundred of them for just an hour day, and we have sixteen tons of content to deliver. Well, you haven't met Angela Andrews, a high school science teacher who *does* find the time to have ongoing written dialogues with all her students. You're about to see how she is working smarter and her students are learning better as a result.

On this activity, we'll give you a challenge and a promise: No matter what you teach, you should try writing letters with your students a few times a year, spending just ten to fifteen minutes of class time on each round. The benefits will be higher class morale, deeper understanding of the material, better-targeted instruction, and a more personal, meaningful relationship with your students. Talk about differentiation. This tool helps you know, reach, and teach every kid as an individual. Indeed, we think that written correspondence between kids and teachers may be the most neglected and potentially powerful teaching (and classroom management) strategy of all. There are lots of teaching ideas in this book, and this one may seem the most unlikely. But these letters can change *everything* in your classroom, quickly and deeply. Teachers who have adopted these letters invariably say: "How did I ever teach without them?"

Play by Play

Getting Started

SCIENCE

Angie Andrews teaches chemistry to juniors and seniors at Elmwood Park High School, in an inner-ring suburb of Chicago. Her students are a diverse bunch, as the once-monolithic Italian immigrant community is now being infused with Polish and

Mexican newcomers. Angie's student load is 130 kids per year, much like teachers around the country. But unlike most science teachers, Angie exchanges personal notes with her students about once a month, in an attempt to get to know kids better and to teach them more effectively. Here's how she does it—and why.

"The first time we do this in September, I just give them the first fifteen minutes of class," Angie explains, "and I keep the topic pretty open. I say:"

> Tell me what's going on with you in chemistry class—how are you doing with the ideas, the homework, the tests? What can I do to help you learn this material better? How are your other classes coming? What else are you up to in school this year—any clubs or teams? How about your life outside of school, anything you want to tell me about? Now, please stick to appropriate topics and language. I don't want to hear about your partying on the weekend—I'm not trying to be your buddy here. And if you tell me anything about someone being at risk or in danger, I will contact the appropriate other adults—social worker, counselor, and so on. OK? Take ten minutes.

Angie reports, "The first time we do these dialogues, they always ask me: 'Why are we doing this?' And I say, 'Look, there are twenty-eight of you and one of me, and I've only got eighteen weeks in this semester to get to know you—so I can be a better science teacher for you.'" Angie laughs as she recollects: "Some kids will actually gasp out loud when I say that; they just go, 'Wow.' Sometimes one kid will say something negative, like, 'This is stupid.' But someone always pipes up and says, 'Shut up, she's just trying to help us, you jerk!'"

After the writing time is up, Angie collects the letters and presses on with the chemistry lesson. Later, during a free period, she starts reading them through to see the range of responses. Ian Guerrero wrote:

> So I'm basically going to write you a note. So . . . about Chem II, I'm kinda lost in here. DAMN THESE SMART PEOPLE. Kinda getting lost over this subject. I'm not too sure I want to be a pharmacist now. Bio II was really fun and I enjoyed the subject matter. . . . One of my friends thinks you are hot (except for the pregnancy thing). Kinda weird. As a senior and 1st time running on a team, I want to make a huge impact (in a positive way) in EPHS. I want to be all-conference for track, impossible but a dream I chase. . . .

Molly Loutos gradually honed in on some good teaching advice for Angie.

> I am really glad that I understand most of the things we do in Chemistry. I just don't understand things at first, but once I practice I eventually get it. I think the white boards make it a lot easier for me to do things. For some reason I actually do the problems better when we work on the white boards.

Sean Padilla shared some larger life issues.

Something that has been troubling me lately is time management. It's becoming harder and harder to find time to finish all my obligations between homework, my extra curricular activities, and clubs at school, and working a job on the weekend. Everything always gets done, but the quality of my work has taken a dip down.

Putting the Writing to Work

How does Angie use these dialogues? First of all, she writes a short answer at the bottom or on the back of each student's note and hands the notes back a day or two later. The kids avidly devour her responses, looking for the quick personal connections that she invariably offers.

My sister and I fought like that, but now she is my best friend (after my husband!).

OK, I will try to slow down. I thought that this stuff would bore you all since you've already done it in Chem I. I'm glad to hear you like this class—it is my first time teaching it. ☺

It's nice to have students with such ambition.

I am sorry to hear about your aunt. Take a deep breath and do what you can do with all the effort you have.

Thanks for that great suggestion—remind me to get out the white boards if I forget, OK?

You'll look back at high school and laugh at its simplicity.

Stick shift rules!

Reader, think about how long it would take you to write brief responses like these. Thirty seconds each?

Back in class, Angie will bring up an important chemistry topic that's appeared on several students' notes—like today, when several kids have asked about "sig figs," or significant figures, the policy by which students are required to work out chemical equations to a particular decimal place. "Do we need to go over why this is so important?" Angie asks, and several kids nod. She goes to the board and conducts a quick minilesson: she jots examples on the board, making an analogy to the measurements her carpenter husband makes at work. "He can't just round his measurements off to the nearest inch—or foot," she explains. "The house might fall down."

Benefits of Teacher-Student Dialogue Journals

1. You get to know students.

2. Students get to know you.

3. People who know each other generally like each other.

4. You get a chance to be playful and human, and to be reminded how funny and delightful young people are.

5. Mutual acquaintance creates investment in the working relationship.

6. You hear from shy kids who never speak up.

7. You get diagnostic feedback about the subject matter: what's hard, what needs review or reteaching, what's easy.

8. You get cues for individualizing instruction.

9. You find out about learning styles and how to reach different ones.

10. You get help matching kids in pairs or forming small groups.

11. You hear kids' often astute self-assessments.

12. You can factor personal issues into assignments, schedules, grading.

13. You provide kids with models of competent adult writing.

What Can Go Wrong?

As Angie herself notes, there may be skeptics in the class who don't take this opportunity seriously at first—or ever. As long as they don't disrupt everyone else's writing time, it's their loss. But most scoffers get sucked in when they see the teacher is serious and that the letters get read, answered, somehow used in class.

If time is the big constraint, don't give up on this whole idea. Try doing letters with just one class at a time. Or have just ten kids a week write you letters (that would mean every kid would get two letters a year from you, still a very special occasion). Just set up a schedule that you can live with, so you feel serene and unpressured enough to offer the quick but personal responses Angie has modeled.

Do you believe in the idea but just can't find the time to answer every single kid separately? Instead of skipping the whole activity, have kids write the letters and then skim through them. Write just one whole-class letter in response, copy it, and hand out it to everyone.

Dear 4th Mod History,
Thanks for your inspiring and amusing letters. Based on what Ned, Jane, Jerry, Julie, and Natasha say, we need to go back and look at the Turner Compromise again. On the other

hand, it seems like everyone has a handle on the last unit. . . . Yes, Brad, I do drive a fifteen-year-old pickup truck. I call it Nellybelle and I bought it in college. . . .

Try to work each kid's name into the letter somehow so they all know they have been heard.

Oh, by the way, did we mention that Angie Andrews is a *first-year teacher?* It is so good to not know what you can't do.

Variations

In the fall, Angie keeps the writing prompt pretty open, because her main goal is to get to know young people as learners and as individuals. Later in the year, she sharpens her prompt, focusing more closely on chemistry. Her midsemester dialogue topic has three parts:

1. What connections do you see between chemistry and your own life, now and in the future?

2. What makes chemistry hard?

3. What can I do to make it more understandable?

Angie listens hard to what kids have to say and makes midcourse corrections accordingly.

We are big believers in letter writing for classroom management. When teachers tell us about discipline problems they are having in the classroom, they often mention talking to the kid out in the hall, calling the parents, deducting points, or sending a discipline referral to the dean. How about writing a letter? We've found that a personal note handed to a misbehaver on the way out of class is often more effective than any kind of face-to-face encounter, which usually just triggers kids' need to openly defy authority. Instead:

> *Dear Mark,*
> *Today I noticed that you came to class without your materials and without having done the reading—again. That meant you couldn't contribute to the small-group discussion. Your group needs you to be ready every day; they are losing lots of good ideas every time you're not prepared. Will you address this, please?*
> *Mr. Daniels*

We caution against sending only negative letters, although one-off notes can work in discipline situations. But it's better if they happen as a part of a wider, multipurpose correspondence focused on the content of the course. In Smokey's first class, he tells students that everyone will be getting a variety of notes as the course goes on—they might be newsy, they might have questions, and they might be behavior oriented. That way, the other kids don't taunt recipients of a teacher missive, going, "Oooh, Brenda got a letter!"

Works Cited

Atwell, Nancie. 1998. *In the Middle: New Understandings About Writing, Reading, and Learning.* 2d ed. Portsmouth, NH: Boynton/Cook.

Bodanis, David. 2000. $E = mc^2$: *A Biography of the World's Most Famous Equation.* New York: Berkeley Books.

Carr, E., and Donna Ogle. 1987. "K-W-L-Plus: A Strategy for Comprehension and Summarization. *Journal of Reading,* 626–631.

Graves, Donald H., and Penny Kittle. 2005. *Inside Writing: How to Teach the Details of Craft.* Portsmouth, NH: Heinemann.

Hyde, Arthur. 2006. *Comprehending Math: Adapting Readiang Strategies to Teach Mathematics, K–6.* Portsmouth, NH: Heinemann.

Smith, Roland. 2002. *Zach's Lie.* New York: Scholastic.

Steineke, Nancy. 2002. *Reading & Writing Together: Collaborative Literacy in Action.* Portsmouth, NH: Heinemann.

Wilhelm, Jeffrey. 2001. *Improving Comprehension with Think-Aloud Strategies.* New York: Scholastic.

Public Writing

So far in this book we have mostly talked about short writing activities that focus on thinking, learning, and exploring subject matter—but not on the *product,* the writing itself. Now we switch gears, big time. For the next few chapters, we will be showing you ways to help kids develop papers for your courses that are

- ≈ *substantial* in length, not short
- ≈ *planned,* not spontaneous
- ≈ *authoritative,* not exploratory
- ≈ conforming to *conventions,* not informal
- ≈ directed at an outside *audience,* not written for the writer
- ≈ composed in *successive drafts,* not a single attempt
- ≈ *crafted, copyedited, and correct,* not unedited
- ≈ *ready to be assessed* by their audience

In other words, we are shifting toward intentional, highly polished pieces that can go out into the world, connect with real readers, get some work done, and stand up to scrutiny. For this kind of writing, we expect students to take the time, do the thinking, and invest enough effort that they can say: "This is my best." We're not talking about perfection here—even adult professional writers struggle to get it right—and we naturally adjust our expectations to kids' developmental levels. But in public writing assignments we very explicitly require workmanlike, prideful products.

Like all dichotomies, the one we've been making between writing to learn and public writing actually has wide areas of overlap. There are obviously *short* pieces of writing that are very highly crafted and precisely aimed at an audience (think poetry), and there are long, long pieces of writing to learn, like some people's diary or journal entries. Most importantly, short WTLs often become the seed or kernel of a longer, more polished piece that, after further development, revision, and editing, goes public. But still, the typology is useful and important. It reminds us that not *all* writing needs to be polished, and not *all* writing needs to be graded by a teacher. But it also helps us to explain to kids rationally and even firmly why some other kinds of writing need to be very, very good.

> *In public writing assignments, we explicitly require workmanlike, prideful products.*

Traits of Public Writing

Students need to thoroughly understand what it means to put aside the powerful, personal tools of writing to learn and enter the arena of formal public prose. Now they are putting their words before the public, composing texts to be read by classmates, the teacher, or more distant readers. No matter the age of the writers we work with, we always teach the distinctive features of public writing directly:

Substantial: Selections of public writing tend to be longer and more meaty than a journal entry, an exit slip, or a to-do list. Each subject area has its own subgenres of text, and those typically have standards or expectations for length. Some historical profiles may customarily need ten pages, a lab report may need eight or ten separate paragraphs covering the steps of a procedure, a statistical analysis of stock market trends would have to match the space available in the magazine that is going to publish it, and so forth.

Planned: Public writing is highly intentional, pragmatic, and consciously arranged. Public writers will usually create not just a schedule of their work but also an organizational plan, specifying what topical slots will need to be filled, what sections might be created, and even whether to use, for example, a comparison-contrast model versus a chronological narrative. This is a quite different mindset from the let-it-rip attitude of WTL.

Authoritative: Most public writing is expected to be definite, confident, and assertive. While there is always a place for both-sides-of-the-story pieces, writers are generally expected to know something, to be ready to announce it, lay it out, define the issues, and offer their best interpretation. In other words, public writers are often taking the stance "I've looked into this issue carefully, and here is what you need to know."

Conventional: Public writers can't be idiosyncratic scribblers, writing to teach or amuse themselves. The *audience* is everything. The goal is to reach and teach, inform, or persuade some real readers out there. That means public writers have to adhere (mostly) to the conventions of the genre they are working in. They don't want anything to interfere with their connection to readers, and so they are careful to meet all expectations about form, tone, and style and to generate as little static as possible with their texts.

Composed: Very rarely do even the most renowned public writers whip off a piece of writing that's clear, correct, and convincing from the jump. On the contrary, skillful authors *compose*—that is, they typically employ a sequential process of drafting, rewriting, revising, and editing that's much more methodical than magical. This tried-and-true approach is often spread over many days and different work sessions. Writers gain insight as they see and resee their own work, ponder the responses of early readers, and patiently build up an increasingly solid, effective text.

Edited: Public writing must be correct, or its reception from readers may be compromised or even undermined completely. It is the author's responsibility to make sure that spelling, punctuation, grammar, usage, and presentation are not just correct but exemplary, even felicitous. To help young writers in school produce this kind of highly polished text, we must make sure they have just as much help as professional writers do along the way, including the use of spell checkers and peer editing groups to achieve developmentally reasonable levels of correctness.

Graded: The most important grade any piece of writing can ever get is the response it evokes from its intended audience. Do readers change their minds as a result of your words? Do they take action? Do they ask for more information or commence their own inquiries? Of course, in school we teachers may also choose (or be required) to assign grades, marks, or rankings to kids' written work. If we have made our assignments well, given kids real choices and responsibilities, and provided a supportive writing community that helped at every stage, our grading need not excessively distort either the process or the product, and at its best, it can help young writers to reflect upon their efforts and lay plans for even better writing to come.

Making Public Writing Possible

How do we get young people to live up to these high standards and exacting criteria? Maybe you are thinking of all those slapdash papers, half-baked essays, and plagiarized reports kids have submitted in response to previous assignments. Maybe you're thinking, "*These* kids are supposed to turn into proud, scrupulous public writers? As if!"

Yet some kids *do* write well, if sporadically, don't they? It's kind of astonishing when a teenager bursts out in powerful prose. It kinda knocks your socks off, like: where did *that* come from? And you are about to see in the samples that pepper the next three chapters that kids from all over the country, students just like yours, are producing writing across the curriculum that's not just satisfactory but spectacular. Where do these beyond-expectations texts come from, and how do we make them much more common? What are the factors and conditions that dial down kids' slovenliness and ratchet up their pride? Here are some key classroom factors that make the difference:

- **Choice:** When kids have some control over their writing topics, the feeling of ownership is enhanced and the chance for deep engagement is elevated. In all of the subjects we teach, we can help kids find relevant and personally interesting topics that *also* fit into the units and topics we must cover. Why have we teachers traditionally asked all the kids to write on the exact same topic anyway? We are the ones who have to *read* them, after all, and then we are bored after the first three papers. Notice, incidentally, what a terrible audience this makes us for our young writers—we become readers who cannot be *informed.* This makes the writing experience *fake,* and thus much harder for kids to invest in.

- **Time to Write in Class:** This goes back to our earlier comments about *going deeper into a smaller number of topics* (page 10). If we want kids to think like historians, scientists, mathematicians, artists, or literary people, they need to write in those disciplines and genres. And while doing so, they need support along the way; they cannot become good writers by taking our printed instructions home on the bus and guessing their way through writing homework. As we show in the next chapter, kids needs side-by-side coaching, modeling, and mentoring through all stages of the process. We cannot leave them alone to write any more than we'd leave them alone to dissect a fetal pig or cook up some chemical reactions. Ka-boom!

- **Response:** Most professional writers show their early writing to trusted friends, colleagues, or editors along the way, before it's done, to get confirmation,

What About Plagiarism?

When the three of us were going to school, if you wanted to plagiarize a term paper, you at least had to copy it, by hand, out of the *World Book*. Now, these spoiled kids today, all they have to do is cut the material directly from a website and print it out. At least when *we* were cheating, we worked at it.

All jokes aside, it sure seems easy for kids to plagiarize today. It's also easier for us to catch them by typing a few of "their" lines into www.myessays.com or just even www.google.com. But catching kids in the act isn't new either. Smokey fondly remembers the freshman student who turned in Robert Frost's "Stopping by Woods on a Snowy Evening" as her own work. When challenged on the poem's originality, Megan doggedly dug in her heels and stuck to her story of authorship. When showed the Frost poem on the page of a literature anthology, right on the table before her, she simply grumbled, "Well, I can't help it if this guy thought up the same poem I did!" So yeah, it seems like plagiarism is always with us.

Let us shock you with two opinions about plagiarism by middle and high school students.

- Lots of it is innocent.
- Most of it is teacher caused.

By *innocent,* we mean that most kids really do not understand the abstract idea of intellectual property or the procedures of attribution attached to it. Oh sure, they know they are doing something wrong when they dump borrowed text into a science report. But they don't know what's *right,* what's kosher, what's required. We can repeat the phrase "other people's words" a thousand times, but long experience tells us that kids just don't get it. We must do more than threaten and brandish lists of consequences; we need to take the time, develop the lessons, and *teach* this very complex and delicate practice of using other people's words and ideas. How? Kids should be *practicing* this process, in class, with real short-text sources, lifting quotes, making proper citations, and getting it right *before* they ever embark on a big assignment full of attribution challenges.

When we say *teacher caused,* we mean that some of our assignments are so plagiarism friendly that they are almost irresistible to the normal adolescent ethical system. "Why did Lincoln free the slaves?" Who in her right mind isn't going to Google *that* topic? And who has the titanium character to resist a little cutting and pasting? Instead, why not ask kids to "compare the end of slavery in the United States to the end of apartheid in South Africa"? Whoops, no free Internet help there! Now all a student can rely on is some real thinking—and possibly some hard-digging, original research, some side-by-side outlining, and some fresh, original drafting. There are countless examples of plagiarism-proof topics across the curriculum:

EASILY PLAGIARIZED	FORCES ORIGINALITY
Describe the functions of the different parts of a cell.	Compare the parts of a cell to the parts of a car.
Explain the importance of vectors in mathematics.	Show how vectors are involved in the game of chess (in the layout of a city, etc.).
Why was the Twenty-fifth Amendment repealed?	Under what circumstances might the Twenty-fifth Amendment be reinstated?

We also address plagiarism prevention in many of the formal writing activities coming up in Chapters 7 and 9. If we teachers know how easy and tempting it is for kids to outsource their thinking to the Internet, it is up to *us* to assign, or help kids choose, topics that require real research.

suggestions, and advice. This vital feedback loop helps writers do their best work, avoid pitfalls, revise and rewrite effectively, and better gauge the potential reactions of an audience. In school, we have long clung to the dysfunctional norm of withholding feedback until the kids' papers are "turned in," done, finished, and ready for grading. Following this protocol, students' work is *sure* to be filled with tangles, errors, and shortcomings; after all, the normal ingredient of feedback has been amputated from the composition process. And then we teachers collect the "finished" papers and spend hours marking them up, telling students what they *could* have done to make their work more effective if we had let them. How dumb is that?

The necessary alternative is a collaborative classroom community where both teacher and fellow students (with careful training and guidelines) become advisers along the way, where all writers, like adult professionals, have a supportive team on their side, helping the writing get better *before* it is released to its final audience. More on this is coming up in Chapters 6 and 8.

Good Models

In order to learn to write, you need to *read* samples of exemplary text in the field to which you want to contribute. In English classes, the students are undeniably exposed to examples of great writing. You gotta admit, when kids routinely read Shakespeare, Jane Austen, Mark Twain, Toni Morrison, Tim O'Brien, and Annie Dillard, they are marinating in marvelous, skillful language. But in history, science, math, and other subjects, the available writing models usually aren't even classic voices in the field, but *textbooks* that transform the stunning achievements and memorable personages of the discipline into gray, soporific gruel. No textbook we know of has ever won an award for its style, voice, or artfulness—or for keeping anyone up reading way past bedtime.

And yet, every topic taught in American schools—the U.S. Constitution, the migration of birds, the origins of Boolean logic—has wonderful writers covering it, writing and publishing every single day, but not in committee-written, thirteen-pound public school textbooks. Instead, the great writing—and the models our students urgently need—are appearing in *Discover Magazine, American Heritage, National Geographic, Time, Newsweek,* and other publications. And, increasingly, great writing appears on literate and lively subject-specific websites that our teenage students can log onto any day.

Indeed, today's teenagers should be reading the same current trade nonfiction that thoughtful, curious members of the adult community are reading. Kids should not be getting ready to be real readers someday—they should be immersed in everyday, grown-up text *right now.* In *Subjects Matter* (Daniels and Zemelman 2004), the reading companion to this book, we recommend 150 current trade nonfiction books that are great mentor texts for budding middle and high school writers. The lesson here, as we think about content-area *writing,* is that kids need examples, models, templates, samples of what good writing in the field looks like. This also means that smart teachers always save examples of great student writing (with permission of the authors, of course) to show future students what they can do—and what is expected.

> *Students should be reading the same current trade nonfiction that thoughtful, curious members of the adult community are reading.*

The Process Approach

The best way we can help young writers to create extended and effective texts is to show them how real writers operate and to coach them in the footsteps of actual authors. Ideally, we're showing them how working historians, social scientists, chemists, mathematicians, engineers, or literary critics operate as authors. And what all these writers have in common, across all these disparate fields, is that they approach writing as a *process,* as a craftlike series of steps and stages that leads from gathering and organizing material and ideas, through drafting and revision, through editing and proofreading, to an ultimate rendezvous with readers. Of course, there are many twists and turns in this craft, and often writers loop back to earlier stages of the work—as the writing researchers say, *making recursions.* Still, while it is not perfectly linear, the

> ## The Writing Process Goes to School
>
> Our colleague Tom Newkirk has recently raised some important questions about the so-called process model of writing, the approach we are relying upon here. Newkirk argues that, especially with younger children, harnessing students to the same strategies and steps that adult writers use may be asking too much. He notes—and we agree—that younger writers sometimes do their best work in sudden, quick drafts, rather than when marched through the more mature step-by-step process that a grown-up writer might employ. Newkirk reminds us that the idea of apprenticing kids to skilled adult writers is meant to be a *metaphor*, not a literal instruction. And we've seen too many classrooms where the process model has morphed into something rigid and mechanical: "Monday we prewrite, Tuesday we draft, Wednesday we revise," and so on. Anyone who has taught adolescents can feel the truth of Tom's concerns—sometimes kids work in mysterious, ungrown-up ways and yet create sensational papers, reports, essays, and stories. We need to let kids be kids, just as we help them acquire the tools and work habits of grown-ups.
>
> So we add a small note of caution here, even though we have seen the staged process, write-like-a-real-writer model succeed across all secondary subject areas around the country.

creation of a text has a predictable trajectory from idea to finished copy. After all, you can't edit a nonexistent draft, and you can't organize material you haven't got yet.

What does that mean in terms of helping kids do great science reports, historical analyses, or critical papers? How do teachers make this process approach work? If we want kids to write well, we must

- ☞ set aside time and . . .
- ☞ conduct activities . . .
- ☞ at each stage of the writing process.

That's exactly what the next chapter is about—how we content-area teachers can create those supports in all of our subjects.

Work Cited

Daniels, Harvey, and Steven Zemelman. 2004. *Subjects Matter: Every Teacher's Guide to Content-Area Reading*. Portsmouth, NH: Heinemann.

CHAPTER six

Supporting the Writing Process

Picture two teachers giving an assignment for an extended writing activity the way all too many of us may have experienced in school. Here's Stan, teaching U.S. history:

OK, everyone, you're doing a project on the Civil War. Read the textbook chapter and choose some aspect of it. Do some library research, and write it up. Ten pages, word processed, double spaced, due two weeks from Friday. Good luck.

At another end of the spectrum is Sherry, in biology:

We've been studying cycles in the biosphere—the water cycle, the carbon cycle, and so forth—and now we're going to do some writing to share what we learn with one another. First you'll read an article about Biosphere II that shows how complicated the cycles really are, and then we'll divide into groups to brainstorm some of the questions that might be interesting to investigate, and then we'll share the questions and regroup according to the ones people want to investigate, and we'll go to the library computers, where I will expect each of you to find three articles related to your group's question. You'll read each article and take notes on it using a guide I will hand out and then everyone will explain their articles to the other kids in their groups and each group will make a chart on butcher paper to see what information you've got, after which. . .

Stan follows the old, standard assign-it, turn-'em-loose, collect-and-grade-it cycle that has frustrated teachers with poor results for many years. It provides no support for the kids, who may have very little experience researching and writing about their research. So unless the students have been unusually prepared by their previous schooling, Stan is likely to be disappointed when plagiarized, disorganized papers come in. Sherry, on the other hand, while trying to be more helpful, lobs all the instruction and guidance at once, with no step-by-step explanations, no modeling, no interim support or monitoring. The young writers are easily overwhelmed as information sails past instead of helping them.

Stan and Sherry are composites of some teachers we have observed over the years, though many others are much more savvy than these two. Those more effective educators know that for students to write successfully for a public audience, it is up to us to show how it's done by competent adults and to coach them stepwise in chunks they can handle. We should give kids freedom to choose topics or subtopics they can get excited about, but also support them as they go along.

But students need to be open to our help. So the very first step in building a classroom where good writing gets done and deep learning accompanies it is to create a climate in which students are willing to tackle new and challenging tasks, ask for and get help, and really explore ideas, instead of just dutifully completing each step. In this chapter, therefore, we look at ways to build a positive climate for writing and then examine just how to guide and support students as they compose more extended pieces for a public audience. Most of you reading this book are not writing teachers, and we're not suggesting that you work in depth on every step of the process. But as you consider the various kinds of support we describe, we think you'll spot activities that will really help kids to learn your subject more deeply—as they dig into their writing.

Want to Jump Around?

If you'd like to jump ahead to see ten effective activities for students writing to a public audience, go directly to Chapters 7 and 9. Then come back here to learn more about the support that helps those activities work smoothly.

Creating a Supportive Environment

So what are some essential approaches for building an environment in which students craft good, thoughtful writing that builds learning in your subject? An effective teacher models and talks with students about seeking to understand a problem and striving to explain it clearly and convincingly to other people. She demonstrates, herself, how writing helps her make sense of the topics she's studying and how each student's writing can help the rest of the class learn as well. She explains that the writing she assigns is not just another kind of test to check up on whether they read the assignment or not, but a tool to help them learn. And she answers some crucial questions that always lurk somewhere in students' minds.

Why are we doing this?

The answer to the question *What is this writing for?* is one of the most crucial in the entire process, because it permeates all of the students' actions and choices. Sure, students get graded on their public writing. But if they believe its main purpose is just to display what they've memorized, or worse, to call them out on things they didn't get, they'll always play it safe, take few chances, and stick with what they already know, however circumscribed that may be. No risking anything new or ideas that appear too complex.

> *The answer to the question "What is this writing for?" is one of the most crucial in the entire process, because it permeates all of the students' actions and choices.*

Think back to your own experience as a student and be honest: perhaps you took that stance yourself. Trouble is, students learn little from such writing, so it can be a waste of everyone's time—and as a result, teachers avoid assigning much of it. So kids need to hear from you, repeatedly:

> *I hope that as you do this project, you really get to explore new territory, something you never knew about, or if it's a topic you're already fascinated with, perhaps there are parts you don't yet understand. That means you might have questions about it. And you might need help explaining it to someone else through your writing. I hope that you ask me for that help and that you tell us what some of your questions and confusions are. In many fields, those questions are what lead to new and exciting ideas.*

Then the kids need to see this in your actions and your responses to their work.

To whom are we writing?

In the real world, people write *to* someone else or sometimes to themselves. In school, writers only infrequently address either of these kinds of audience. Students usually write *for* the teacher, though not really to inform or persuade him about the topic. As our colleague Peter Elbow once said, if you're a student yourself, "'Getting an A is results,' you may say, but see how you feel if you write your teacher for a contribution [to your political campaign] and get an 'A' instead of a check" (1981, 220). Students generally figure the teacher already knows a lot more about the subject than they do, so they aim simply to show what they've learned. But true public writing is far more motivating because students actually have to inform or persuade someone about something—not pretend to, but really *do* it: teach the rest of the class about weapons used in the Civil War; help younger children learn about the solar system; write an alternative section of the math book to help next year's algebra students learn how to factor a complicated expression; campaign for healthier food in the cafeteria. Having a real audience not only clarifies the writing task but also guides particular choices of wording, length, and organization, and it changes the teacher's role from judge, jury, and executioner to team coach who helps players become more successful out on the field.

How do you actually write this stuff?

Along with making clearer what the writing is for, we need to help kids see how it gets done. This is where modeling is a key teaching tool. Students need to see how a competent adult actually creates lines on a page. Modeling a writing task by talking your thoughts aloud as you project your draft for students to see—often called a *write-aloud*—not only shows the kind of thinking and organizing and explaining that smart writers use but also allows you to lead the way in taking some risks, yourself, just as you are asking the students to do. And as you do it, you are simultaneously teaching about your subject. **We cannot overemphasize the value and effectiveness of this strategy.**

Matt Olson provides just this sort of demonstration for his sophomore chemistry classes at the South Shore School for Entrepreneurship in Chicago. When Matt's students were about to write letters on nutrition and body chemistry, to be sent to chemistry classes at another high school, Matt especially wanted to help them organize their paragraphs. So he showed them his own process for composing a couple.

To be sure that the kids were involved and not just watching passively, Matt first had the students help him jot notes on the board. Here are the notes for one paragraph, on energy intake and output in the human body:

- When you eat—exothermic—gives energy out
- Energy going to waste—50%

☞ Energy to cell respiration—35%

☞ Energy to growth—15%

Matt then wrote on an overhead with predrawn blank lines for a topic sentence, supporting ideas, and a conclusion, which he asked the students to use to organize their own writing. Here's Matt's write-aloud (his thoughts are in italic, and his writing is in regular font):

> *(Now I'm going to give some detail. I guess this next paragraph is about where the energy goes. So that's the topic—"where the energy goes." I've got to give some sort of starter sentence. So when I look at my notes, I see three different things.)*
> So in my chemistry class *(and it is my chemistry class!)* I learned *(I'll give my readers the details later)* that the energy in food is used 3 *(I'd better spell that out)* three ways. *(I took the notes beforehand, so this makes it easy.)* The majority of the energy in the food I eat goes to waste. *(Hmm. I'd better give some examples here.)* Some examples of waste are *(I guess I should use the scientific term.)* fecal matter, sweating, and heat. *(Hmm. Three examples are enough. We brainstormed a lot more, like twelve, but three are OK. Next I'll tell them where the second most energy goes.)* The second most energy goes to cellular respiration. *(Maybe I could have left out examples for waste, but they might not understand this one, so I'd better make sure to explain.)* Cellular respiration is when oxygen is used to produce the energy needed to run, play, breathe, and *(I guess I'll say . . .)* live.

While Matt displayed his own thought process here, he finds that his students usually need to be more actively involved, so he likes to combine his thinking with some group composing. "The kids want to be part of the process," Matt observes. "Otherwise, they begin to tune out." Matt embraces this as an aspect of culturally relevant teaching. Perhaps in some settings, some students may be more willing to passively learn from the teacher's process, but that's not what works best for Matt. Such adaptations are always a part of the work of highly effective educators.

By the way, if you're getting nervous about the amount of time that such steps require and whether they will suck time away from teaching your subject, just remember: as Matt Olson's write-aloud shows, when you model writing like this, *you* **are** *teaching your subject,* showing students how to think like a scientist or historian or mathematician about the material you teach.

Are we competing with one another, or are we supposed to help each other? And if we're supposed to help, how do we do that? We're not the experts in here.

Students are more likely to invest in thoughtful and well-developed writing in a classroom where mutual support is valued. Writers need someone who will tell them if their sentences make sense, but who is basically on their side, instead of just trying to pick their arguments apart. The teacher can do some of this, but her time is limited, and she should not become a bottleneck holding up kids' work. Besides, students will actually learn what makes a good explanation as they listen to one another.

However, it's easy for a stronger student to simply do the work for a partner—or for a weaker one to feel that he just doesn't have the needed expertise. So we must show students how to help each other. When Federal-Hocking High School math teacher Sue Collins, in Stewart, Ohio, assigned an algebra problem for students to solve and write about, she asked them to work in pairs. The problem: two groups of hikers, one heading up a mountainside with stops to rest, and the other descending the next day; do their paths ever hit the same spot at the same time of day, and if so, when? Sue noticed that in one pair, John was doing all the work, simply completing the steps for Alex. This was not meaningful help or true collaboration. So the next day, she discussed with the kids how to help by asking questions ("Did you look through the problem to see what information it gives you?" "Why don't you try writing that step out in words?"), rather than just giving the answers.

MATH

Sue makes sure that when she gives pairs or groups a task, she moves around the class quickly at first, to see how kids are doing. This way she can give guidance more strategically. "It takes a lot of energy to do that, but it's well worth it," she observes.

What if I make a mistake or get confused?

Kids expect the red pen to come down hard. And traditionally, teachers often think they must spend hours at home marking up the papers. But we're here to tell you that you don't ever have to do that again. Years of research have shown that it's completely ineffective. Students don't learn from it; it sends a negative signal that you're about fault finding, not helping them learn; and the truth is, you're more likely to shy away from giving writing assignments rather than sink loads of time into marking mistakes you may be a bit unsure about anyway.

> *Years of research have shown that marking up papers at home is completely ineffective.*

Instead, make it really easy on yourself. Focus on just one aspect at a time and help students notice it in their own writing. The Collins Writing Program does this in a classroomwide or schoolwide fashion (see www.collinseducationassociates.com). An advantage of this program is that it enables subject-area teachers who lack knowledge about teaching writing to get started without more in-depth training. However, many teachers prefer to establish just a couple of their own goals based on students' specific strengths and weaknesses, which is much less mechanical and more efficient in the long run. This shifts teachers' response from a "Gotcha!" mode to a focus on learning and

Building a Positive Climate for Writing

Establish constructive purposes for student writing. Show students that your aim is to help them learn, not just to catch them making mistakes. Demonstrate this in as many ways as you can think of.

Find real audiences, beyond the teacher, for students' writing. Identifying real audiences and communicative purposes for writing develops students' engagement—and converts your role from judge and jury to supportive coach.

Demonstrate for students the processes that real writers go through. Compose aloud with projection equipment to make the process visible. Keep in mind: This is one of the most effective strategies you can use to help your students improve their writing and understand how expert practitioners in your field think. It lets students see your thinking and your struggles, and it shows them processes they can use. It also demonstrates that you are willing to take the same risks you are asking of them.

Teach students how to help one another, and organize classroom activities so they can do so. Guide students to become good questioners and to give help by asking their partners about the process they are using, rather than providing all the answers. Kids step up when given responsibility, and they learn from giving help (by articulating what they're learning) as well as from receiving it.

Show students that it's safe to ask for help. One way to do this is to focus on just one or two aspects of their writing at a time and track their improvement.

improvement. Not only does the teacher *tell* students that she wants to help, but she has an organized way of doing so.

Helping with Specific Stages in the Writing Process

Content-area teachers will rarely have time to teach all the aspects of composition; we've got our subjects to cover! Still, the more we understand the writing process and the qualities of good writing, the more we can help our students. Besides, many strategies for supporting writing just happen to help kids learn the content. So here we review major steps in the writing process and activities for supporting them.

We're talking now about longer, in-depth assignments, not the brief two-minute think-and-jot strategies described in earlier chapters. To guide those shorter efforts you'll mainly encourage students to think and share ideas, demonstrate that it's safe to do so in your classroom, and perhaps model to show what you are asking for. But for longer pieces, many students have no other image of how to proceed than to just jump in at the beginning and plow ahead until the end. When they're stuck, they're stuck. Instead, the steps and strategies we outline will help students cope with the challenges they may face along the way. Be aware, however, that many of the following steps can overlap, shift in order, or call for the writer to return to one or more as she discovers more about her topic.

- **Before-Writing Activities** that raise some big, important questions, so that students are writing to address an issue or explore a topic that matters
- **Gathering Information,** concepts, viewpoints, or data, so that these budding writers have something meaty to serve up to their readers
- **Organizing** the information or steps in the argument so a reader can readily follow the writer's line of thinking (Some writers carry out this step before the next one, while others need to get it all down first.)
- **Getting Ideas Down** on paper
- **Letting Early Drafts Rest** so the writer can come back to the work with fresh eyes
- **Reviewing** the work to see whether it really says what the writer wants to say and whether it's clear, well organized, complete—or perhaps includes extraneous material; this often includes getting feedback from a fellow student, a peer response group, or the teacher
- **Revising** ideas and explanations where needed
- **Polishing,** fixing grammar, correcting spelling, getting the piece ready for a wider audience
- **Publishing** to get students' writing out into the world and in front of real audiences, where the results matter

There have been many books written on each of these steps (take a look at Heinemann's website, www.heinemann.com, as well as our own Works Cited sections). But we want to move along shortly and show you ten kinds of writing activities for a public audience that will promote kids' learning. So we'll settle for quick sketches of a few of our favorite activities for each step, to whet your appetite and give you a good start.

Before-Writing Activities

To get them thinking about a potential topic, you need to give students a meaningful and thought-provoking context in which their writing is part of a discussion or an expression of concern. After all, that is what leads any of us as thinking adults to use our brains more actively, and it will boost the task beyond just a dutiful recitation of memorized facts. Here are two very different strategies for giving writing a sense of purpose and social meaning *before* students even hear what the assignment will be. We want them to go into it with their minds turned on.

Anticipation Guide

Kick-start conversation so that before students write, their discussion gets them really thinking about the topic they will shortly be putting down on paper. Remember: this comes *before* writing, and it isn't a writing activity *per se,* but it can make a huge difference in the writing that is to come.

The anticipation guide is easy to use. Project a couple of questions for everyone to see—controversial or open-ended if possible. Have students jot their own individual answers—true or false, a couple of phrases, a reason or justification. In small groups, students compare answers and discuss, and finally the groups report on their discussions to the whole class. Record the main responses, projected for the class, and save these for later comparison, after students have researched and written about them.

In a biology class, for example, a teacher jotted the following on the board:

- ⇝ How much soda pop do you drink per day?
- ⇝ Based on what we've been reading, name two things you think it does to your body.
- ⇝ Do you think we could get the students in this school to drink less of it?

The kids then did some reading on nutrition and relevant aspects of body chemistry from their textbook and from a couple of articles on the Internet. For writing, they chose some aspect of teen nutrition to write about and proposed a plan for how to improve diet and health in their school.

Four Corners

This is a kinesthetic, visual, and verbal way to surface varying opinions on a topic or approaches to a problem. Again, controversy—in civil form—is a great igniter of student expression that will shortly end up on paper.

To begin, the teacher poses a question or writes it on the board, worded so that there are three or four possible answers –such as a Likert scale, or a range of solutions to a problem. Students then move to the corners of the room to indicate their response. For example, those agreeing with choice one stand near the door; choice two, by the windows; and choice three, at the back of the room (post numbers on the wall before class to help avoid confusion). Once there, the groups talk (quietly) about why they chose that answer. A spokesperson or a few volunteers from each group explain the group's thinking. Then the teacher invites people from the different corners to talk directly to others across the room.

Gathering Information and Ideas

Gathering information is the most natural part of the process for a content-area classroom; we want kids to write in order to learn more of our content, right? So they should be encountering new information to share with classmates as well as the teacher. Individuals or small teams can each focus on a different aspect of the topic, informing and educating one another, rather than all reciting the same material just to show they read it. There's no clever activity for getting this done (but if you've got one, write to us and we'll include it in the second edition of this book!). It just takes astute management so kids don't get bogged down or end up plagiarizing. Here are some ways various teachers handle this.

Advance Preparation

Make a list of the main topics students can choose from, so you can have information available in advance and aren't overwhelmed trying to help students find it on the spot. Have materials ready for kids to browse, either as article copies to hand out, websites for kids to visit, or media center materials that the librarian has laid out.

Jigsaw Reading

Individual students each read a different article and report to each other in small groups on what they've read. Students can then exchange articles as needed to get the information they realize will help with their chosen topic.

Using the Internet

Be prepared with strategies to ensure that students don't simply copy the first page of three websites that they find. Especially effective is an evaluation form requiring students to analyze the quality of the information on a website, so they really have to think through what they've found.

Organizing

Some writers love outlines. They can comfort you as you face the chaos. You may think as a teacher that they're absolutely basic. But many students find them useless and just dive into the wreck to start groping their way. How many of us will confess as adults that we always completed the required outlines after the writing was done? Of course, some fields feature

> **Want to Jump Around?**
>
> The I-search project in Chapter 9 (pages 236–251) will help you guide students to research more wide-ranging topics and give you strategies to ensure that as they use the Internet they don't simply plagiarize from the websites they find.

a standard order for a technical report, so the teacher can simply lay it out for the students. That's what biology teacher Melissa Bryant does when her students research and present reports on various human diseases and their treatment. But if there's not a prescribed structure for a project, we may need to help students figure out an order that will helpfully guide readers through the material. And we need to help them find some kind of order and sequence that supports the development of their ideas and words. Thank goodness word-processing programs with their ability to move blocks of text around have made organizing or reorganizing much easier than it used to be. So what to do, instead of requiring traditional outlines?

Looking at Samples

Reading and working together on a couple of student samples provides a good, quick lesson in organizing. Dig through your files or your basement and locate a couple of student papers from a previous year that each unfold differently. Perhaps one begins with an example or a scene (if this is a history class, say), while the other first lays out an argument or thesis. If they're short, you can put them on overheads. Students can read these and discuss the pros and cons of each. An alternative pair for comparison can be created if you take one paper, make a copy, snip it apart into discrete sections, and paste up the pieces in a different order. Kids can then compare the two and consider whether and how the alternatives work. Either way, the more students look at their work as readers, themselves, the more readily they can understand what's needed to make their explanations clear.

MATH

Or share with students examples of high-quality writing in your field and analyze their characteristics together as a class. That way, you're exposing kids to additional material on your topic as well as teaching how good arguments are organized in your field. How did mathematician John Paulos, for example, organize his ideas as he wrote a short chapter on using probability and randomness to win in a negotiating session, for his book on math in everyday life (1995, 30–33)? What did he do to create an effective opening? How did he organize his baseball pitching and hitting example to make his ideas clear? *Are* they indeed as clear as they could be? How did he write his conclusion? Is it a good one? What kinds of words, sentences, and ideas grab the reader's attention and keep the piece interesting? (And by the way, is it really crazy for a U.S. trade negotiator to roll the dice to decide what he should say next? Or might it actually be a winning strategy?) It's much more meaningful and effective for students to create their own outlines and lists of criteria—and to create several options—by analyzing examples of good writing together than for the teacher to just prescribe a required structure for the writing.

We're not just saying to use fewer advanced outlines. We also need to move students away from the flat and usually lifeless five-paragraph essay, which clings to life in high schools but really nowhere else in the literate world. Janet Angelillo, in discussing how to help students with essay tests, is passionate about this:

> The formula—plug in this sentence here and that sentence there—actually mocks students' intelligence because it does not give them the opportunity to play with ideas and unfold their thinking. In fact, five-paragraph essays are just too easy and simplistic for students; they can do much more. (2005, 87–88)

This does not mean you wink at disorganized writing. On the other hand, it does not require the teacher to become an expert on all sorts of essay structures. You are simply helping kids to learn how to organize their writing from the really strong writers in your field.

Getting Ideas Down: Drafting

Once students have the information they need, they start writing a draft, right? Well, maybe. But this is still an easy place for writers to get stuck. Where to start? What order to give to it all? How much to explain about each part? We wish writing were a nice neat process, but often it's not. Here is one strategy that will help.

Four-Card Stud

This is a prewriting trick Steve learned from composition guru Don Murray long ago, but it's still as useful as ever for helping marshal ideas.

Once students have decided on their topic, hand out four 4-by-6-inch note cards to each student (or have them tear an 8½-by-11-inch sheet of paper in quarters if you don't have the cards). Ask them to jot a phrase naming their topic at the top of the first card. Then they quickly brainstorm words and phrases associated with the topic on the rest of the card, in any order. After a couple of minutes, it's time for the second card. Tell everyone to circle one word or phrase on the first card that he thinks he can tell more about—and then do that telling on the second card. Allow just three or four minutes for this, because it's really only a start. The third and fourth cards work the same way: students circle another word or phrase (on the first card or any succeeding card) and write a quick explanation about it on a separate card. Continue with more cards if there's time.

Now the student has a stack of cards with a list of subtopics and possibilities and a number of chunks, one of which might make a good beginning and others that can become parts of a draft. Most students find the small cards easy to fill, while the listing and expanding help break through writer's block. Instead of just one beginning that the writer has plunged blindly into, she now has a set of possibilities to choose from and a good start on the whole piece. Extraneous chunks can be set aside, and another round of cards can always generate still more material.

Letting It Rest

Standards, curriculum guides, benchmarks, scope and sequence charts, and test prep may press in upon us. But there's no way around the human fact that real understanding usually takes time. How often has the right word for a crossword puzzle, or the answer to a tough math problem, or a thoughtful solution to a difficult family or career challenge come to us only after we've slept on it at least for a night? Writing is especially like this because the more you mess with the words, the harder it becomes to see them as a fresh reader would. But a few days or a week later, after a little mental rest, the errors and confusions can jump out at you. So how can we teachers build this in when our days are already so packed with all the topics and skills we're expected to cover?

One way is to simply plan a break. Don't add more total time for the project; just schedule enough time to get a draft done and have the kids put it away for a couple of days—or collect the papers if you think the kids may lose them. You probably have plenty of other stuff to teach and won't have any trouble filling the intervening class periods. Arrange for a final day of editing and polishing to come after a weekend or a few days after you've started the next unit. Talk with the kids about this, so they'll understand that there's a method to the zigzag. This is an important piece of life learning for them, and it emphasizes the value of a staged approach to writing, with scrupulous polishing at the end. And the writing will get better as a result.

≋ Want to Jump Around?

Any of the activities back in Chapters 3 and 4 can easily help students pull together material for a larger project. KWL charts, double-entry journals, nonstop writes, and the rest all help students get their ideas down as they read and begin to explain the topic in their own words.

Or turn to Chapter 8, on classroom workshop, which outlines a larger classroom structure that enables the teacher to help students with individual needs and challenges as they write. Students work on their writing during class time while the teacher conducts conferences with individuals or small groups. Students keep their work in individual writing folders, and the teacher documents student progress and conference topics using carefully designed record-keeping forms that simplify the task of tracking all the individual work going on. This structure takes class time, but it enables the teacher to provide individual help when students get stuck while drafting.

Reviewing and Revising

Reviewing and revising is an especially challenging part of the writing process, because language is enormously complex, and there are more aspects to it than any of us can possibly teach. We explain things to each other every day, and we're sometimes understood and sometimes not. We think we're saying one thing to our partner and what he or she hears is entirely different. Thus, the highly profitable self-help-book publishing industry (one of the latest, as we write: *You're Wearing That? Understanding*

Mothers and Daughters in Conversation). And one student may struggle with one aspect, like how to provide good concrete examples, while another rambles among an overabundance of irrelevant details.

Furthermore, students tend to repel the very idea of revision: "I'm done; it's not great, but please don't rub my nose in it!" Too often revision is only about what's *wrong* with a piece. Or the student's few changes are superficial—a couple of spelling errors, a comma or two. So the first step that writing gurus usually suggest is to distinguish between revising *ideas* and polishing *conventions*. We start with revising ideas first, since that connects more with our subject-area teaching anyway.

> There's no way around the human fact that real understanding usually takes time.

Audience and Purpose

Thinking about the audience and purpose for a piece of writing provides the key to revision: "What am I trying to say and why? And will they get it?" But we can build the basis for this before kids ever get to the revision stage. At the very beginning, make sure that assignments include—or students have chosen—a specific audience and purpose for the piece. Are they composing a short feature article for a newsmagazine, a pamphlet to convince people to adopt healthier eating habits, or a detailed argument that takes one side or the other about a controversial event in U.S. history? When it comes to revising, one of these may call for condensing an explanation, another for expanding it.

Make It Real

Writers need to write for someone whom they desire to reach. We can't explain it any better than we did once upon a time in an earlier book:

> Providing a real audience is one of the most organic ways for a teacher to create a reason for students to revise. Until the student writes for a real audience besides the teacher, revising is in a sense just an exercise, guided mainly by the teacher's authority to demand particular standards. A committed poet may invest much time getting the words right just for his own satisfaction, but for most of us, it's the need to communicate that forces us to reconsider what

Want to Jump Around?

We especially like the writing activity called RAFT, in Chapter 7 (pages 159–166), to help give focus to revision. It asks students to choose a *role*, an *audience*, a *format* such as a letter or article or debate dialogue, and then the particular *topic* they will explore—all of which define what the writing task really requires.

we've said from a particular reader's point of view and try to make it clear for that person. (Zemelman and Daniels 1988, 178)

So it's a good idea to go beyond just *imagining* a possible audience and actually plan to circulate those pamphlets in a doctor's office or send the letters to an author or a newspaper. Recently we listened to a group of students on the radio enthusiastically describe how they were seeking to convince a state governor to exonerate a young man who was wrongly convicted of a crime years earlier. You can be sure those students worked long and hard composing their arguments as cogently as possible.

Small-Group Feedback

Students take turns reading their work (or parts of it) in small groups, and the listeners provide feedback on how the ideas were presented. You'll see such collaborative activities in almost all the public writing models we introduce in Chapters 7 and 9. This peer conferencing can require a bit of guidance, so you can provide a tip sheet that directs students about which aspects of the writing to attend to and how to give helpful feedback. For example:

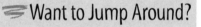
Want to Jump Around?

Think you don't know how to conduct a writing conference with a student? It's really just a short human conversation. For specific detail on what to say, how to coach, and how to make good conferences work, go to Chapter 8, on classroom workshops (pages 198–202).

- Point out the strong parts first.
- Focus at this stage on the ideas, not the grammar or mechanics.
- Try to help the writer explain his own point of view rather than change it to yours.
- Identify any spots where you were confused or desired more explanation, but leave it to the writer to decide how to address those needs. Explain to the writer how you understood the information, but don't try to fix the piece for him.

One-on-One Conferences

There's no substitute for individual conferences with students as they draft their writing. These enable you to help with problems that vary from student to student, and to do some good teaching about your subject. Yes, it takes class time, but it's an opportunity to do some of your most powerful teaching. Kids may snooze through a lecture, but they will long remember the one-on-one talks you took the trouble to have with them.

Polishing

Just about everything we've said about big-idea revising goes for the polishing stage as well, except that this really comes at the end of the process. There's not much point (besides the rote practice) in fixing up sentences that might just end up on the cutting room floor. Polishing is for getting ready to go public. And if you've created a context in which the kids are engaged in what they have to say, and have real audiences and purposes for their writing, they'll be much more willing to do this work—though sometimes adolescents require one or two embarrassing experiences for the public exposure to take effect. We're talking about teenagers here, who haven't always fully developed their understanding of consequences for their actions. Here are a few additional thoughts about helping students polish up their grammar and mechanics.

Reading Aloud

Students pair up and each takes a turn reading his piece to his partner. Often, all the partner needs to do is sit and listen, because writers spot all sorts of errors when a real human being is sitting there taking it in ("Oops! Wait. Let me fix that."). Encourage the students to stop as they go along to make quick editing marks. A variation is to have the partners swap papers and each read the piece back to its owner.

Quickie Minilessons

Don't ever feel guilty or pressured about not teaching everything about writing. Focusing on just a couple of challenges is more effective anyway. If you've got a pet peeve about spelling or commas or whatever, and you observe a majority of your students getting it wrong, provide a short demo. Using projection equipment, jot a sentence containing the error and ask everyone to figure out what's wrong. Make the correction with the class. Then provide another sample sentence with the same problem and ask the class to try fixing it on their own, after which kids can compare their solutions. Leave a sample on the board and remind students that you'll be watching for this as you circulate and as you read the papers later. Stay with this item until you see that kids have gotten the message and are on top of it. Now you've really taught something, without eating up a lot of time.

Schoolwide or Grade-Level Campaigns

Either the Collins Writing Program or the 6 + 1 Traits framework from the Northwest Regional Educational Laboratory can help students and teachers throughout a school focus on just a few issues at a time. Such a formal program can be rather lockstep, however, so your school or department or grade level might want to develop its own list of key writing mechanics to address. On the other hand, don't fall for the temptation to develop an extensive school style manual, thinking it will "solve" editing problems once and for all. We know many schools are proud of their manuals, but unfortunately, they rarely get used extensively. They lose the concept of focusing on and learning a few important skills at a time and instead become more of a blaming mechanism than a teaching tool.

Publishing

When only the teacher sees the final outcome of a writing assignment, it's no wonder that students will care only about the grade. But there are lots of natural audiences out there who would be tickled to hear from your students. This places you in the role of publisher rather than critic. It creates motivation, and naturally it's fun for kids to get real responses from the real world.

So just who are these audiences? Here are a few.

- **Your Own Class:** Sharing should be a teaching and learning event for all, rather than a situation in which kids sit there bored while the teacher listens and grades the presentations. If reports are delivered aloud, students can take notes and pose questions. If papers are swapped and read silently, kids can jot responses to each other.

- **Adult Panels:** Increasing numbers of schools have students make oral presentations to visiting panels at the end of a quarter or semester. The panels often include parents and community members who are supporters of the school, along with other teachers and students as well.

- **Other Students in Your School or Elsewhere:** Classes down the hall or across the country can correspond with each other, learn from each other, and discover that they have a lot in common as learners, especially if they live in different kinds of neighborhoods. The Internet makes this far easier to arrange than it used to be.

- **Special Interest Groups and Organizations:** It's hard to find a topic that isn't a hobby, preoccupation, or focus of advocacy for some group out there. On the Web, you can find groups that investigate prime numbers, groups that reenact Civil War battles, organizations that help graduating scientists find jobs, you name it. Many will be pleased to hear from and happy to respond to students who have taken an interest in their particular obsession.

- **Targets for Advocacy:** Government and business leaders are naturals for this. But students can also create pamphlets on controversial issues, such as food safety, obesity, diet and fast food, gun control, restrictions on teenage drivers licenses, to circulate to friends or members of the public, and they can then re-port back to the class and the teacher on people's responses. While not all top-ics lend themselves to this approach—it might be hard to get public reaction on whether Socrates should have so easily submitted to drinking his cup of hem-lock—it's surprising how many subject-area topics do raise controversies when probed deeply enough. Wait a minute: hemlock means capital punishment. Maybe it's controversial after all.

☞ **Experts in Particular Fields:** "Here's what we're learning. How does this figure into your work?" A chemist might not want to answer each student's letter, but she might gladly write a response to the whole class. And it's not a bad idea for kids to realize there is a good reason for someone to know about molar mass out in the real world, and that the jobs using this knowledge pay *really* well.

☞ **Contest Judges:** We're not enthusiastic about writing contests. The problem is that with just a few winners, it's too easy for many students to conclude that they have no chance of winning, so why even try. We're out to help all our stu-dents learn, not just a few. So if you can design a competition where there are genuine prizes and recognition for all, have at it.

The list could go on, but you get the idea.

Assessment

Assessment is one of the knottiest topics in our profession and one of the scariest for content teachers when it comes to writing, because of the possibility of a huge time drain and our uncertainty about evaluating the skills. And the puzzles are many. How do we learn about students' actual learning, rather than just whether the writing got done and looked good? How do we make the assessment of writing part of a learning process, rather than just a way to rank students? After all, ranking encourages the achievers but discourages the strugglers. How do we keep kids engaged in the actual content, instead of just thinking about getting the test over with? We can't address all of these questions without writing a separate book (though we can refer you to one of our favorites—*Classroom Based Assessment,* by Bonnie Campbell Hill, Cynthia Ruptic, and Lisa Norwick [1998], which has informed many of the ideas in this section). But here are a few essentials that fit well in a content-area classroom.

Individualized Goal Setting

It's not difficult to have students set individual goals for their writing, so their effort and your assessment focus on specific improvements the kids aim for. This does require some time at the start of each quarter. Ask students to write down three or four things they think could most improve their writing. At least one should be about learning content, rather than improving mechanical details. Then in brief individual conferences (while the class is writing or reading or completing math or science problems), go over these with individuals and add one or two key expectations of your own, based on each student's work. The lists of goals go into individual folders kept in your room, to guide you and the students as learning proceeds through the quarter.

Marking Papers

You don't need to mark all the errors, even within one aspect of writing. If you see a pattern in a student's paper, mark two or three instances and ask the student to find the rest and return the paper to you. This way, the student is learning from your input and putting it into practice, you're avoiding the time drain, and you're addressing the research that says kids don't learn from intensive paper marking.

Responsibility Sheets

Along with the individualized goal sheets we've suggested, have each student keep a list of writing skills he has learned. All you need on a form are some lines and a column for the date that each skill was learned. As their work improves, students should add their newly learned skills to the list and then consult it when they are revising and editing the next paper. Again, this helps turn assessment into learning, rather than judgment after the work is over.

Rubrics

Many teachers use rubrics to provide students with a list of the things they will look for. This does take the mystery out of writing, so that students are not left guessing and they understand what you are asking them to do. The 6 + 1 Traits program has become very popular as a result. Rubrics can, however, pose a danger of straitjacketing the work, which means you might be spending hours poring groggily through dozens of nearly identical pieces. It's easy enough, however, to add lines to any rubric to recognize students' individual thought, creativity, and unanticipated learning. You wouldn't want your rubric to punish the kid who discovers a great way to explain something effectively, that doesn't fit the 6 + 1 Traits or some other set program.

Long-Range Reflection

What do students think they are learning? How does it all add up? Where's the improvement? We can ask students to stop periodically, look over their work (kept in folders with their goal sheets and lists of learned skills), and tell us in writing how they see it. This way, assessment is no longer a one-way communication or a series of disconnected events. Students can contemplate their learning and think about where they need to go next. This is not just about writing, but about how students are learning from all that we teach.

Truly Not Leaving Kids Behind

At one school we admire, the teachers have figured out how to keep grades from becoming millstones weighing some students down and leading them to drop out. At Young Women's Leadership Charter School in Chicago, teachers provide specific course outcomes, but in any area where a student does not succeed, she can return to it, even after the course is finished. The student's ultimate grade point average reflects all that she has learned, rather than an average of earlier weaknesses and later growth. Thus, there's always an incentive to improve as opposed to a permanent label that makes struggling kids give up. Such an approach requires a whole-school structure, in which students must complete an increasing number of outcomes for promotion from each grade so kids don't procrastinate. It's not idealistic; it's being done, and we put it out for you to consider because it shows how careful design can make an evaluation system actually encourage learning rather than just rank and label kids. (See Farrington and Small 2006.)

One Thing at a Time!

We've thrown a lot at you. Writing is complex, and writing teachers can spend the whole year helping kids master its many steps and stages. We wanted to put a lot of it out on the table, to help you understand what's involved. We know content-area teachers who take students through a very full process, and you can read about one in Chapter 8. But we also know that teachers everywhere struggle with overstuffed curriculum requirements and the pressure to cover huge amounts of content to prepare students for the standardized tests. How can you find class time for all this?

One good approach is to start small. Begin by picking out one or two of the strategies we've described and getting yourself and your kids comfortable with them. Perhaps you might start simply with an anticipation guide before giving an assignment or by building in some one-on-one conference time after students' drafts are completed. Once that first strategy is working well, and you realize it is doing a better job than some other method for teaching the same material, you can let go of that old trick and make a little more room in your schedule. Then go ahead and add another piece to your writing toolkit. As your students find enjoyment in the energizing writing activities you've introduced, you and they will want to do still more. Whatever your choice, now is a good time to begin.

Works Cited

Angelillo, Janet. 2005. *Writing to the Prompt: When Students Don't Have a Choice.* Portsmouth, NH: Heinemann.

Elbow, Peter. 1981. *Writing with Power.* New York: Oxford University Press.

Farrington, Camille, and Margaret Small. 2006. "Removing Structural Barriers to Academic Achievement in High Schools: An Innovative Model." Paper presented at American Educational Research Association Annual Meeting, San Francisco, April 10.

Hill, Bonnie Campbell, Cynthia Ruptic, and Lisa Norwick. 1998. *Classroom Based Assessment.* Norwood, MA: Christopher-Gordon.

Paulos, John. 1995. *A Mathematician Reads the Newspaper.* New York: Random House.

Zemelman, Steven, and Harvey Daniels. 1988. *A Community of Writers: Teaching Writing in the Junior and Senior High School.* Portsmouth, NH: Heinemann.

CHAPTER Seven

Shorter Public Writing Projects

In This Chapter

Now we can take off the sweats and the gym shoes. It's been a great workout with writing to learn, but it's time to dress up for a formal occasion. Time for writing that is planfully constructed and carefully polished. We're going to help kids write for maximum public impact, whether the reader is just us or their classmates, or they are writing for a publishing opportunity around school or in the community. Up ahead are six projects that require precision of thought and scrupulous editing but can also be playful, creative, and engaging. Watch out, though, one of them is about eyeballs. Eeewww.

People Research:
Surveys and Interviews

What It Is

You've already heard us beat up on traditional research papers a few times. We're not being negative, nor are we seeking revenge for all the note cards we had to copy out of dusty library books back in the day. We are just worried because this particular kind of research is highly abstract and exceedingly difficult. Take it from us (and we have several graduate degrees and dissertations between us): So-called library research is one of the hardest cognitive tasks anyone can attempt. It has taken us *decades* to get good at it (assuming that we are now doing it well). Locating information, keeping track of data, figuring out what's important and not, trying to find categories and patterns, remembering and attributing sources, and just keeping your physical materials straight is a huge task for any graduate student, not to mention a sixth grader or a junior in high school. And no matter how we try to liven it up, kids often feel (incorrectly, but steadfastly) that the research procedures we prescribe are arbitrary, rigid, and mechanical.

Another problem with traditional term papers is that they often spawn really bad writing. "In this term paper, the writer will explain three main things about volcanoes to the reader. The first thing the author will explain to the reader is the origin of volcanoes. . . ." And then *we* have to read them! OMG! Not fun. Wouldn't you rather have your students turn in something like this?

Going Blind: A Medical Interview

I was expecting to see large posters of sliced eyeballs. I had imagined goopy, globular eyes with sticky whites and hard pupils . . . but there were no three-dimensional dissections or "Do I have Glaucoma?" dioramas. Instead, Dr. Richard Levinson's office was sparse and clean. There was a plastic Gatorade bottle resting next to a day calendar on the cumbersome mahogany desk. A pair of glasses perched on top of a box of ball point pens with a visible irony. The blinds were open, and the room was flooded with clean, bright light. I had asked Dr. Levinson to think of a "special case" he had encountered in his work as an eye doctor before I came to visit him at his office in Rose Medical Center. I was expecting lots of gory detail, maybe bloody tears and Technicolor pupils. The story I ended up with was much less palpable. Instead of some disgusting ocular carnage, it was psychologically engaging . . . the kind of "what would I have done?" that makes for a good, sad story.

The patient was a healthy, thirty year old woman. She was married, had two children, and enjoyed cross-country skiing and travel. She had come to Dr. Levinson because her vision was rapidly deteriorating. Everything was dark, she said, and blurry. It reminded her of the paintings Monet had done when he was going blind. Shaking blood red bridges and melting water lilies. She was worried that if her vision problem continued to progress as it had been she would go totally blind. She said it had begun with blurry vision while she was reading, and had continued to worsen. She denied any history of ocular infection, injury or surgery. Her medical history was positive for hypertension and "an irregular heartbeat." Unfortunately, she could not initially recall the names of any medications she was taking.

Dr. Levinson knew that loss of vision could be attributed to a number of causes, and that the most likely was a tumor putting pressure on the ocular nerve. He ran a CAT scan, an MRI, but found no tumor. The only thing of interest were several oddly shaped pigmented corneal lesions. The appearance of the lesions is called corneal verticillata or vortex keratopathy. These cell deposits look like symmetrical patterns of powdery yellow, a dust storm behind the woman's pupil. The tornados themselves don't have any impact on vision; however, they are also produced as side effects of certain medications that can have other impacts on vision. They are also a symptom of Fabry's disease.

Obviously, Sara Sisun is a particularly talented young writer. But can we just take a minute to savor what kids can accomplish when our assignments *let* them excel? How many more Saras are out there? We won't know until we try some different kinds of writing—and research.

Just Ask Somebody

So traditional term papers plunge students into the hardest kind of research too soon. It's like trying to teach a beginner how to pole vault by setting the bar at world-record height and then saying, "Go ahead, learn how to jump!" A better way to teach a complex skill, like research, is to set the bar at a reachable level, so the learner can first master that, and then move it steadily up. So, before we send kids off to the library (or onto the Net) to research abstract ideas, we should first give them lots of practice gathering and analyzing data that are concrete, tangible, human, and fun.

There are two main types of concrete research that you can adapt to any subject: questionnaires and interviews. Both involve simply *asking people for information*. Now talking to people is a lot more real-seeming than digging through books in a library, but it can also yield tons of useful data to be sorted, sifted, interpreted, and reported, in words and graphics, either written down or told out loud, or both.

Questionnaires and Surveys

At Burley School in Chicago, Steve Wolk's seventh graders do a whole unit on designing and administering surveys. They study the tools of the genre by reading a variety of surveys in newspapers and magazines. They learn about different item types and scoring systems. Then they design and administer their own instruments and put them to work. Jaime, Adam, and John investigated people's attitudes toward poverty; Elizabeth, Pedro, and Andro studied whether people thought female soldiers should be allowed in combat. After collecting data from respondents in the neighborhood, students sifted and categorized the information during a classroom workshop, turning their results into reports, graphic displays, and presentations.

How can your students create curriculum-related questionnaires? Just look for the big teaching topics that have evident applications in life: the use of *statistics* to sell products or mislead votes; the contradictory *scientific research* about global warming. (You can also use the Wiggins and McTighe screens on page 11 for selecting promising survey topics.) Here's a fun one for social studies: Reword the Bill of Rights and make it into a ten-item Likert-scale questionnaire (strongly agree, somewhat agree, and so on). Then tally how many respondents support these bedrock constitutional provisions. Break it out by age, sex, race, occupation, religion, socioeconomic status, educational level, political party, you name it. A similar recent study showed that many Americans, especially teenagers, think that our civil rights are "too liberal."

Interviews

The simplest kind of "ask someone" research is conducting interviews with selected informants. Math students might interview ten adults about what kinds of mathematics come up in their jobs and then present their findings using quotations, bar graphs, pie charts, and other appropriate representations. In social studies, family history projects that feature interviews of elders are an excellent example of "ask someone" research. For guidance on setting up these inquiries, see Steve's book *History Comes Home* (Zemelman et al. 2000). For a science class, kids can interview selected community members about their attitudes or their (self-reported) behavior concerning any timely topic: recycling, energy conservation, or evolution (if you dare!).

When kids are doing interview research, either note taking or tape recording (or both) is critical to ensure that data is accurately captured. Professional ethnographers often use an interview *protocol,* a set of pre-chosen questions or topics they will raise with each informant in order to keep the scope of each interview parallel. Kids will need to develop tools like this, probably with the questions on the left side of the page and plenty of room for notes on the right. In-school interviewing practice with classmates is a must before hitting the field.

Play by Play

For the classroom procedure section of this activity, we'll simply let Sara Sisun's biology teacher, Charles "Doc" Coleman, tell us how he structures the medical interview assignment at Colorado Academy in Denver. As you read these excerpts from Doc's assignment sheet, notice the steps and structures he designs for students; you'll see many of the supports that we have mentioned earlier—student *choice* within the assignment, plenty of *time* to write and revise, *modeling* by the teacher of the genre at hand, structured *peer collaboration in the classroom,* and more.

Please keep in mind that the plan for this activity could work with *any occupation.* Not all middle or high school students can find a doctor, dentist, nurse, or pharmacist to sit for an interview. But this assignment works equally well with postal workers, bus drivers, store owners, landscapers, and even teachers. And, of course, the underlying structure of this research project, which later incorporates library and Net resources, can easily be adapted to all kinds of interview projects across the curriculum.

The Medical Interview—Doc Coleman, Colorado Academy

Expectations for This Assignment

- To practice interviewing skills
- To organize and distill ideas and research to create an essay
- To research a specific topic using the Internet and library resources
- To discover details about a profession that has connections with biology (medicine)
- To appreciate the forces associated with decision making in the face of uncertainty

You will need to find a doctor who is willing to meet with you for a short interview. (See me if you should have trouble finding a person to interview.) Ask if it would be all right if you taped the conversation. The purpose of the interview is for you to have a glimpse into what it is like to be a doctor. What are some of the pressures doctors feel? Where does the joy in the vocation come from? In this regard you could ask:

- Do you recall a particularly interesting case? Why was it especially interesting?
- Did you ever encounter a situation that gave you second thoughts about becoming or being a doctor? What happened?
- Have you encountered a particular disease or condition that stretched your abilities in some manner?
- Can you think of a particular case that made you glad you became a doctor?

After your interview you will use the Internet and library to flesh out details about whatever condition or disease your doctor has described. Here is what the start of your essay might look like:

continues

Setting the Scene (some dialogue, scene descriptive details)

Dr. M sat across from me in Starbucks. It was a warm spring morning, and she was dressed for jogging. I thanked her for meeting me and handed her the assignment to read. She held it out and squinted a little. I guessed she didn't have her reading glasses.

"So you want to know about an interesting case? Something you can research on the Net and also make real through your conversation with me? I'm glad you phoned first to give me a heads up. I've been thinking about it."

The episode recalled by Dr. M had occurred years earlier when she had been an intern. Feeling important and confident on the outside, while nervous and anxious about her responsibilities on the inside, she had found herself alone in the emergency room on a weeknight. It had not been a very busy evening, and she was in the midst of suturing a cut arm, when a man had pushed his way into the room. He was dark haired, had an ashen complexion and was dressed in an expensive-looking suit. He gestured wildly, was disoriented and mumbling guttural sounds. An orderly took charge and was ushering the man to the waiting room when he collapsed. His heart was racing, his breathing was shallow. Then his eyes had begun to bleed. Blood had almost spouted from his tear ducts. Dr. M conveyed to me her mounting panic, as new and alarming symptoms came quick and fast. And all the while they were unable to communicate with him. He was unresponsive to questions, while keeping up a barrage of frightened noises. Was something wrong with his throat? Was he a deaf mute? They were acting like vets, unable to gain any useful information beyond the anguish in the patient's eyes.

Internet Research

The symptoms described above probably do not exist for a specific illness. I made them up! In my model above, Dr. M will continue her description, finishing by giving the patient's condition a name. You will then move to the Internet and flesh out some details regarding this illness.

You can avoid plagiarizing by doing the following: Read your supplementary material several times until you have a clear understanding of it. Put away the material and ask yourself, "What did I just read?" Answer this question aloud, ideally explaining it to someone. You may be asked for clarification and you may have to go back to the source. Finally, write down the gist of the topic. Whatever you include in your essay must be attributed to the source in your bibliography. Use *NoodleTools* (www.noodletools.com) to see how to make reference to web publications. Be sure to document, document, document!

Your Audience

You are writing to inform and engage your biology classmates and college freshmen. These are readers who are aware, somewhat sophisticated, but

continues

not experts in the area of medicine you are describing. So you should be careful with word choice, especially when writing about scientific issues about which your reader may not be familiar. You must use clear language. Unfamiliar words that you want to use must be explained or defined. Acronyms must be decoded when they are introduced.

Your Voice

While you write your piece, you should be aware of your voice. It should be yours. Don't ape a style you have just read. Use *your* language and style. Journalists who have churned out many, many articles can fall into a clichéd style whose formula produces stale writing. These writers are called hacks. Often the beauty of student writing is the freshness of its voice. Be careful of trying to sound like one of the models you have just read. Figurative language will enhance your essay, but be careful of using clichés.

Peer Response

This process will take place in class after you have completed the first draft of your essays. While peer editing, you will look at three aspects of your partner's draft:

Revision can involve significant re-working of your writing. Perhaps the opening doesn't sufficiently grab the reader's attention and needs re-working. Sections might be more effective elsewhere in the piece; other bits might be best deleted altogether. There may be details that need to be expanded.

Editing is less invasive and takes place after the revision. Here you will consider word choice and order, spelling, and sentence structure.

Proofreading is the last step. Here you look for those little errors that are easy to skip over, things the spell check misses: *the* for *then, you* for *your*, etc. Make sure that the final format conforms to the requirements with regard to line spacing, margins, font and type size.

For the revision process, double space your work. This will provide space for your revision partner's suggestions. Comments such as "I don't like this paragraph" are not really helpful. Comments such as "In this sentence, this word seems too strong" or "This section seems out of place, could you move it closer to the beginning?" are more useful. Examples of what you should be looking for in this revision exercise are as follows.

1. Is the description of the doctor and his/her situation clear? Can you picture the scene?

2. Does the introduction "hook" the reader? Do you want to read on?

3. Is it easy to follow and understand?

continues

4. Is the word choice appropriate?

5. Are there terms that are not explained? (This is of vital importance since this is a biology essay, very likely containing new words.)

6. Can you pick out errors in any aspect of the scientific content, for example, biological details or confused logic?

7. Is there an effective "wrap-up" or conclusion? Does the story link back to the opening scene to form a satisfying ending?

8. How do the connections or transitions between paragraphs work? Can the reader follow where the story is going?

9. Are the sentences correct with regard to syntax, spelling, word order?

10. What details can you personally connect with in the writing? Does the writing feel "real"?

11. Watch out for clichés. Is the word choice "fresh"? Give examples.

12. Is the sentence structure varied, or do they all sound the same?

13. Do you have other suggestions for the writer? (use the back)

The final essay that the writer hands in will include this draft with your peer revision notes. If you do a conscientious job at this you will receive a bonus of up to 5% on top of your own essay grade.

Length

For this paper 750 to 1,000 words will suffice. If you get carried away you may extend this to 1,200 words. Type your essay and double space. Include a bibliography that lists where you have found your information. Use www.noodletools.com to help you with this.

The Grading of Your Essay

As with your first project, I will be looking for the following:

Style: Sentence variety, mechanics and grammar, word choice, clarity of expression. (20%)

Content: Research on topic, documentation, your understanding of your topic, how you weave your interview into the description of the medical problem. (65%)

Presentation: Are you aware of your audience? Do you engage the reader? Is the essay well organized? Has the essay been well proofread? Are there spelling errors? Sentence fragments, etc.? Is the writing clear and easy to follow? (15%)

Faction

What It Is

Faction is the marriage of factual research and imagination. The most popular genres that capture this kind of writing are historical fiction and science fiction. In the best examples of these, the writer meticulously researches a topic and then weaves a story around the facts that educates the reader while entertaining him as well. Take a look in the back of Michael Crichton's *Jurassic Park*. Crichton just didn't let his imagination run wild when it came to DNA, chaos theory, and velociraptors. He did a ton of research first and the references are there to prove it! Also, though these genres are fiction, many pieces—Gore Vidal's *Lincoln* comes to mind—strive for a nonfiction tone and an accurate depiction of reality, what might have really happened. Now, we know you are not going to have your kids write whole novels in history or science class. But the principles of the genre can be applied to very short, guided research assignments as well (two to three typed pages, double spaced) such as a diary of or interview with a famous person or a witness to a historical event.

When to Use It and Why

Faction offers tremendous potential as an alternative assessment, guided research project, or extension activity. In addition, if you pursue this project repeatedly, students can progress through the year from highly guided to more independent forms of research. Finally, faction gives students the chance to personalize their learning, connecting it with other parts of their lives, as they pull from their prior knowledge and experiences in order to create a believable fictional subtext.

At a time when you wish to use an alternative assessment, a student's faction can serve as an addition to or a replacement of a unit test. Have students review the material you've covered, creating a character that would lead a reader through the important facts in an interesting way. Within the writing, students could be required to underline or italicize information from the text or their notes, placing extra emphasis on the research and rereading that students should do when reviewing for a test.

You can also use faction as a short guided research project. Give students a series of three to five articles on a specific topic (see the Taino diary shown later in this section). Kids read and discuss these articles in class. As each article is distributed, students add the bibliographical information to a list using APA (American Psychological Association) or MLA (Modern Language Association) style. After completing all of the readings, students reread the material from the perspective of a character linked to the material, highlighting information that would be significant to that character. Finally, students write one or two diary entries, creating a fictionalized life based on the facts of the article. This time, rather than underlining the facts, students indicate their research via the use of citation.

The most advanced form of faction is a type of independent research paper. If students are already familiar with this kind of project, with guided research, and with how to cite sources and create a reference page, then creating some interesting, original writing should not be the insurmountable challenge that the typical research paper often presents. Here students start with a list of topics from the teacher. After receiving some brief background information (if this is a science topic, for example, your kids may not be quite as familiar with the world's greatest scientists as you), students pick their topics. Though you might not want two students using the same topic, it's unlikely they will approach their faction in the same way. We believe that whenever possible, letting students choose their topics will lead to more investment and a better product.

Play by Play

Topic Search

How your students choose their topics depends on the ultimate goal of the project. If you want to guide students through the research process via a fixed set of texts, all students will be writing from the same collection of information. On the other hand, if students are doing independent research, there are several routes you can take. First, you might develop a list of possible topics. Dan Schwarz, a colleague at Andrew High School in Tinley Park, Illinois looked at his calendar, saw spring break coming up in a couple of weeks, and realized there were a lot of topics related to the Roaring Twenties that he wanted to cover in his American Literature class before reading *The Great Gatsby*. With the help of Kate Schwartz, the American history teacher across the hall, he developed a list. Each student had to choose a different topic, and woe to those who were absent that day: Dan made the choices for them! Students went out, did their research, presented to the class, and all of those topics got some attention. Mission accomplished!

1920s Research Topics

American economy in the 1920s	Al Capone	Harlem Renaissance
stock market crash	Henry Ford	popular dances: Charleston, jitterbug, black bottom, shimmy, breakaway
racial violence and the Ku Klux Klan	Scopes trial	
	red scare	
	F. Scott Fitzgerald	Elliot Ness

jazz music	Charlie Parker	art deco
Birth of a Nation—film	Charles Lindbergh	Fats Waller
flappers	Admiral Byrd	vaudeville
prohibition	The Cotton Club	silent movies
organized crime, gangsters	popular music	Rudolph Valentino
Herbert Hoover	Ziegfeld Follies	the great migration
inventions of the 1920s		

If you do not need to cover this many subjects, then more than one student can choose the same topic. But beware: Teacher-created lists set up a common excuse from kids when their projects are not up to par: "But I didn't like anything on the list." So unless you *need* a list (as in Dan's case), don't make one; let the kids find their own topics instead, of course guiding them toward a good choice by using one of the following strategies:

➤ Have students review the chapters studied in the textbook, paying special attention to the items highlighted in bold. They should make a list of those topics they would like to know more about.

➤ Find two or three good websites related to the general topic you'd like students to research. Have students review the sites, in class or on their own, once again making a list of intriguing items they'd be interested in researching further.

In either case, be sure to devote some in-class time for students to talk about their potential choices to each other and to the whole class. Oftentimes, when students just hear the ideas of others, it gives them new insights that hadn't occurred to them before. Also, you'll need to help students narrow down topics that are especially broad, reminding them that these papers will be only one or two pages, double spaced.

Identifying the Audience

There are three audiences for this paper. Obviously, the first two are you and other students. To identify the third one, you and your students need the answer to this question: Whom might this faction influence, living or dead, real or imagined? For example, for an indigenous person's diary written in response to Columbus' destruction of her land, people, and culture, the audience might be those who could have helped her people at the time or future generations who need to be reminded of the atrocities Columbus committed against the Arawak tribes.

Gathering Information

For something this short, students do not need to do a ton of research. Two or three good sources are more than adequate. Of course, the qualifier is the word *good*. For us it means sources with worthwhile, detailed information. For our students, it often means the first three hits on Google. If you've managed to model a guided research faction using sources similar to what they might find online or in your school's media center, the kids already have a head start picturing what good sources should look like. Additionally, your willingness to do a little preliminary planning can make a world of difference. Be sure to talk to your media specialist about which databases and websites might be most useful. Also, any Internet searching you can do ahead of time will save many headaches. There is nothing wrong with giving the kids a list of five or ten website or database sources from which to start. There's even nothing wrong with telling them that two of their sources need to be from your list. Those additional, and perhaps questionable, sources they find on their own can serve as extras.

Also, as long as we're talking about sources, let's not forget those old standbys: encyclopedias and almanacs, many of which still exist in print in your media center. And, hard as it is to believe, there are still lots of *books* lounging about, just waiting to be picked up by your eager young researchers. The media specialist knows about these forgotten relics and will be more than happy to steer you and your students to them. As a matter of fact, she might even put them on a cart for easier access.

Prewriting

There are several steps in this preliminary phase. First, as soon as students find a source and print off a copy for themselves, they need to record all of the necessary bibliographical information. Second, as they read the information, they need to react from the perspective of their faction character. This means underlining information that stands out in relation to their character as well as jotting in the margins of their copy what their character might have been thinking in regard to this info. Finally, they need to flesh out the details of their character:

- age
- social status
- occupation
- education
- background
- gender

- goals, hopes, dreams
- impact of the researched information upon the character's life

Drafting

When students are completing this assignment for the first time, it's important to begin the writing in class, by either handwriting in the classroom or typing in the computer lab. That way you can circulate, reading over shoulders and answering questions when students get stuck. Also, once students have been working for about thirty minutes, have them stop and read aloud what they've written in small editing groups. Reading aloud is a very effective revision tool because the writer immediately hears phrases that work and those that don't, especially wording that might not signal a need for correction as readily during silent reading. Finally, if you're using computers, have the students save their work in a way that allows them to access it from home. Tell the students that a typed, double-spaced rough draft is due two days from the first writing day.

Revising

Since this is a research paper, students need to revise for two specific functions:

- sufficient evidence of quality research
- imaginative yet accurate characterization and attention to incident and detail

Instead of trying to revise for everything at once, it's better to split the revision into two separate days with some space in between. If you began the writing on Monday, the typed-up rough draft is due on Wednesday, and research is the focus of the revision. With their research and their typed drafts in hand, students should underline specific research facts and details woven into the paper. After students have completed this part, demonstrate the proper use of parenthetical citation. Using an old paper that's been transferred to a transparency, underline the facts. Above each underlined item, write the parenthetical citation using the specified APA or MLA format. Then have the students work on adding citations to their own papers. Finally, tell the students to reread their papers and place stars by areas that have little factual content. This session ends with the following revision assignment:

Create a new draft of your paper, revising for research information and citation.

- **Research Information:** Return to the areas you starred. Add information that reflects a greater depth of research and interesting factual detail.

☞ **Citation:** Type in your parenthetical citations at the end of the sentences they refer to. The period goes *after* the citation.

Two or three days later, students should return with a new rough draft. Ideally, the embedded research information is improved and the citations are in place. Now it's time for some feedback about the *story*. With their editing groups, students should take turns reading their factions aloud. Remember, the more the kids read their stories aloud, the more they will improve them. After a reading, the group discusses several questions and the writer records her group's feedback on the rough draft.

☞ What words really showed action or visual detail?

☞ What was your favorite part?

☞ What parts made you want more information or ask questions?

☞ At what point did you care most about the character?

After one paper has been read aloud and discussed thoroughly, it's time to move on to the next.

Editing

No matter what the paper, the basic editing procedure stays the same. The most important thing to remember is that since editing is detail oriented, it's best to have the kids work just with one partner. Here are some ideas to try.

☞ As you evaluate student writing over time, keep track of the errors that keep cropping up most frequently. Simply make your own chart of the items that you see most often. Review with kids how to find and correct the top three or four errors on your chart and focus the conventions part of the grade on those particular errors rather than every error that could possibly be made.

☞ Talk to the English department and see what punctuation and grammar conventions are featured that year. If freshman year is the year of the semicolon, spend five minutes in class reviewing its use and then include its correct usage as part of the grade.

☞ Have partners work only on the first page of each paper, trying to really clean it up, making a list of errors found. Students can then finish their editing individually. Because writers do not invent new errors on every page but repeat the same errors over and over, it's *very* important for them to refer back to the lists. As an alternative, you can have each student create an individual responsibilities list, starting with his three most frequent errors. Students should consult their list when revising and turn in a copy of the list to you with their paper so you can see how they are progressing on it.

☞ Have the other partner instead of the writer read the paper aloud. Someone unfamiliar with the text is more likely to catch errors or awkward wording versus someone who has been looking at her words all week. Have you ever repeated a word twice when writing and not even noticed it? We rest our case.

☞ When checking for spelling errors (for some reason they still occur even in this age of spell check), have students read aloud, placing a finger on each word as they read. Before moving to the next word, they need to determine if it's the *correct* word choice (think *there, they're, their*) and if it's the *best* word choice (getting rid of words like *you, things,* and *stuff*).

☞ Require students to have two other adults—not teachers, we all have enough papers to read already—proofread their papers, marking and signing off on them.

The bottom line is that most final-draft papers are still going to have some errors. A perfect paper requires an attention to detail that few kids or adults, for that matter (see how many errors you can find in a single edition of your local newspaper!), possess. It's important that your grading reflect the proper use of standard conventions, but the bulk of the points need to focus on style and content. As teachers, it's more effective for us to help kids improve a step at a time rather than aim for a level of perfection that will only discourage us from giving writing assignments.

Sharing the Writing

Sharing will be determined by your purpose. If the goal is to review the material in lieu of a test, the sharing might be limited to the teacher and the partners the writer peer edits with. However, whenever you can expand readership beyond the grader, the writing will improve because students will be more invested when communicating with a real-world audience. As long as the pieces are short, it's never a waste to spend a couple of days hearing students read their work aloud. It's amazing how even an average paper can sound much better when heard through the writer's voice.

Another possibility, particularly if you plan to do several pieces of writing in the course of the semester or year, is to have students keep a writing folder of all their finished pieces. At the end of the course, each student polishes and submits one piece for a class magazine, which is distributed on final exam day. Students always enjoy seeing their friends in print, the magazine becomes a souvenir, and having something to read keeps them quiet for the rest of the period when they'd otherwise be driving you insane on the last day of class. Plus, the magazine holds a treasure trove of writing models for next year's classes!

What Can Go Wrong?

The biggest problem that arises is when kids don't follow the process, going straight from idea to final draft, usually all in the twelve hours prior to the assignment's due date. Our society often fails to value the process by which a product is attained. Even though Michael Jordan is retired, many Chicago-area students still worship him. However, they worship his accomplishments, seldom reflecting upon all of the hard work and continual practice Jordan undertook. There are no shortcuts to becoming one of the world's best basketball players or turning in a high-quality faction paper. Therefore, it is absolutely essential that project steps get checked in along the way via stamps, points in the grade book, or a teacher-initialed checklist. To make this work, students *must* turn in the interim pieces or checklist with the final paper. Honoring the process is the single best way to avoid the thorny issue of plagiarism, a crime almost always committed during a moment of deadline desperation.

How Do I Grade This?

Figure 7–1 shows a possible rubric you could use to score a faction paper.

Example

The following is an example of a faction project used in an American history class. After reading several entries from Columbus' journal along with several other pieces detailing the consequences of his exploration, students wrote their own journal entries from the perspective of the Taino tribe, the first indigenous people Columbus encountered. Here is what Alyssa wrote.

HISTORY

April 13, 1494—In all the fourteen years I have been alive, I have never experienced so much fear, torture, and depression than I have over the past two years. My loving people are dying, many at a time, and we are all anxious, never knowing what these evil people will surprise us with next. Yesterday, I jolted awake in the middle of the night to see several dozen of my fellow people (men, women, girls, and boys) boarding twelve enormous ships (Bigelow, 1998). Ironically, these were the same ships we so naively first welcomed to our lush island some time ago. Now these ships carry us to slavery (Bigelow, 1998). Helplessness crawls deep inside of me, and it tears me apart inside knowing there is nothing we can do to stop them. I am petrified that if I do one thing to displease these white men or if they catch any of us trying to escape our village, they will ship me away just like all the others.

<table>
<tr><th colspan="12" style="text-align:center">Faction Evaluation</th></tr>
</table>

Faction Evaluation

Name _____ Date _____ Hour _____

Main Character _____ Genre _____

• Main character is fully realized, using emotion and detail	10	9	8	7	6	5	4	3	2	1	no
• Replicates genre clearly and accurately	10	9	8	7	6	5	4	3	2	1	no
• Extensive use of notes, text, and research—details evident	10	9	8	7	6	5	4	3	2	1	no
• Complete works cited page; citation used correctly	10	9	8	7	6	5	4	3	2	1	no
• Original and interesting; imaginative *yet school appropriate*	10	9	8	7	6	5	4	3	2	1	no

© 2007 by Daniels, Zemelman, and Steineke from *Content-Area Writing.* Portsmouth, NH: Heinemann.

Figure 7–1 *Faction rubric*

Minding my daily chores, a white man came charging into my home like a bear. He slammed me to the ground, claiming my family was planning to escape the village by canoe. I gasped and struggled to force words out of my bloody mouth. I slurred to him that I didn't know what he was talking about, but secretly I knew my family was planning an escape and my people were preparing for an attack upon the ship Isabella (Bigelow, 1998). He slashed at me until I felt paralyzed, making sure my family would think twice before trying to leave. Then he strutted away. My entire body throbbed, and my heart raced with panic, but I was thankful to still be living with my family and friends.

My people have made it through these two excruciating years. My parents say that our people are like boulders on the beach, pounded by waves yet enduring. Our people are putting up the best fight they can, but I know the truth. Millions are dying of disease, slavery, and murder. In time my people will come to an end (Zinn, 2003). It hurts to think we once lived in a "thriving place" (Barreiro, 1998, p. 107). We estimate we have been in existence for fifteen hundred years, years in which we all were well fed and rarely experienced conflicts within our villages (Barreiro, 1998). I'm afraid we are not thriving anymore.

Works Cited

Barreiro, Jose (1998). "The Tainos 'Men of the Good.'" *Rethinking Columbus* (pp 106–107). Milwaukee: Rethinking School Ltd.

Bigelow, Bill (1998). "Timeline: Spain, Columbus, and Tainos." *Rethinking Columbus* (pp 99–102). Milwaukee: Rethinking School Ltd.

Zinn, Howard (2003). "Columbus, The Indians, and Human Progress." *A People's History of the United States* (excerpt). New York: Harper Collins Inc.

RAFT

What It Is

As defined by Doug Buehl, RAFT is an acronym that stands for **r**ole, **a**udience, **f**ormat, **t**opic (2001). Keeping their research, reading, or a recently studied unit in mind, students deepen and express what they've learned by writing a piece that is based on their own choices for each of these four characteristics. In other words, they create a faction that is built around the answers to four questions.

Role: Who am I? What is my personality? How will I react to the information from my new viewpoint? Roles are often dependent upon the content. In science, roles might include a scientist or a recently dissected earthworm. In American history, roles might include people living during a past era or inanimate objects that have witnessed history.

Audience: Who needs to read this? Whom am I trying to persuade? What is the goal or purpose of the writing? What kind of emotional reaction do I want from the reader? The decisions of role and audience are intertwined. That dissected earthworm's audience might be fellow earthworms being persuaded to give up their lives for the advancement of scientific knowledge.

Format: What is the format? There are many possibilities: news story, letter to the editor, journal entry, travelogue, speech, and so on (for a vastly expanded list of genres, see pages 207–208).

Topic: What is the subject I am covering? What information do I have to share? What is the focus of my chosen format?

While we like to see students taking on the decision making, it's also possible, when structuring any RAFT assignment, for the teacher to make these decisions or for teacher and student to negotiate them.

When to Use It and Why

The RAFT is most suitable as a closure activity, a way for students to demonstrate what they have learned during a unit of study or during their own research. Though a RAFT might contain information similar to what might be found in a formal essay, its format enables students to share their knowledge more creatively, using the voice of their role rather than the drab and depersonalized diction that characterizes most essay test answers. When students have opportunities to make choices and connect more of their full selves with the work, they are almost always more engaged and more likely to assimilate the material they've studied.

Play by Play

Topic Search

As always, the topic search is dependent on the goal of the assignment. In the case of research, a teacher might give a list from which to choose or a broad category that limits the possible subtopics. Sometimes, as evidenced by the science examples we show later, the topic is nonnegotiable. Nevertheless, the possible roles and audiences can still usually be brainstormed and individually chosen by the kids.

Identifying Role, Audience, and Format

Unlike the student who is composing a typical essay or report, the writer of a RAFT piece specifically plays a role other than himself and, therefore, the writing must aim to appeal to a specific audience that is far removed from the classroom. Here is where the class needs to brainstorm together. For example, if students are to review the reasons patriots felt that severing ties with England was necessary, what roles might they take and what audiences might they address? Also, which formats might best meet the needs of the intended audience? Here's how these characteristics—role, audience, and format—might line up:

ROLE	AUDIENCE	FORMAT
Ben Franklin	French Delegation	Letter or speech
Quill pen	Future historians	Memoir
Abigail Adams	John Adams	Dinner table conversation
Patrick Henry	The Sons of Liberty	Speech, Q & A session
Samuel Adams	Boston Tea Party protesters	Motivational speech
Thomas Paine	Average-citizen fence sitters	Emotional essay
Tradesman	Other indentured servants	Pub argument
Recent immigrant	Relative back in England	Letter to relative
Minuteman	Men needed for recruitment	Recruitment speech

After brainstorming, it really helps for students to talk in groups of three or four to figure out the list's implications. What personality, social status, and attitudes are reflected in each role? How would each role interpret the information differently? How might audience affect the style and format of the writing? For example, though Abigail Adams supposedly exercised strong influence on her husband's decisions, during the 1700s it would have been completely inappropriate for her to address him publicly. However, she could have certainly written him a heartfelt letter stating her viewpoint related to the colonies' possible independence from England. Before groups end their discussion, each member must decide on her role, audience, and format as well as her answers to the questions the group was directed to consider.

Gathering the Information

Now that students have made decisions regarding role, audience, and format, they need to return to the material, rereading through the eyes of their new role, taking notes on important information, and thinking about how their viewpoint influences its interpretation.

Prewriting

Some prewriting was already done when students did their initial brainstorming and searched for information. At this point, it can be very helpful for students to see some samples related to formats they are somewhat unfamiliar with. While letter writing needs little explanation, examples and a tip sheet for writing genres like dialogue, memoir, and speeches will be necessary. However, since collecting this background information might seem overwhelming, there's nothing wrong with limiting students to the formats for which you have samples. But before discarding some of the formats, do a quick Internet search. Some U.S. history sites are filled with links to letters, speeches, news articles, and other written artifacts from various historical periods. Many of these examples are accompanied by instructions. All you need to do is find, print, copy, and distribute them!

Drafting

Nothing fancy here. Once the previous steps are done, let the kids loose to work. Remind them that they must be true to their role, audience, and format as well as reveal what they know about the topic. Within the constraints of your schedule, provide in-class writing time, during which you can coach, confer, and provide the kinds of during-writing support outlined in Chapters 6 and 8.

Revision

Students should work in editing groups, where writers read their papers aloud. Here's the feedback the listeners need to give:

- Which lines really fit the role? Which ones didn't?
- What details reflect the role, setting, or time period?
- Without being told, can the listeners tell what effect the writing is supposed to have on the intended audience? What suggestions do they have for making the effect more powerful?

After meeting in their groups, individual writers need to reread their work silently, reflecting on how well they covered the topic. Sometimes students get so wrapped up in the creativity aspect that they forget that the writing also needs to reflect significant research. As they reread their drafts, they need to underline the hard facts that demonstrate their research. Then they need to return to their information sources, reviewing their readings with the goal of inserting further topic details. Before editing, students should make their changes and additions, returning to their groups with a clean copy ready for editing.

Editing

Work on this stage of the process often depends on the particular mechanics of writing that a school or grade-level team has chosen to stress. Pick just a couple of items to watch for in a given assignment. As we've suggested earlier, marking up dozens of errors on every paper not only discourages students and deters subject-area teachers from assigning writing but is unhelpful because it doesn't allow kids to perceive any pattern to their problems. One focus that might be especially apropos, if many students have chosen conversations, is a review of dialogue writing: use of quotes, dialogue tags, when to put the punctuation inside versus outside the quotes, and how to indicate speaker changes with paragraphing.

Sharing the Writing

Since RAFTS are filled with creativity, voice, and variety, it's definitely worth having the kids read them out loud to the rest of the class. Also, be sure to submit the really clever ones to your school's literary magazine!

What Can Go Wrong?

The biggest problem with this assignment is that kids get carried away with the creativity and forget that they also have to show what they know about the topic. Stoke their enthusiasm as they really get into their roles, but keep reminding them to return to their information sources.

How Do I Grade This?

Figure 7–2 contains a rubric that could be used for grading a RAFT paper.

Examples

Here is Liz's interview with one of the survivors of the Donner Party.

> **Role:** Interviewer
> **Audience:** Those curious about Donner Party survivors
> **Format:** Talk show interview
> **Topic:** James Reed's accounting of his Donner Party experience

RAFT Evaluation

Name _____   Date _____   Hour _____

Role _____   Audience _____

Format _____   Topic _____

• Role is clear; fits format and audience	10	9	8	7	6	5	4	3	2	1	no
• Choice of format appropriate; replicates format conventions accurately	10	9	8	7	6	5	4	3	2	1	no
• Extensive use of notes, text, and research—details evident	10	9	8	7	6	5	4	3	2	1	no
• Original and interesting; imaginative *yet school appropriate*	10	9	8	7	6	5	4	3	2	1	no

© 2007 by Daniels, Zemelman, and Steineke from *Content-Area Writing*. Portsmouth, NH: Heinemann.

Figure 7–2 *RAFT rubric*

Survivor of Donner Party Tells It All!

1846 was the year when the American migration went west. Many went west to get a fresh start in a wide open land to get away from the overcrowded cities. 20,000 Americans already lived west of the Mississippi River, but many more still rushed further west to start new lives. Among the ones who traveled west was the Donner Party. The Donner Party consisted of 87 people in all, including men, women and children. Leading the Donner Party were George Donner and James Reed. The excited travelers could not wait to get to California, but they had no idea that they were in for a horrible journey and that many would not reach their destination. Nearly half of the Donner Party died, and some resorted to eating the dead in order to survive. I am fortunate to interview James Reed, leader of the Donner Party and one of its survivors.

Hello Mr. Reed. How are you?
I am fine, thank you.

Before traveling to California, where did you come from and what did you do?
I was born in Ireland but lived in Illinois. I was a wealthy businessman. I lived in a nice home in Springfield with my family.

I understand that you are a survivor of the Donner Party. How do you feel about being one of the few that survived?
Well Liz, I feel very fortunate to be alive. I am very lucky that my family also survived, but I do feel sorrow for those who did not make it. My stepmother died

HISTORY

because she was too weak and could no longer carry on. Overall, more suffered than survived.

How many children do you have?

I have four children whom I love dearly. I am fortunate to have them and my lovely wife, Margaret.

Why did you, along with George Donner, decide you wanted to take Hastings' Cutoff?

We believed Hastings' Cutoff would offer us a shorter route over the mountains, so we took it for the sake of the women and children. We received letters from Hastings that encouraged us to take the cutoff, and we trusted him so we took it.

Why do you think it took so long for the remainder of the Donner Party to reach its destination?

I believe we were unfortunate at the time. I regret taking Hastings' Cutoff because that was a big factor in our delay. Also, there was horrible weather. We tried to walk through many blizzards and storms. The pass was completely blocked by snow twenty feet tall. It was so cold that many could not continue on. It was impossible to get all the wagons through.

What happened between you and Mr. Snyder at the Humboldt River?

It all started when I saw Mr. Snyder beating an ox. Since he was injuring the animal and we desperately needed it for hauling one of the wagons, I tried to stop him, but I only made things worse. I tried calming him down but that did not work. Instead he took his anger out on me, punching and hitting me until I stabbed my knife into him in self-defense. He died. I did not mean to kill him, but I did. I was protecting myself. I could not let him kill me.

What happened to you after you killed Mr. Snyder?

After I killed Snyder, I was banished from the party and rode off to California by myself. I had to leave my wife and children behind. Actually, I was very fortunate. I was banished instead of being put to death.

How did you feel about leaving your family and what did you do?

I felt terrible leaving them. I knew I had let them down. I owed it to them to get them safely to California. Once I arrived in California, I raised money and organized a rescue party. As soon as the weather permitted, we traveled back to where I thought my family and friends were stranded.

Were you successful in finding them?

Yes, but I went five months before I knew whether or not I would ever see my family again.

How do you feel about the Donner Party members who turned to cannibalism in order to survive?

I do not really blame them. This was the only way for some of them to survive, and I believe that they should not be criticized. You really don't know what the situation is like until you've been in that position.

Do you know what the process was for eating the dead?

My family told me that the survivors labeled the body parts so no one would accidentally eat the flesh of a family member. Flesh was cut off the bones and roasted over a fire pit. It was hard for those survivors to eat the only food available to them, but they managed.

What are you doing now and how do you like California?
I'm working to support my family by farming and ranching. We have a nice home here. We're all happy to be together once again.
Thank you very much Mr. Reed. I really appreciate your time.
You are very welcome Liz.

The next example is an assignment from Tracy Sukalo's biology class.

Thank-You Note Assignment

Let's pretend that you are the nucleus. You have just spent many long hours controlling all the activities that take place within the cell. As you sit down to rest after a tough day's work, you begin reflecting about all the great things that are happening within your cell. There is plenty of energy, materials are transported effectively, there is careful monitoring of what flows in and out, all waste is properly broken down. You've got fantastic organelles working inside your cell! These organelles are doing a great job for the cell, and you want to show them your appreciation.

SCIENCE

Your Assignment: Choose any organelle in the cell that you would like to thank for its contributions. As the nucleus, write a creative and thoughtful thank-you note to this organelle. Make sure that you tell them how their specific job is helping the cell. Also, it is important for the nucleus to describe why the cell does not function properly without this particular cell. You must include the following:

1. The name and function of the organelle and how the cell would be different without it

2. Facts and details about the organelle

3. A minimum of two creative paragraphs

4. Your thank-you note should be in letter format or in the form of a greeting card written in first person as the nucleus.

Here is Brianna's thank-you to an organelle.

Role: Nucleus
Audience: Cell Membrane
Format: Letter of appreciation
Topic: The Cell Membrane's contribution to the nucleus and other organelles

Dear Nuclear Envelope,
I would like to thank you for being a part of our cell. We have grown very close over the past couple of days. You are considered part of our family now. You are a layer of two membranes that surrounds me, the nucleus. That is why I feel so close and protected by you. You are like an older brother to me. You have thousands of dots of nuclear pores that are not only adorable, but serve a very good purpose. They allow material to move in and out of me. I really appreciate that. If it wasn't for you, I would not have any

visitors and I would become a very lonely, old nucleus. Just like messages, instructions, and blueprints moving in and out of central office, a stable stream of proteins, RNA, and other molecules move back and forth through your nuclear pores.

You are like my faithful partner in crime. You are the secretary and I am the boss. I really appreciate all the work you put into your job. If you didn't do your job, I would either be bombarded by materials I wouldn't be able to handle or nothing would come visit me at all. That would make me very upset, so because of you my days are much better. You also have very good judgment on whom you allow to come have a meeting with me and whom does not pass your gate of approval. Hopefully, you will not choose to leave or retire anytime soon because I would never be happy again. I will never lay you off because you are such a good employee. If someone or something was to stop in our lobby, they would be able to see that you have been "employee of the month" for the past several years. No other organelle has topped you yet, so I would just like to take a couple of minutes to recognize you and your achievements. Thank you for the loyalty you have offered to me and our cell as a whole.

Sincerely,

Brianna Nucleus

Brochure

What It Is

Ever go on a driving vacation and stop at an information center? Even if your intention was just a quick pit stop, it was probably pretty hard to walk past that rack of colorful brochures without grabbing a few. The inviting graphics and quick-read nature of commercial brochures are easily adapted to classroom topics as well. In this kind of writing, students must condense text to the most essential information yet write in an interesting style aimed at an audience that might know nothing about their topic. Then the kids have to come up with a graphic design inviting enough to get someone to pick up the brochure in the first place!

When to Use It and Why

Brochures, like many of the other public writing examples we have discussed, work well as summative activities for a unit or line of inquiry. They can be used as a review activity before a test or (as we prefer) as an alternative assessment in lieu of a test. Jeff Janes, a science teacher at Andrew High School in Tinley Park, Illinois, finds brochure writing a great way to get kids to reread their notes before a test, something some students might otherwise choose to omit from their to-do list. He also says that brochures give the less sciencey kids a chance to shine. While the ones who enjoy the math and formulas sometimes grumble, those who are more talented in writing and art breathe a big sigh of relief and get right to work. Also, when those kids use the media they feel most comfortable with, it's surprising how much science they actually learn that wouldn't necessarily be reflected on a traditional test!

SCIENCE

Play by Play

Topic Search

In the case of brochure writing, whether or not there is a topic search depends solely on the purpose of the assignment. When Jeff uses the brochure assignment as a way for kids to review their notes, he tells them exactly what he wants covered so that their writing will prepare them for the test. On the other hand, if the brochure is a research vehicle, students should be given a list of potential topics from which to choose or an opportunity to be guided in some effective brainstorming (see the section on the I-search paper in Chapter 9 [pages 236–238] for further topic search ideas).

Identifying the Audience

Though other students and the teacher will be part of the audience, the point of the brochure project is to present the information in an interesting and understandable way to people beyond the classroom. When his students work on their brochures in Introductory Physical Science, Jeff says, "Imagine that your brochures will be distributed to middle school students who don't have much of a background in physical science. You need to write the information in a manner that would be understandable to them."

Gathering Information

In Jeff's most recent brochure assignment, students needed to review specific information about the eight types of chemical reactions they'd studied to write about one of them. They needed to include the following:

1. the name of the type of reaction

2. the reason scientists chose that particular name (For example, why is endothermic called endothermic? Why is single replacement called single replacement?)

3. its symbolic form, should one exist

4. a chemical equation demonstrating this type of reaction

5. a real-world example (it can be the word equation of the reaction described in item 4 , or another example)

6. its relationship to at least one other type of equation

Prewriting

Before students get started on their first brochure of the school year (Jeff likes to repeat this assignment two or three times within a course), Jeff takes them through some rudimentary steps. First he has them fold a standard letter-size piece of paper into a brochure and think about what would go on each of the panels. Though Jeff demonstrates a six-panel version, additional panels are fine with him. It's the information and creativity he is most interested in. Then he focuses them on the front panel, the one that will need to visually attract readers as well as introduce them to a topic they may be unfamiliar with. Finally, he has students think about the layout and artwork. What kind of special effects might they use? Lettering using shading or back shadow are examples. How will they organize the layout so that the reader sees the most important information first? Jeff finds it useful to show the kids samples from previous classes. Displaying commercial brochures you've collected will also give them many layout ideas.

Drafting

Though MS Publisher, as well as other desktop publishing programs, offers a variety of brochure templates, Jeff insists that the kids do their brochures the old-fashioned way, by hand. They create their own artwork and they neatly print the brochure information. Text and graphics are physically cut and pasted into the layout. However, before creating the final text that will be glued in, students write a draft first in their notebooks so that they can edit and revise it before neatly transcribing it and permanently gluing it into place.

Revision and Editing

Since the writing is short, students can easily combine the revision and editing steps as they work with a partner. First, they read through each other's text, ascertaining that the required information is present. Next, they look at the way the information is written. Does it sound like something copied straight from the notes or textbook, or does it sound like an enthusiastic scientist trying to entice the reader to learn more? Also, is the information written so that a middle school student could truly understand the content and be able to explain it to someone else?

Finally, once the content is in good shape, it's time for students to proofread and edit. First, partners trade brochure text and the nonowner slowly reads the information aloud while the writer carefully listens for words, phrases, and sentences that don't sound right. Afterward, writers give their text a second editing, starting at the very end of the paper. Starting with the last word in the paper, they put their finger on each word and piece of punctuation as they read it aloud. Before moving on, writers need to determine the following:

- Is that the correct word (for example, *it's* or *its*)?
- Did I spell the word correctly?
- Do I need a piece of punctuation there? If so, is that the correct punctuation?

Reading backward slows the writer down enough to find errors that he would otherwise skip over.

Once students have perfected their text, they are ready to put it all together and create a final-draft brochure.

Sharing the Writing

On the day the brochures are due, the kids trade with each other, reading several, seeing how the same information was presented in a variety of imaginative ways. The kids enjoy seeing what their classmates have come up with while also reviewing for the upcoming test. How cool is that? Afterward, students take their brochures home and use them to study for the test. Interestingly enough, the kids who really make the effort to put the concepts into words that nonscience students can readily understand are the same ones who best display their own knowledge of the unit when they take the test.

What Can Go Wrong?

As mentioned earlier, Jeff is a stickler for doing this project by hand. In the past, he found that kids who did the work on the computer often cheated. They had no trouble finding clever, good-at-science friends or siblings who were perfectly willing to sit down and whip out a computer-generated brochure. Since Jeff can recognize everyone's printing (the kids have to print on all their lab reports), he immediately spots unfamiliar handwriting. Also, there's something to be said for the thinking necessary for conceptualizing and drawing original graphics versus slapping in some generic clip art.

Another problem Jeff runs across is that the kids who really enjoy the precise nature of scientific equations and math sometimes balk at having to do a creative project. However, he just tells them that their discomfort is an indication that they need more practice in this kind of thinking; after all, the best scientists do not just repeat the experiments of others—it is their ability for imagining new possibilities that leads to scientific breakthroughs.

Variation

Even though a computer-generated brochure has the potential for plagiarism, those templates are pretty cool. If you want to give them a try, the following ideas might curb the copying problem.

☞ Want to Jump Around?

Lisa Evans addresses the creation of computer-generated three-fold brochures for the geometry portion of the family fair discussed in Chapter 9; see page 233.

☞ Have students work in class to write and revise the text, checking in the final handwritten version before typing anything into the computer.

☞ Retain the requirement of original graphics. The kids can scan them in and then use them just as they would clip art.

☞ Take the kids to the school computer lab and lead them through the process of creating a brochure using a template. If you've already made one of your own, you'll be able to show them some tips and tricks as well as oversee the original creation process.

Brochure Evaluation

Name _____ Date _____ Hour _____

Does each chemical reaction brochure contain the following information?

PANEL #1	#2	#3	#4	#5	#6	#7	#8	REQUIREMENT
								1. The name of the chemical reaction
								2. The reason scientists chose that particular name
								3. Its symbolic form should one exist
								4. A chemical equation demonstrating this type of reaction
								5. A real-world example (word equation or other example)
								6. Its relationship to at least one other type of equation

48 Points Possible for Information: _____/48

2 Points Possible for Overall Quality (Neatness, Color, Enticing Front Cover) _____/2

Grand Total _____/50

Figure 7–3 *Brochure rubric*

How Do I Grade This?

See Figure 7–3 for a rubric you could use to grade your students' brochures.

Example

Figure 7–4 shows the front cover and inside panel of one student's brochure.

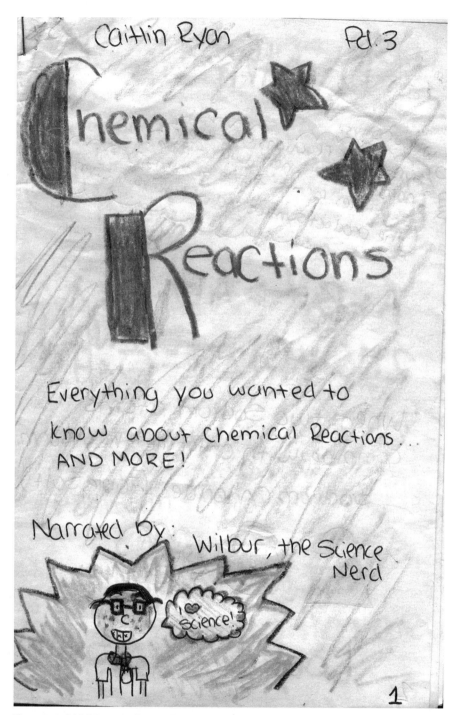

Figure 7–4 *Caitlin's Science Nerd narrator keeps the audience engaged.*

continues

Single Replacement

Single Replacement reactions only use ONE element to take the place of another.

$$A + BC \rightarrow B + AC$$

$$Cu + 2AgNO_3 \rightarrow 2Ag + Cu(NO_3)_2$$

When copper replaces the silver in silver nitrate, this forms... copper (II) Nitrate!

WOW!

crystals are formed!

4

Figure 7–4 *continued*

Newspaper Front Page

What It Is

Although we know that MS PowerPoint is all the rage, we think it's time that desktop publishing gets some attention as well. Nowadays, most desktop publishing programs (MS Publisher, PageMaker, Print Shop, QuarkXPress) have lots of ready-to-use templates that make for pretty quick work in the computer lab, particularly if the kids avoid altering the original layout. Though most of the newsletter templates run four pages, who says you can't just write the front-page articles and leave the inside copy to the reader's imagination? A newspaper front page can contain articles and graphics related to any topic being studied or researched. The goal is for each student to create a couple of short yet interesting articles that leave the reader wanting more.

When to Use It and Why

As with most of the other public writing examples, the newspaper front page is a great summary activity. After the conclusion of a unit, the kids become reporters, reviewing their notes and textbook for the five W's: who, what, when, where, why, and the big H: how. As with the RAFT assignment, the newspaper articles are written from a perspective other than the writer's. Besides straight news stories, a newspaper front page might also include an advice column, editorial, or feature article. All of these choices require both original thinking and content knowledge.

ENGLISH

Also, writing for a newspaper, albeit a fake one, gives students a firsthand opportunity to study how objective news can still ring of subjectivity depending on word choice and how information is presented. In the upcoming *Trojan News* example, students were required to pick a dramatic event from *The Iliad*. Using specific details and style from the text, they needed to retell the story in breaking-news fashion but also create an opinion piece that commented on the event. These students chose to focus on Achilles' slaughter of Hector and his subsequent mistreatment of Hector's body. In the slant of their stories and choice of words (Hector was not defeated by Achilles; he was *murdered*), both articles show clear bias in favor of Troy. Had the newspaper carried the title *Greek Gazette* in its banner, the lead article would have lauded Achilles' heroism while the opinion piece might have supported Achilles' refusal to return Hector's body to his father for proper burial.

Play by Play

Topic Search

For the newspaper front page, the teacher often stipulates the topic scope and article selections. In the Iliad example, students were required to focus on specific characters and a specific event as they composed a news story and an editorial, but the kids still needed to brainstorm additional characters, events, and potential bystanders that they might use.

Identifying the Audience

Part of the brainstorm process is coming up with an article title. That title should reflect the audience. The writer will have to ask this question: How will I need to write these articles so that they hold the interest of _____? In the case of the example, both articles were written to appeal to Trojans.

Another little twist for the project is coming up with an alliterative newspaper name. Though the example seen later in this chapter is called the *Trojan News,* the *Trojan Times, Telegraph,* or *Tribune* would have sounded a bit snappier! Following is an alphabetical list of common newspaper names. In the banner, almost all start with *The:*

Advance	*Gleam*	*Post*
Advertiser	*Gleaner*	*Press*
Advocate	*Graphic*	*Record*
Beacon	*Guardian*	*Recorder*
Bee	*Harbinger*	*Register*
Bulletin	*Herald*	*Report*
Chronicle	*Independent*	*Reporter*
Citizen	*Informer*	*Republic*
Clarion	*Inquirer*	*Republican*
Colonna	*Inquisitor*	*Review*
Commoner	*Journal*	*Sentinel*
Courier	*Ledger*	*Standard*
Daily	*Life*	*Star*
Democrat	*Messenger*	*Sun*
Dispatch	*Mirror*	*Telegram*
Eagle	*Monitor*	*Telegraph*
Enquirer	*News*	*Times*
Enterprise	*Observer*	*Tribune*
Examiner	*Outlook*	*Voice*

Free Press	Pioneer	Weekly
Frontier	Plain Dealer	World
Gazette	Planet	

Gathering Information

Though one option is to have students do further research, depending on the assignment a simpler approach is to focus on the information already available in students' notes and textbook. The trick for the writer is to reread the information with new eyes, thinking about how this "news" could be made most appealing to the newspaper's audience.

Prewriting

Between the brainstorming of the newspaper name and the information review, students will have already done some significant planning. The easiest way to move them on to the actual writing is to distribute photocopies of the newspaper front page template you plan to use. The example included here is from Microsoft Publisher. Students will need to plan their stories around specific lengths that will fit on the template. One story accommodates between 175 and 225 words while the other runs between 75 and 125 words. Though stories can go onto a second page, think hard about restricting the writing to those first-page limits. This is an opportunity to force the kids to make every word count! Plus, having thirty front pages to grade versus thirty full newspapers makes a big difference. In addition to the stories, students also need to imagine what else could go into the issue if it were a full-length paper. For example, if they are using the MS Publisher template, they will need to brainstorm items for the "Special points of interest" and "Inside this issue" boxes, both of which can be found on the left-hand side of the page.

Drafting

Since the articles are short, it makes sense to get the rough drafts started and possibly even finished right in class. Because this project will probably need to be completed in the school's computer lab, it's not worth having the kids type the stories up at home unless they're easily able to transfer the files from home to school.

Revision

For this project, it's important to get the content right before it is dumped into the newspaper template. Like the projects described earlier in this chapter, editing groups need to focus on wording, audience appeal, and skillful inclusion of information (see the description of the RAFT activity, beginning on page 159, for the full process). Writers should take turns reading their papers aloud and jotting down specific feedback.

Editing

Once the content is set, it's time to visit the computer lab. First, students need to type their two stories up in a word-processing program and run them through spell check and grammar check. Probably the most important function a grammar check can offer is converting passive-voice sentences to active-voice ones. Next, the kids need to find the word count of each of their stories, keeping the template requirements in mind. This means they might have to add or subtract and then edit again. If you have extra lab time, let the kids print their stories out so they can do some final partner proofreading with hard copies.

Now that students have two relatively clean-looking stories, it's time to start plugging things in. Students will directly type in the title, date, headlines, and left-hand box and columns. This is another time to edit carefully. Even though today's kids learned to use a keyboard before they learned to walk, it doesn't mean they're good typists. Plus, desktop publishing programs often don't do as good a job highlighting errors as word-processing programs. Blow those pages up big on the screen and have partners carefully read through and correct their headlines and columns.

The last step is to use the Insert command to pull the story text from their files and dump it into the newspaper columns. Once that's completed, the kids can spend the remaining lab time searching for the perfect picture or two to finish off their newspaper front page.

Sharing the Writing

The newspaper front pages are quick and fun to read. They can be passed around in the editing groups and each group can vote on the best story, which the writer gets to read before the entire class. Also, because of their visual appeal, front pages are worth posting on the bulletin board. Just remember that if you want them to be read, they've got to be at eye level since the text print is newspaper size: tiny!

What Can Go Wrong?

The biggest problem when using any desktop publishing program is that the kids will accidentally move a text column, erase a graphics box, or otherwise commit technical goofs. This is going to happen; it's guaranteed! So if you're serious about this project, it's *imperative* that you be familiar with the publishing program before you take the kids into the lab. The best way to do this is by creating your own newspaper front page. You'll have worked through the process and pitfalls, and you'll have a model for the students to follow. Also, when the kids are in the lab, having a computer projector hooked up makes a huge difference. When it comes time to create the front pages, you can guide the kids through the steps visually while you also manage the pacing.

How Do I Grade This?

We've included a rubric for grading front pages in Figure 7–5.

Example

After finishing *The Iliad,* the students in Donna Driscoll's freshman English class paired up and wrote accounts of the Trojan War as if they were reporters from either Troy or Greece. Besides needing to represent specific story details in the context of the news articles, students also had to reflect their bias through word choice and phrasing. Figure 7–6 shows a blank template from MS Publisher; Figure 7–7 shows how one group used the template to create their front page on the Trojan War.

Newspaper Front Page Evaluation

Name _____ Date _____ Hour _____

| SELF | | PEER | | TEACHER | | |
YES	NO	YES	NO	YES	NO	ELEMENT
						1. Do you have a catchy title that uses alliteration?
						2. Do you have an accurate date and volume header?
						3. Have you filled in the "Special points of interest" box?
						4. Have you listed articles and page numbers under "Inside this issue"?
						5. Do you have a consistent serif font style for all text?
						6. Did you use no larger than a 12-point font for the articles?
						7. Do you have a consistent font style for all headlines?
						8. Do your headlines catch the reader's attention as well as pertain to the article?
						9. Are the article headlines slightly larger than the articles?
						10. Did you bold the headlines?
						11. Did you single space the body of each article?
						12. Does a scanned photograph accompany at least one story?
						13. Does the lead (first sentence) of each article grab the reader's attention?
						14. Do your news stories cover who, what, when, where, why, and how?
						15. Do your news stories reflect specific details and elaboration?
						16. Do the news stories reflect accurate depiction of people, characters, events, or content information?
						17. Do the articles reflect the information designated for research or review?
						18. Are headlines free of typos, spelling, and grammatical errors?
						19. Are articles free of typos, spelling, and grammatical errors?

Figure 7–5 *Rubric for newspaper front page*

Volume 1, Issue 1

Newsletter Date

Newsletter Title

Business Name

Lead Story Headline

This story can fit 175-225 words.

The purpose of a newsletter is to provide specialized information to a targeted audience. Newsletters can be a great way to market your product or service, and also create credibility and build your organization's identity among peers, members, employees, or vendors.

First, determine the audience of the newsletter. This could be anyone who might benefit from the information it contains, for example, employees or people interested in purchasing a product or requesting your service.

You can compile a mailing list from business reply cards, customer information sheets, business cards collected at trade shows, or membership lists. You might consider purchasing a mailing list from a company.

If you explore the Publisher catalog, you will find many publications that match the style of your newsletter.

Next, establish how much time and money you can spend on your newsletter. These factors will help determine how frequently you publish the newsletter and its length. It's recommended that you publish your newsletter at least quarterly so that it's considered a consistent source of information. Your customers or employees will look forward to its arrival.

Caption describing picture or graphic.

Special points of interest:

- Briefly highlight your point of interest here.
- Briefly highlight your point of interest here.
- Briefly highlight your point of interest here.
- Briefly highlight your point of interest here.

Inside this issue:

Secondary Story Headline

This story can fit 75-125 words.

Your headline is an important part of the newsletter and should be considered carefully.

In a few words, it should accurately represent the contents of the story and draw readers into the story. Develop the headline before you write the story. This way, the headline will help you keep the story focused.

Examples of possible headlines include Product Wins Industry Award, New Product Can Save You Time!, Membership Drive Exceeds Goals, and New Office Opens Near You.

Figure 7–6 *MS Publisher template*

Volume 23, Issue 3

March 11th

The Trojan News
Special Final Issue

Achilles vs. Hector *written by Michael Bianco*

Today, horse-taming Hector was killed at Achilles' hands. Hector, not wanting to return to the walls of Troy waited outside to face Achilles man to man. But when Achilles arrived his heart was filled with fear and Hector attempted to flee. With strength given to him by Apollo, Hector ran around Troy 3 times, with Achilles close behind. No Greeks threw anything at Hector by order from Achilles. Eventually Athena put an end to it. By turning into one of Hector's brothers, Athena tricked Hector into stopping and facing Achilles. Hector tried to make a deal with Achilles to return his body to his family, but he would have none because of his anger and sorrow.

Achilles threw first, but it missed its mark, because Hector bent down beneath the spears path. Fortunately Athena returned Achilles' spear. It was Hector's shot now and he threw his spear, but it was turned harmlessly away by Achilles' bright shield. Needing another spear, Hector looked to find that his brother was not actually with him. Knowing his fate was sealed, he drew his sword and charged Achilles. But Achilles sprang forward as well, and seeing an

The war continues to rage on, but without flashing-helm Hector, we will eventually meet defeat.

opening in Hector's armor, speared him in the neck. Hector could still speak, dying as he was, and prayed to Achilles to no effect. So ended the fight between Achilles and Hector. City-wasting Achilles was victorious.

More on Hector's Death

It had been confirmed. Our great hero is dead. Hector was murdered by Achilles in a blind rage. According to all reports that we have at this time, Achilles has denied Hector's dying wish, that he be given a proper funeral in the city he once defended, high-walled Troy. I personally think that this sense of revenge for Patroclus has turned Achilles into a bloodthirsty savage, comparable to the citizens of Thracia. There are rumors that Priam is going to go to Achilles to get Hec-

tor's body back, but I just hope that the old king returns alive. Achilles has been dragging Hector's body around Troy for the past five days. One of the witnesses of the death of man-killing Hector says that is brother, Deiphobus, was there one second then gone the next. We suspect that this was one of the gods. I think Achilles would not have won that battle without the help from heaven. If Achilles has any shred of honor left within him, he will give back Hector's body.

Figure 7–7 *Michael captures the Trojan spin in his reporting of the war.*

Web Page

What It Is

More and more, teachers are asking students to display their writing on the Web, or through other technological media, rather than just turn in a sheet of paper. One great advantage to web-page publishing is that the work becomes widely accessible to the whole class and, potentially, everyone else in the web sphere. And if there's enough time, students can add links and subpages to make their presentations much richer, with more interactive pathways that the viewer can use to explore the subject. This leads students to think in new ways about the information, breaking it into smaller chunks and integrating pictures, drawings, sound, and links with other resources, instead of writing out one long paper. Often, teachers turn to the computer faculty for help with the technical side of the work.

When to Use It and Why

Creating web pages connects kids with the new literacy that they may already use outside of school every day. And kids can teach each other about it. Every class inevitably has four or five students who are already skilled at designing killer websites.

Because the process of learning to create a web page can be time-consuming, teachers often save web-page publication for big projects that take place once or twice per year, instead of trying to employ them for smaller efforts. The public nature of the outcome, however, makes the work highly motivating for students. They know that their friends, family, and who knows who else will be seeing the results. In the past, locating and connecting with real outside audiences for students' writing took lots of extra work for teachers, but the Internet simply erases that obstacle.

≋ Want to Jump Around?

See the section on the I-search paper in Chapter 9 (pages 236–252) for general strategies to make research projects effective.

Play by Play

Getting Started

The first step when students create web pages is doing research on their topics, just as you would have them do for a more traditional report or project. The more that can be done on the Web, of course, the more links the students will find for their web pages, offering readers relevant websites to consult.

You can reduce students' tendency to plagiarize from other websites by making clear that they can include links, but what goes up as text on their pages must be their own work and cannot be simply copied from other sites. The rule: "If it comes from another site, then just link to that site. There's no point in recopying it on your site."

If you can team up with the computer faculty in your school for the technical side of creating web pages, then you won't need to invest time in training students to carry out the actual creation of their pages. It's likely that some of your kids have already taken courses that provided this skill, and your more tech-savvy class members will probably be eager to coach the rest of the class. If you're on your own for this, computer teachers recommend you use Dreamweaver, a basic, what-you-see-is-what-you-get web-page construction tool, which includes its own tutorial for learning to use it. We've also found free Dreamweaver tutorials on the Web. The one we like best is at www.brevard.edu/aam/support_documents.htm. It's sponsored by Adventure of the American Mind, a partnership between the Library of Congress and the Education and Research Consortium of the Western Carolinas. Brevard College, as part of the consortium, provides this particular resource.

Working the Room

Sonja Coble, who teaches at Federal Hocking High School in southeastern Ohio, uses web pages for an integrated science class, when the students are studying ecology. She requires students to each create an animal ad page that promotes a creature ordinarily considered undesirable or repugnant—mosquito, snake, rodent—to help kids learn that all the animals in an ecosystem play an important part in it.

SCIENCE

What about time? Sonja explains that once students know how to use a program like Dreamweaver and have their researched material in hand, the time required to create a simple web page itself, without lots of links, subpages, or bells and whistles, is really quite minimal—half an hour to an hour. Since Federal Hocking High runs on block periods, she schedules half periods for several weeks to complete the animal ad project. The other half of each period is devoted to the ongoing content of the course. Not only does this avoid project fatigue, but Sonja finds that students begin to make use of the additional concepts they are learning as they work on their projects.

The other big webpage project that Sonja Coble helps students to complete is their graduation portfolio, which students can choose to put together electronically. The Federal Hocking faculty has created an in-depth guide, requiring the seniors to display their accomplishments in three areas: career readiness, democratic citizenship, and skills for lifelong learning. These teachers take their commitment to the large goals for their work very seriously. A sample first page for a student's web-page portfolio is shown in Figure 7–8.

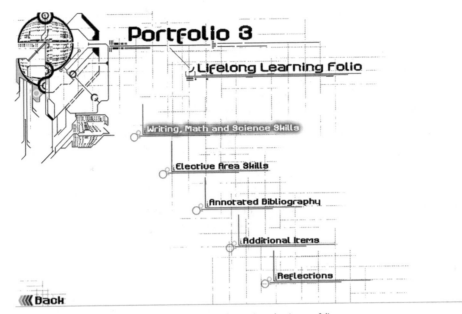

Figure 7–8 *Homepage for a Federal Hocking High School senior's graduation portfolio.*

What Can Go Wrong?

Providing for student choice helps avoid one of the most common concerns that teachers have about research projects, namely the level of student commitment. Still, students need to be kept on track. Sonja conferences with individuals as they work and sets deadlines for each stage of the project—choosing a focus, completing the research, creating the graphics, drafting a script, and getting the final product completed.

Web security is a big issue for schools. It's an ongoing struggle to block connection from inside the school to undesirable websites and chat rooms, and to prevent hacking and worms and viruses from the outside. In fact, CIPA, the Children's Internet Protection Act, requires schools receiving federal funds for Internet connection to utilize filtering and virus protection programs. We're not techies, ourselves, so you'll need to check with your school or district information technology person if you're having trouble with this.

Variation

Sonja Coble has on occasion linked a webquest together with the web-page project. At home.frognet.net/~coble/webquest/student.htm you can see the directions she provided to students for one such webquest on stone circles, the structures that various ancient peoples used to astronomically track movements of the sun, moon, and stars and to determine the timing of the seasons. As you will see, Sonja provides a detailed explanation of the steps in the process. Here is what steps two and three look like:

2. You need to look at some ancient stone circles and complete the *Think Sheet*. You can do this by accessing some of the following websites or by looking up your own at Google or Yahoo.

    ☞ *The Stone Circle Webring Site List* *Updated*

    ☞ *The Megalithic Map*

    ☞ *Stone Pages*

    ☞ *The Big Horn Medicine Wheel*

    ☞ *New England Antiquities Research Association*

    ☞ *The Gungywamp Society* *Updated*

    ☞ *America's Stonehenge*

    ☞ *The Prehistoric Web Index of Ancient Sites*

    ☞ *Archaeoastronomy, Middle East & Africa* *Updated*

    There are some books in the classroom to help you out too. You may not remove these from the classroom, as they are shared resources. You may find them very helpful, so don't forget about them! They are:

    ☞ *Skywatching* by David Levy

    ☞ *Abell's Exploration of the Universe* by Morrison, Wolff, & Fraknoi

    ☞ *Ancient Astronomers* by Anthony F. Aveni

    ☞ *Stone Circles, A Modern Builder's Guide to the Megalithic Revival* by Rob Roy

    You may also want to look in the library for additional resources.

    The Think Sheet also helps you figure out how to find the information you need for your next step.

3. You and your teammates will need to determine which alignments you will use in your circle. Research and calculate where your alignment choices will place your stones. At this point you may want to create a couple of draft sketches of some of your circle ideas.

Sonja also provides a template for the students' websites, a log to track the progress of their work, and a grade sheet to lay out how the various steps of the project are evaluated.

Works Cited

Buehl, Doug. 2001. *Classroom Strategies for Interactive Learning*. Newark, DE: International Reading Association.

Zemelman, Steven, Yolanda Simmons, Pete Leki, and Patricia Bearden. 2000. *History Comes Home: Family Stories Across the Curriculum*. York, ME: Stenhouse.

CHAPTER eight

Running a Writing Workshop

I n the chapter after this one we describe four kinds of bigger public writing projects that work well in all content areas. But in these longer, more formal activities, the students need support to get the most out of them. And the most powerful structure for helping them do that is called *classroom workshop*. In this setting, kids get writing done right in the classroom, where the teacher can observe, provide one-on-one help, and *teach* in a focused, step-by-step manner. This is education in the tradition of the artisan shop, where an experienced craftsman guides apprentices as they create real pieces of furniture, blown glass, paintings, or other finely wrought objects.

"But wait a minute," you might say. "This is a big order! You're asking me to actually schedule writing during class, when I already must fill every moment covering material for the test next April? I'm supposed to help individual kids and keep everyone else on task at the same time? And then I'll need paperwork to keep track of each student's work. You'd better start talking hard and fast if you're going to convince me."

OK, give us a chance and we'll do our best. Some reasons workshop is valuable:

1. It ensures that kids actually get writing done.

2. It lets you instantaneously see what they are succeeding with and what is tripping them up, whether in the writing or in the content you are teaching.

3. It allows you to individualize instruction so you can help, explain, or teach a lesson to just the students who need it, just when their issue is on their minds.

4. It's actually much more efficient than whole-class instruction—you can decide whether to help one student (while the others are working), a small group, or everyone, based on what you observe on the spot.

So workshop is a pretty nifty, flexible way to get things done. But is it really worth the time? To figure that out, you have to think about your overall goals. Most secondary content syllabi include far more than can possibly be covered in the semester or school year they are shoehorned into. And suppose you find the kids aren't getting something. Do you rush on, chased by the calendar (meaning you actually "wasted" the day or three you devoted to that concept since the kids didn't learn it anyway)? Or do you pause to really help your students and fall further behind? Fact is, we struggle with coverage versus depth every day. We can tell ourselves we must get to it all for the standardized test, but if the kids don't learn from a quick buzz-through, they still won't do well on the test.

> *We can tell ourselves we must get to it all for the standardized test, but if the kids don't learn from a quick buzz-through, they won't do well on the test anyway.*

The *National Science Education Standards* document (National Research Council 1996) addresses this challenge head on:

> Emphasizing active science learning means shifting emphasis away from teachers presenting information and covering science topics. The perceived need to include all the topics, vocabulary, and information in textbooks is in direct conflict with the central goal of having students learn scientific knowledge with understanding (see Chapter 2).

Is It Worth It?

We posed a question to history teacher Nikoletta Antonakos, at Deerfield High School in the Chicago suburbs: With all the historical periods and parts of the world you have to cover for your world history course, how do you justify spending class time on writing workshop? Her answer:

> Writing is the essential work of historians. It's what they do. And it's important for students to learn that history *is* interpretation. They need this in order to analyze what they're reading, whether it is a primary source or the analysis of an established historian. If students don't try to write interpretations, they won't

understand the work behind them. And individual conferencing with me is *so* essential to this process.

If you agree with us that going deep is a vital part of your work as a teacher, the question is: How much time for in-class writing? We're not saying that kids are in workshop every day. It's a matter of balance. Over the year in the world history classes taught by Niki and her partner, Hilary Quagliana, students use frequent half-period workshop sessions to do at least some of the writing for ten three-page essays on key focus questions. About two weeks in the third quarter are devoted to a research project, with a time allotment as follows:

- one period for in-class research work
- three half periods devoted to writing up an expanded outline
- the rest of the time for instruction on the analytical thinking that Niki and Hilary emphasize

In this project, however, the students do not actually write drafts or turn in completed papers. Instead, they stop when they have finished the research and incorporated it into a detailed outline of their analytical argument. The teachers have decided on this strategy because they have a more long-range, full-year plan for developing the kids' writing. The students have written short papers earlier in the year. Now, in step-by-step fashion, these thoughtful teachers want the kids to focus on the research and the analysis itself. Then, the full research, argumentation, drafting and polishing of a five-page research paper, toward the end of the year, completes the cycle. And it takes between two and four weeks of workshop time alternating with several days of direct teaching or kids discussing their topics in small groups.

So the answer is, yes, workshop takes time, no way around that; but it's not your entire curriculum, and it's worth every minute.

How Does It Work?

So what does workshop look like up close? To find out, let's visit Niki Antonakos' world history classroom as kids dig into their research projects. We flag the key features of this well-structured approach as we go, and we outline them later, for more of a bird's-eye view. Niki begins with a balance of choice and assignment. Students each list three geographic areas or places they think they are interested in, and she assigns one of the three, to be sure the papers cover a variety of places and cultures, instead of all focusing on Darfur. Each student then searches news and information on the Internet to identify a contemporary problem or issue to study; the purpose of the paper is to examine the historical roots of a political or social problem.

HISTORY

This process *builds engagement* before the students launch into their research. Jake Brown explained that he is researching the ongoing breakup of Yugoslavia because a good friend emigrated here from Croatia. Alec Levy wants to learn about the Chernobyl nuclear disaster and its aftermath in Ukraine because, he said, he is troubled by the local people's passivity—why didn't they do something about their plight? In fact, one of the best things about classroom workshop is that *students get to choose their own topics.* Even when choice is limited within a range, as Niki's assignment is, students are far more motivated when they exercise some control over their work. And the negotiation between student choice and teacher assignment allows Niki to guide students to take on tasks appropriate to their particular stage of development.

The students need a variety of kinds of instruction as they proceed with their research. Niki provides a worksheet, reproduced in Figure 8–1, on how to develop a hypothesis about the historical links to a social problem before they start probing their country's history. She uses a *brief minilesson* to explain that this is important as the first step in the process of interpretation, and she shows them how to use the worksheet.

With the help of an extensive list of websites and databases and a cartful of books and encyclopedias that Niki and the library staff have compiled, students start combing for historical background, and because they are in the library computer lab together, Niki is able to offer individual help wherever it's needed. This means, of course, that the *teacher moves around the room* to confer briefly with individuals and provide guidance, thus ensuring that all students are productive. For example, Sam Block was stumped trying to find information about Singapore until Niki guided him to the *New York Times* article archive, using her password to get him to it. Much of the instruction has added up over the year, however, to ensure the students are successful at this challenging research effort. The kids draw on the numerous lessons on note taking, structuring arguments and interpretations, organizing their information, and paraphrasing instead of plagiarizing, which their teacher conducted for the shorter papers earlier in the year. Niki teaches the kids to use note cards, but not in the old, grinding traditional way. Instead, different colors of cards help to distinguish between various kinds of information and to remind students when they need to give credit to their sources so they aren't plagiarizing.

Niki Antonakos works intensively with her students on developing and supporting the theses, arguments, and assertions that make up the heart of their historical writing, not just for the final research paper but as a central task in all of the writing assignments throughout the year. The outlines that she requires focus on this effort. She provides lessons and guide sheets (one example is shown in Figure 8–2), and *models the work* for them, completing examples as a whole class and then in pairs as shown in Figure 8-3. For the final research paper, for example, she spends a period modeling

World History Research Paper   Name _____

Hypothesis/Links Worksheet

What could possibly have led to this state of affairs?

Place: (ex: U.S.A.)

Identify: What is the current issue? (ex: War in Iraq)

Generalize:

1. **What type of issue is this?** Consider political, economic, social, cultural characteristics. (ex: international affairs)

2. **What is its general scope?** Describe the issue in general terms. (ex: International power of the U.S. is exercised once again in U.S. leadership of a coalition against Saddam Hussein).

Brainstorm: What conditions in the past may have caused this issue to emerge? In other words, what do you think happened in the past that continues to affect the present? You may need to think of the conditions that are needed for the opposite to have occurred, and then ask why these conditions are absent. (ex: U.S. confronted by Hussein's repeated violations of UN resolutions; UN not powerful to do anything).

Hypothesize/Think Deeper: Where could this phenomenon come from? Could there have been something in the past that set a precedent for this state of affairs—perhaps a significant event or action by a leader or group? (ex: U.S. emerged as leading power after WWII, and since then has been prominent in world affairs. U.S. battled for "spheres of influence" with USSR in other places; maybe it had a vested interest in this region, too. Then there is the whole oil source question. That and the Cold War might be two roots of U.S. active interest in Iraq's stability/compliance with UN.)

Check this in with Ms. Antonakos, then

GO RESEARCH! Armed with your hypothesis, you can begin to research the history of this place. Do not worry if your hypothesis comes out all wrong. By thinking about the issue and its possible roots before you research, you will have sharpened your critical thinking skills.

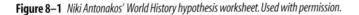

Figure 8–1 *Niki Antonakos' World History hypothesis worksheet. Used with permission.*

Unit 3: Expansion & Diffusion

FOCUS QUESTION

A Focus Question is one that synthesizes what we have been learning about a particular civilization and era and which "focuses" on a particular theme or concept.

In answering such a question, you must

1. think about the meaning of the question, what it assumes is fact and what it requires you to know

2. take some preliminary notes listing what you think the assumptions and required facts are— include some of the important terms from the relevant chapters

3. *still in note form:* synthesize what you have learned by making some connections between these facts you list and the bigger issue the question raises

4. begin formulating a general, one-sentence answer to the question (this is your thesis statement!)

5. divide your answer into sections appropriate to the parts of the question

6. create an effective answer to the Focus Question by writing one paragraph for each of the sections; the answer should begin with the thesis statement (which you most likely will revise as you go through the process of writing); no conclusion is needed at this point

Sample FQ: How did political and economic stability create the conditions for the rise of a rich culture in classical Rome?

assumed facts: there was political & econ stability in Rome
there was rich culture in Rome
there is some link between the two

required knowledge:
- how pol/econ stability was created/maintained
  - Pax Romana after great conquests, begins w/ Augustus
  - great geog. position for trade
  - earned $ from conquered lands, too
  - use of citizenship as a tool for stability
    - connect that to idea of civic pride
  - legion used to maintain borders w/ settlements
    - built roads, other infrastructure . . .
- how this created wealth & time to be spent on culture
  - $ not needed as much to wage battles
  - stable economy means good tax revenues
  - individuals & institutions likely to have more to spend on culture
- various elements of Roman culture (sp. exs.)
  - theatre/spectacles (coliseum)

sculpture (realism, subjects include warriors & politicians)

Figure 8–2 *Niki Antonakos' Guidesheet on Answering Focus Questions. Used with permission.*

WORLD HISTORY I   Outline By _____

OUTLINE PEER REVIEW SHEET   Reviewer's Name _____

1. THESIS: Does it refer to a current issue, a root cause and a hint at how the two are linked?

Does it read logically/clearly?

Does it map the paper?

2. ARGUMENT: Does the outline have distinct, clear
   • assertions that are related to the thesis and are distinct

   • subpoints/subassertions

   • tie-backs (summary of the argument of the paragraph, tying back to assertion and/or thesis)

3. EVIDENCE:
     Does the support included
   • prove each point made

   • have a distinct purpose (or is there too much of the same)

Is there a lack of support for any of the subpoints? (be sure to mark on the outline, or note here)

Are quotes/specific evidence cited? integrated well?

4. OTHER COMMENTS

Figure 8–3 *Niki Antonakos' peer review sheet for research outline*

how she would develop an outline on causes for World War II, since she has just returned the tests on that war from their previous unit of study.

As students begin drafting their papers, she holds thorough *one-on-one conferences* with each kid, going over their outlines to help them see if they've created solid arguments and backed them up with supporting information and explanations. In these conferences, she does not instruct students on what to fix or how—that's their job. Instead she asks lots of questions: "How do you know that?" "Why do you think that was happening?" "What else do you know about that?" Often, the kids know the answers but haven't realized the need to include them. Niki explains, "I get students to express what they know and don't know. I ask questions to get them talking, making connections. Using their knowledge more extensively motivates them." A period for small-group discussions and another for peer editing deepen this work still further.

Niki's teaching partner, Hilary, also has students employ drawing to examine their arguments, using a tree diagram in which the roots and trunk represent parts of the history while the branches and leaves are aspects of the current issue. Students share these in small groups, and the drawing and discussion help them make new connections between ideas and figure out what questions still remain.

While Niki has chosen a very sharp focus for her conferences, other teachers use one-on-one sessions to address any area for which the students request help. Or the teacher may inquire about a student's progress on a particular goal or the application of a concept that has been introduced in a minilesson. Toward the end of the project, the conferences will be more about organization of ideas, editing, and polishing.

When it comes to *record keeping,* many teachers employ *writing folders* for students to keep track of their work and to maintain a record of their individual needs and the teacher's responses. Keeping the folders in a file drawer in the classroom helps make sure they don't get lost or pilfered, though students are often expected take individual papers, or parts of them, home to continue their work. The folders contain notes, brainstorm lists, drafts, and *individual goal sheets* (see Figure 8–4, on p. 200 for an example) to list skills each student has committed to mastering, along with notations and dates to record progress on these goals. (And what if you don't have your own classroom? One teacher we know wheels around a cart with all the folders stashed in plastic banker's boxes on the bottom shelf.)

Another, more centralized approach is to make shorthand notes on little sticky notes as you observe students working and lay these into squares on a sheet of paper labeled with students' names. Peel them off later and repaste them on a separate sheet for each student to create progress records with minimal labor.

Niki finds she can keep things a little simpler. She just makes sure students save their writing on the computers and uses folders for hard-copy drafts, on which she jots her comments, along with peer review sheets (an example of which is shown in Figure 8–3). She checks these folders every step of the way.

Niki's students conclude their projects with oral presentations to *share their learning*. The information and analyses are presented not just for the teacher to grade but for the listeners to learn from, and they are expected to take notes, since their final exam will include questions about the topics the kids have investigated.

How does Niki evaluate these research projects? Actually, it's surprisingly easy, she says. While she employs a rubric for the shorter papers during the year to pinpoint the specifics she considers important, she finds this unnecessary for the final project. Her conferences with kids and the notes she jots on their outlines not only give her all the information she needs to formulate a summative grade but also communicate to the students more effectively than any letter grade or points on a chart about how they are doing. After all, how many kids actually contemplate the comments on a final paper when it's returned with a letter or number at the top? But under Niki's system, these world history students learn from their teacher's feedback all along the way. And that is precisely what Niki is aiming for.

What do the students think about this kind of classroom? Alec appreciates the support he gets from his teacher. Jake observes that "she pulls the information out of you." Caiti Case explains that at first the independence made her nervous: "Am I doing things the right way?" However, she found that when she was confused, the help she got not only solved her problem but gave her confidence and built her trust in the teacher and the process. We really didn't need to ask the kids, though. When these students are working in the computer lab on their drafts, they are a cheery, busy, focused bunch, typing away, asking each other for help—and there is always a student in the middle of the room with the teacher, their heads bent together, poring over an outline.

To Review

So in sum, what are the main features we've seen in this very active and engaged classroom workshop?

- ☞ **Building Engagement:** The teacher takes time to introduce the project, build students' interest in it, and create purpose for their writing.
- ☞ **Choice:** Students have the opportunity to make choices for the focus of their efforts.
- ☞ **Individual Goal Setting:** Students set some of their own goals for learning the subject matter and developing their writing.

- **Students Working Independently in the Classroom:** The teacher allows time for writing right there with her, providing a window into kids' thinking, and an opportunity for them to get writing done in a supportive setting.

- **Brief, Focused Teaching:** Brief, focused minilessons help students learn concepts and writing strategies one at a time, at a rate that makes them easy to digest.

- **Modeling:** The teacher helps students understand the task by demonstrating how it's done, showing how a competent adult tackles ideas and composition.

- **Teacher-Student Conferences and Observation:** The teacher moves about the room and holds short conferences with individual students.

- **Conference Records:** The teacher creates easy-to-maintain records of her observation of the students' efforts, to help her track kids' progress and needs.

- **Writing Folders:** Each student keeps a folder that holds his work, enabling both student and teacher to longitudinally track progress.

- **Sharing the Results:** Students have an immediate, real audience for their writing, so that it contributes to everyone's learning.

Yes, But...

Since this is obviously *not* the traditional lecture–assignment–quiz cycle of instruction, teachers may have quite a few questions about how to make it work effectively and how it can fit into their crowded schedule. Let's address some of those right now.

OK, how do I fit this time-consuming activity into my schedule?

First of all, start modestly. Don't tackle a huge weeks-long project if you aren't confident it will pay off in students' learning. Make sure the work covers some of your own (and your school's) goals for learning in your subject, not only in the writing but also in the reading used for minilessons and demonstrations. Throughout the workshop process you have numerous opportunities to incorporate important material. And when holding individual conferences with kids, you are teaching lessons that will be remembered far longer than many of your best lectures.

But finally, classroom workshop does take time, and it must be viewed as a trade-off. You may have to make room by letting go of something else. You may not be able to achieve as much total coverage of your curriculum, but check off the items in the writing assignment and minilessons and remember that now you don't have to address those at other times. Anyway, we're not proposing that you abandon all your favorite lectures, class discussions, problem-practice sessions, or reviews. Make your own decision about how to balance these activities. However, we've found that the depth and engagement of more extended inquiry and writing is more than worth the time it requires. Writers of science and history standards stress that without this depth, there is little meaningful learning. Even if we must prepare students for standardized tests, racing over the material doesn't get it into their heads. *Mentioning* ideas is not the same as *teaching* them.

> *Writers of science and history standards stress that without depth, there is little meaningful learning.*

The workshop sounds fine for English or history, but what about math or science?

OK, how about some examples of classrooms where it's happening. Harshaw Soni uses classroom workshop for the writing of lab reports in seventh-grade science at the Young Women's Leadership Charter School in Chicago. She finds that when students complete the writing as part of the lab period, the work gets done and she can help students follow the report format that she requires. In fact, plenty of science teachers have no doubt been using workshop for years and just haven't given it any high-falutin label.

SCIENCE

Jeff Hoyer, at Deerfield High School, also provides plenty of write-up time in his biology labs and says that the students focus more on the thinking and analysis than when they do the write-ups as homework. A more extensive project takes place in Jeff's environmental science class. Jeff focuses a major two- to three-week project on the *Sand County Almanac,* by Aldo Leopold, a Thoreau-like classic collection of observations of nature. Writing in class helps students connect various passages in the book to concepts learned in the course and to contemporary environmental issues. The kids then write their own versions of Aldo Leopold's "land ethic" and are required to actively apply it in some part of their own lives.

Want to Jump Around?

Go to the "Social Action Paper" section of Chapter 9, on page 216, for a more complete account of the *Sand County Almanac* activity, a shorter version of which could easily be conducted in any biology or environmental science class.

In Dorne Eastwood's seventh-grade math classroom, in Chicago's Northwest Middle School, workshop is an everyday practice. Dorne uses the *Connected Mathematics* curriculum, which helps students explore math through real-world problems instead of abstract exercises. Following each problem, students write reflections in their math notebooks on how they approached the problem, what they learned, and what they're still struggling with. Small groups compare reflections and talk over the various strategies they used to solve a problem. Dorne estimates that in each fifty-minute class period, kids are working on solutions and writing about them for ten to twenty minutes. Conferences take particular skill, Dorne

MATH

observes, since she doesn't want to take over the thinking. She first asks what the student knows about the problem. Usually, this does the trick, as verbalization becomes realization: "Wait a minute! Now I get it . . ." If the student is totally stuck, she asks probing questions, usually about another, similar situation. To any teacher who has used conferences for English or social studies, this will sound completely familiar.

How do I make sure students stay on task and get their work done while I'm conducting conferences? Will I lose control of what is happening with the other twenty-nine kids?

One of the best things about workshop is that it allows you to keep abreast of students' work much more immediately than if you simply waited until an assignment was due and then felt your heart sink when kids turn in halting efforts or nothing at all. But yes, you do need rules for maintaining order and working productively. Conduct a mini-lesson early in the year to establish basic ground rules. Better than simply announcing a list of regulations, ask kids to brainstorm the rules *they* think support a productive, collaborative workshop. Then select a few key ones to post on the wall. A list typical of the sort that students will create:

- ☞ Stick to your work.
- ☞ Place a sticky note at the edge of your desk if you need help from the teacher.
- ☞ If you are stuck and waiting for a conference, go back to revise or edit other work in your folder, or do your reading.
- ☞ Use low voices and sit knee-to-knee if you are conferring with a fellow student.
- ☞ If you are finished with an assignment before workshop time is over, go to the file cabinet to get a list of additional writing ideas.

And as you move around the room for conferences, you can readily see who is doing the work and who may need some prodding.

I'm not a writing expert! And I don't have that much experience with writing myself, so how would I know what to focus on and what sort of advice to give?

We totally understand—and we're not suggesting you assume the English teachers' responsibilities. The content-area writing projects we're recommending are meant to help students explore your subject more deeply by thinking through a topic, communicating about it, and hearing and responding to each other's written ideas. So you will probably focus most of your teaching on your content rather than on composition or grammar. You may decide to offer help and comments on one or two writing skills that especially interfere with kids' communication. These are likely to be about content, ideas, clarity, and organization—qualities that you can evaluate simply by being a reader with expertise in your subject. And very shortly, to conclude this chapter, we'll provide some suggestions on how to conduct conferences with students so that they do most of the work and the thinking rather than depend on you to fix everything.

What do I do about assessment? If the students have chosen individual topics and individual goals for improvement, how do I keep track of it all without spending gobs of time on mountains of paperwork?

This is where the folders, regular observation of kids as they work, teacher-student conferences, and kids' oral presentations are really helpful and make assessment more of a meaningful record of your teaching and students' learning. As Niki Antonakos finds from observing and talking with students, you'll know a great deal about their effort well before papers are handed in. The individual goals listed in their folders and the concepts you've stressed in your minilessons help focus your evaluation on just a few key things that students are trying to learn. You do, however, need easy ways to keep track of the data. Teachers who use classroom workshop regularly develop their own forms to facilitate record keeping. A typical form is presented in Figure 8–4.

Teacher-Student Conferences: A Powerful Way to Support Students' Writing

Providing individual help is one of the key strategies made possible by a workshop classroom. Conferencing is an art worth developing because it addresses students' specific, individual needs, instead of neglecting them for whole-class instruction or consuming whole-class time on the problems of just a few kids. And conferencing is teaching that kids remember because of the individual attention it provides.

What does a good conference look like? It's a brief, two- to three-minute session in which the teacher sits side by side with the student and first poses some key questions:

- What are you working on?
- How is it going?
- What help do you need to move ahead?

After the student talks and a problem emerges, another question will lead the conversation further. You have many choices, depending on the situation. Some possibilities:

Writing Goals and Progress on Them

STUDENT:	TEACHER COMMENT:
GOALS FOR QUARTER:	
Assignment 1	
Progress on goals	
Concepts/skills from minilessons	
Items observed in conferences	
First draft—other specifics	
Final draft—other specifics	
Assignment 2	
Progress on goals	
Concepts/skills from minilessons	
Items addressed in conferences	
First draft—other specifics	
Final draft—other specifics	

Figure 8–4 *Record-keeping form*

☞ So what do you think you can do about that?

☞ What else do you know about this?

☞ Tell me some more about why you decided to talk about. . .

If the student figures out a good solution, you're finished! You may simply conclude, "That sounds great. So what will you do now?" If she's still stuck, you draw on your content knowledge and experience as a writer to offer a specific suggestion. And don't worry. With the information gained from the student, plus your own knowledge, this advice will come easily to you.

Of course, there are some challenges to making conferences work:

1. **Time:** How do I keep the conferences short? How do I get to everyone?

2. **Focus:** What do I focus on, especially if a student has a plethora of writing problems?

3. **Data:** How do I keep track of what I've observed and taught during all the various conferences and not get overloaded with record keeping?

Let's look at these one by one.

Time: Keeping Conferences Short and Getting Around the Room

Don't try to use workshop conferences to solve a student's every problem. Ask what she's working on, or what she needs help with, and focus on just one thing. Don't try to read a student's complete draft or have him read a long section aloud to you. Instead, have the student explain what he thinks the problem is. And if you see that many kids are struggling with the same issue, plan a minilesson instead of trying to teach it twenty or thirty times. If you have trouble keeping track of time (as Steve usually does), use an egg timer.

Choosing a Focus for the Conference

Often an experienced conferrer starts by asking what the student needs help with. She has shown kids how to review their work to see what they need help with, as well as aspects they've handled well, which is an excellent skill, anyway, for independently

---

Tips for Controlling Time in Conferences

☞ Focus on and teach about just one aspect of the thinking or writing.

☞ Don't try to read whole drafts of student work; have the student point to a key spot to look at, or choose one based on the focus of your teaching.

improving one's work, catching avoidable mistakes on tests, and becoming a more reflective learner. And instead of hunting for errors, the teacher is responding to a request for help. An alternative: have the student flip open his folder to his goal sheet, review the list, and see how he is doing on it.

Niki Antonakos, on the other hand, is very single-minded in her conferences. Her aim, which she pursues calmly but intently, is to teach students to construct good, thoughtful arguments, and to go beyond mere facts to interpret their meaning. Students can, of course, always ask her for other kinds of help as well.

Keeping Track of Your Observations and In-Conference Instruction

This is where small sticky notes are a godsend. As you move around the room, carry a clipboard or notebook with a sheet on top that lists all the kids and provides space for stickies next to each name. After each conference, jot a couple of words on a sticky note to name the conference topic and indicate what transpired. Slap the note into that student's space and move on. After class or at the end of the week, transfer the notes to separate sheets for each kid and, presto, you have written records for overall evaluation of progress later. And don't forget the "Writing Skills I've Learned" sheet that students can keep in their in folders—a sheet like the one shown in Figure 8–4, or a shorter list that the student and teacher agree on. This becomes a responsibility guide, a reminder of the aspects of writing the student should check each time he tackles an assignment, and a document to consult when you come back for another conference later on.

Taking the Plunge

Are you ready to try this? That's great. But if you tend toward the risk averse, like many normal human beings, then don't try to implement every element of workshop at once. You might start just with offering choices among writing topics and then helping kids make good choices. Or begin by instituting folders for the students' writing and gradually figure out what kinds of record-keeping forms should go in them. Maybe you'll start off with short in-class writing tasks to try moving around and providing individual help. It's OK to build your workshop gradually and get the machine revved one part at a time. Just ask Niki Antonakos' kids and they'll tell you: workshop really works.

Work Cited

National Research Council. 1996. *National Science Education Standards.* Washington, DC: National Academy Press.

More Ambitious Public Writing Projects

In This Chapter

1.   Multigenre Project

2.   Social Action Paper

3.   Learning Fair

4.   The I-Search Paper

These are the big ones. Meaty and extensive projects, no bones about it. Done as described, these are great alternatives to the Dreaded Term Paper. But they require careful teaching and plenty of time for research, drafting, response, revision, editing, and sharing. During these projects, you'll draw heavily on Chapter 6, "Supporting the Writing Process" and Chapter 8, "Running a Writing Workshop." For assessment ideas, you'll want to look back over the adaptable tools introduced on pages 157, 163, 171, and 178 for some of the activities in Chapter 7. The challenges are great, but so is the potential. Projects like these can be breakthroughs for kids. When the moment is right for the young people, and the teaching has been right on target, there's a chance that kids will say: "This is my best." What a beautiful sound! Every time you introduce one of these projects, savor the fact that many of the resulting papers will end up in family files, trunks, or scrapbooks and will be saved for a lifetime.

Multigenre Project

What It Is

The multigenre project is something new and different. Really. Instead of writing one long paper, in a multigenre project students create a collection of five, eight, or even twelve different shorter pieces centered around a single important topic. These pieces might include some traditional expository-essay text but also student-written newspaper articles, diary entries, poems, letters, interviews, and more. By writing in several different genres, students are challenged to shed light on their chosen topics in rich, *multiple* ways. Forget the junior term paper! Multigenre research engages kids as real creators, not plodding note-card writers and dispirited footnote finaglers.

Our colleague Tom Romano gets credit for developing this welcome variation on the traditional research paper. In his excellent books *Blending Genre, Altering Style* (2000) and *Writing with Passion* (1995), Tom has laid out a model of research writing that's more robust, more demanding, and more real than most of the pro forma research assignments that kids encounter in school. Just recently, one of Tom's disciples, Melinda Putz of Midland, Michigan, wrote the concrete and practical *Teacher's Guide to the Multigenre Research Project* (2005), which shows the way step-by-step. With Melinda's kind permission, we rely on her management strategies for multigenre projects here. Also helping us create this section are Betsy and Charles Coleman of Colorado Academy, marvelous teachers whose kids will shortly show you the excellence that is possible when multigenre projects are well structured and carefully executed.

When to Use It and Why

With plenty of moving parts, Multigenre projects (MPGs) require a good amount of in-class and out-of-class work and strong teacher support along the way. But they're so worth it. Multigenre projects are the very embodiment of the going-deeper-and-thinking-higher mindset. And remember, though these projects feel like a refreshing departure from the old-style term paper, MGPs incorporate all the same cognitive tasks. As Melinda Putz points out: "The student selects a topic, does research as if it were a traditional research paper; collecting information and recording it; synthesizing the information; then presenting it through . . . imaginative writing based on fact" (2005, 2). Kids have to put their findings *into their own words,* and do it across many different text formats. Careful documentation and attribution are required at the end of each project. Spelling, grammar, and style definitely do count—after all, this is formal, public writing. Plus, multigenre projects are 100 percent plagiarism proof. What's not to like?

Play by Play

Getting Started

So how do you launch this challenging new kind of writing in your classroom? Not like we used to introduce research papers! Remember how the mandatory term paper was announced when you were a student? If your school was like ours, the teacher began by handing out a multipage list of instructions, necessary supplies, deadlines, and dire warnings about lateness and plagiarism. And then he talked you through this endless inventory of specifications, until you were mentally breathless and sapped of all initiative. In that version, research writing felt more like a compliance obstacle course (with lots of potentially painful traps) than an exciting intellectual adventure.

So we need a whole new starting place. Multigenre writing will probably be new to students as well as their teacher, so the first thing is to clearly explain—and *show*—the nature of the project. If you get a hold of Melinda's book, the included DVD has a slideshow of Cassandra Folsom's lovely thirteen-part MGP on the Salem witch trials, which includes news accounts, poems, songs, an imagined autobiography, even an invitation to a secret witches' party. Cassandra's project can give your students a great sense of both the structure and the creative freedom in this assignment. The DVD also contains all the forms and handouts Melinda uses to support her students all through the multigenre process.

Naturally, once you start doing MGPs in your classroom, you will want to save your own examples of good student work to help you orient future classes. Or, as we have said a few times before, you could create your own multigenre project on a topic of real interest to you—a fine kind of modeling. However you provide the examples, it is so important to show students what their work should look like and not leave them alone to guess.

When Melinda teaches the multigenre project in her own classroom, she begins with topic searching. She pushes kids to make a genuine personal choice, both in their overall topic and the selection of genres. In fact, kids have to work their way through several guiding questions to develop *two* possible topics, ones that might ignite a little fire in the belly. Then each student spends one class period in the library, doing preliminary research on each topic, both to find out which one really holds her interest and to make sure there is plenty of accessible material to draw upon. As a result of this process, Melinda's kids have confidently taken on a diverse range of topics, including

Barbie dolls	Leonardo da Vinci
the Manhattan Project	temporal lobe epilepsy
Bill Gates	Tupac Shakur
attention deficit behavior	computer programming
Ellis Island	the USS *Arizona*

Mozart
the Underground Railroad
Italian immigration

Ansel Adams
Ben and Jerry's ice cream
dioxin poisoning

Working the Room

Melinda (2005, 91) requires that kids use at least seven different genres in their projects. But look at the alternatives they have to choose from:

wills
letters
campaign speeches
birth announcements
calendars
dialogues
newscasts
questionnaires
obituaries
song lyrics
TV commercials
radio shows
shopping lists
speeches
time lines
news releases
medical records
manifestos
personal data/favorite sheets
surveys
historical fiction
telephone conversations
baseball (or other sports)
    cards
resumes
family trees
dedications
crossword puzzles
cartoons/comic strips
menus
diplomas

requisitions
bumper stickers
magazine articles
memos
myths
parodies
magazine covers
notes to or from the
    teacher
greeting cards
class notes
leases
contracts
textbook sections
parodies
police reports
brochures
diaries
children's books
CD liners
invitations
biographies
telegrams
recipes
interviews
fiction
encyclopedia entries
epitaphs
poems
daily schedules
advice columns

email messages
definitions
fairy tales
catalogs
horoscopes
membership cards
driver's license
advertisements
book jackets
postcards
telegrams
schedules
tickets
contracts
editorials
prayers
bulletins
laboratory notes
journal entries
maps
pamphlets
bottle labels
billboards
graffiti
psychiatrists' reports
tattoos
directions/instructions
wanted posters
plays/skits
eulogies

Quite an inventory, isn't it? Because Melinda offers kids so many choices, she cheerfully accepts the responsibility of providing lots of support and class time along the way, in just the way we outlined in earlier chapters. Her classroom (and her book) is filled with minilessons, guide sheets, discussion structures, and other supports that help kids get the work done step-by-step.

≋ Want to Jump Around?

You might want to skip back to Chapter 6, where we talk about supporting young writers in your classroom, or Chapter 8, where we explain how to set up a *writing workshop*, the ideal classroom structure for multigenre projects.

Just to give you a taste of what Melinda's kids have done with these genres, here are two quick selections. Chris Vickery, whose project concerned the chemical dioxin and how it spreads in the environment, wrote this imaginary internal memo from Ben and Jerry's corporate headquarters.

SCIENCE

Ben and Jerry's Homemade Holdings
MEMO

To: Ben and Jerry's employees

From: Bennet Cohen and Jerry Greenfield

Date: 11/12

Due to implications and accusations brought by the Competitive Enterprise Institute, Ben and Jerry's Homemade Holdings will be changing its policy on the creation of our paper used in ice cream packaging. We will no longer be bleaching the paper since paper bleaching is one of the largest causes of toxic water pollution in the United States. One of the byproducts of the industrial process of paper bleaching is dioxin, a suspected carcinogen. It is known that dioxins in large amounts can cause cancer, and in order to keep our customers healthy and safe, we are not bleaching the paper used in our packages. Each of our new "eco-pint" containers will contain a message stating that our product packaging is dioxin free.

We will still be under criticism about dioxin being contained in our actual product. However, members of Junkscience.com have stated that they believe Ben and Jerry's ice cream is not dangerous to human health. Very low levels of dioxin are not scientifically linked to human health effects. We believe that we are being used as a scapegoat to dodge the real question of how the dioxin got into the environment and food chain in the first place. We are not the ones who should be on trial here, and we are safe and ethical in our method of production with unbleached paper.

We would like to make sure all of our 259 employees here know that we are still just as firmly committed to the environment as we were when we opened our first store in a gas station in 1978.

[Chris found his information in this memo in "Ben and Jerry's Dioxin Controversy," *Wired News,* 18 Aug, 2000. Environment News Service. 5 Nov. 2001 www.wired.com/news/technology/0,1282,38302,00.html] (76–77)

Amanda O'Brien, whose project was about the violent New York newspaper strike of 1918, impersonated a reporter interviewing a few of the rebellious newsies.

Get to Know the Newsies: An Interview with the Brave Souls
By Amanda O'Brien, staff reporter

Amanda O'Brien: Now, I understand at the beginning of the strike, the Arbitration Committee went to the papers, as a last resort to get the demand heard. What went on there?

Boots McAleenan: Well, 'bout six of us went inta de office ta talk wid de men an' Jack waited outside fer us ta report back. I sez ta him, "It's dis away, we went to de bloke wot sells de papers and we tells him dat it's got to be two fer a cent or nuthin'." He says, "Wot are yer goin' to do about it if yer don't get 'em?" "Strike," sez I, and Monix, he puts in his oar and backs me up. The bloke sez, "Go ahead and strike," and here we is dat's all. (91)

In Melinda Putz's version of MGPs, authoring means more than putting smart words on paper—style, presentation, and packaging definitely count. Students need to think very carefully about layout, type, page design, and illustrations, much as today's high-tech workers must do when creating complex documents using text, charts, and photos. Cassandra, mentioned at the start of this "Play by Play" used different sizes of paper, created pseudoweathered parchment paper, and produced a colorful three-page *USA Today*–style newspaper called *Witch Weekly.* The lead story:

Tensions Mounting in Salem

The new Salem Village committee, elected in October, is refusing to collect taxes. These taxes would go to pay the Reverend Samuel Parris salary. The Committee also decided recently that they would change the terms of Parris' contract.

Originally a source of conflict has been the powerful Putnam family's attempts to make Salem Village independent from Salem Town. Those on the western side of Salem Village agree with the Putnams that Salem Town's economic success has only proved to break down family ties and degrade Puritan traditions and customs. (DVD, Folsom, part 4)

HISTORY

Melinda also requires students to connect all seven (or more) of their pieces into a coherent whole. They must set the pieces in a logical order, keeping the reader in mind, and create any needed transitions between documents. Packaging helps create part of this cohesion, too. Melinda invites students to place their whole report in some kind of special container, box, case, or object that works thematically with the chosen topic. This can be a found object (a bright pink Barbie doll case) or something specially created for the project. For his report on the USS *Arizona,* which was sunk at Pearl Harbor, Matt Davey stocked a footlocker with his multigenre papers—*and* all the artifacts that an ordinary *Arizona* crewman might have possessed, even died with, on that fateful day: a jackknife, a bible, a harmonica, big black shoes, a treasured postcard, family pictures, dog tags.

Putting the Writing to Work

Melinda's kids aren't done when they shut down their computers and hand in their packaged projects. As a culminating step, Melinda asks students to get into groups of five and create a sharable dramatic presentation that incorporates something of each person's project. Whoa! Aren't the kids' topics all different? Yes, and that's what makes this such an amazing synthesis assignment. Melinda instructs: "As a group, search for and discuss connections among your topics or subjects. Do they all include people who were in the limelight at one time or another? Did they all overcome some difficulty? Do they all reveal in some way what it means to be an American? Write the many connections you can find between your subjects" (149).

So the kids have to work, share, talk, and plan together to find common strands or complementary themes between, say, Mickey Mantle and astrophysics, and create a performance showcasing a piece of everyone's work. The dramatic format kids typically use is *reader's theatre,* in which key lines of text are taken from each student's project and stitched into a script that is performed aloud in four or five voices. Coauthor Nancy Steineke has written extensively about the practicality of reader's theatre across the curriculum. To grab copies of Nancy's latest student handouts and instructions, go to www.walloon.com and click on "Conference Handouts."

Finally, Melinda always saves time for student self-assessment. "Reflection is easy to skip," she writes, "but don't do it. It's too important. Often if kids take the time to do this, they not only realize where their projects are deficient but also what they have learned and how much they have grown" (130). She provides kids several questions to think and write about, including

> ☞ Are you still happy with your topic choice? Why or why not?
> ☞ What did you learn about the research process from this project?
> ☞ What criteria did you use to decide on the genres to include in your paper?
> ☞ How did you decide on the organization of the pieces into a cohesive whole?
> ☞ Did this kind of project help you get a better understanding of your topic than you might have with a more traditional research paper? (135)

Melinda asks students to write answers to these reflective questions as the last homework assignment during the project, so they can be discussed in class the last day.

Textbook Connections

Multigenre projects can make great use of subject-matter textbooks. As we know from cognitive research, learners understand and remember information only when they *act upon it*. That's why students' passive, silent scanning of textbook pages rarely has any sticking power. But when kids have to recast textbook information into their own words—and in different genres—they are *really* taking mental action. Drawing on facts in the textbook, students can create imaginative texts like the following:

- the autobiography of an equation
- an *exchange of emails* between the mitochondria and the cell nucleus
- a *resume* for Albert Einstein
- a *poem* in two voices: the First Amendment and the Patriot Act
- a *telephone conversation* between Jack and Bobby Kennedy during the Cuban missile crisis

For more ideas, just combine the key concepts in your curriculum with Melinda's genre list—or better yet, let the kids make the matches.

What Can Go Wrong?

The multigenre project presents the same teacherly challenges as any substantial, long-term writing project. You must create a schedule that offers kids plenty of in-class support but still allows you to teach the rest of the curriculum. You have to pull short-attention-span teenagers through this unfamiliar, but very realistic and life-practical long haul. You need to deal with assorted unpredictable questions and problems along the way, while making sure that kids get their sources and attributions right. In other words, nothing you can't handle.

So what unique problems present themselves with MGPs? If kids are going to try writing in genres of text that they have rarely read before, they may not have solid enough mental models to generate good impersonations. There are two ways to deal with this: either take the time to teach a minilesson on that genre to the class (or to an interested small group) or encourage kids to simply switch to a more familiar genre. If you choose the former course, the key is to gather (or have kids gather) several short examples of the target genre and read them over, looking for common features. Then

Want to Jump Around?

Our reflective write model in Chapter 4, beginning on page 96, is more open-ended than Melinda's model and is highly applicable to this final stage of multigenre projects.

meet to list those features and have students work in pairs to surface explicit talk about the formula, practice composing examples, and then share them.

Variation

Since Melinda is an English teacher, and has writing itself as a major curriculum goal, she has the "luxury" of not needing her multigenre projects to cover some required topic. Not all of us share that freedom. At Colorado Academy, another English teacher, Betsy Coleman, collaborates with history teacher Emily Leary on a major unit on the Middle East. Together, these teachers have developed a more structured and focused multigenre project. The students conduct research on Middle East politics and cultures, gathering information and synthesizing ideas, and then they write their own original texts in twelve *assigned* genres, including

SOCIAL STUDIES

1. a **memo** to the director of the film *Osama* (watched in class)

2. an **evaluation** of a visiting Muslim student panel

3. two **letters to the editor** from different points of view

4. a **creative response** to an article on youth in the Middle East

5. a **literary essay** on the graphic novel *Persepolis*

6. a page of **reflections on homework** from writings about *Persepolis* and readings

7. a **persuasive speech** on Islamic fundamentalism

8. a **cartoon strip** addressing the Sunni/Shiia split

9. a **newspaper article** on oil in Middle East

10. two **sets of rules** for women under different versions of Islam

11. a **self-reflective essay**

12. a complete **bibliography** of sources used in all elements of the project

Examples

The kids have delivered fine writing in response to Betsy and Emily's challenging three-week activity. Here are a couple of samples from Elizabeth Kresock's final project.

Item 1: Memo to the Director of the film *Osama*

To: Siddiq Barmak
From: Elizabeth Kresock
CC: Ms. Leary block 1
Date: 11/30/05
RE: Osama
Mr. Barmak,

I enjoyed your movie Osama. The desperation of Osama's family, especially that of her mother, was evident as she is transformed into a boy in order to make money so the family won't starve. It was also clear how the Taliban abuses its governmental power, changing the lives of the citizens desperately. Women are not allowed to work, and families without a male will starve. It is disturbing when Osama is sold and becomes a sex slave. I like how she is able to select her lock, thus giving up the little freedom she had and sealing her fate.

My biggest question about the film is why did you choose to have Osama become a sex slave? Do you believe that this is the fate of most girls under the Taliban regime? Why didn't she escape?

Though I thought the movie was moving, I didn't understand why Osama's legs were covered in blood when she is lifted from the well. It was not until after the movie that I was told that she had her period. I thought that her legs were scraped by the sides of the well.

Your movie was thought provoking and well made. I enjoyed watching it.
Sincerely,
Elizabeth Kresock

Item 6: Two Sets of Rules for Islamic Women

Rules for Muslim Women: According to Islamic Religion

1. Women have the right to inheritance.

2. Women have the right to work outside of the home.

3. Women have the right to be educated.

4. Women have the capability of being a strong influence in her family, workplace, religion, and society in general.

5. Women are able to decide if they want to marry and who.

6. Women have the right to spend money that they earn.

7. Women are permitted to participate in anything as long as they preserve their modesty.

8. Women have the right to remain chaste until marriage.

9. Women have the right to privacy.

10. Women must be treated equally if their husband has more than one wife.

Rules for Muslim Women: According to the Taliban in Afghanistan

1. Women are not permitted to work.

2. When in public, women must be escorted by a close male relative.

3. Women must wear a burqa.

4. Women may not talk to men.

5. Women may not wear make-up or nail polish.

6. Women do not have a say in their marriage or divorce.

7. Women cannot vote.

8. Women must wear light blue or mustard yellow.

9. Women cannot go to school.

10. Women do not have the right to drive.

11. Women must follow the laws imposed by the Taliban.

Item 9: Newspaper Article on Oil in the Middle East

Saudi Arabia Issues Caused by Oil by Elizabeth Kresock

—Riyadh, Saudi Arabia
Oil revenue has skyrocketed in Saudi Arabia since the United States entered Iraq, but Saudi problems grow. Economic and security issues now overshadow Saudi Arabia's wealth. The kingdom has become more reliant on its revenues given the Monarchy's massive spending and the cost of anti-terrorism security. Oil export revenues make up over ninety percent of total export revenues, seventy percent of state revenues, and forty percent of the country's gross domestic product.

Though its economy appears to be flourishing, thirteen percent of Saudis are unemployed, and terrorist attacks have become an even greater threat. The monarchy wants the country's oil revenues as well as protection from the western powers. The House of Saud has not spread its wealth among the people because it is less concerned about the citizens. Saudi Arabia's government has kept the sales of the country's oil for itself, paving their private streets with Italian marble, while the population heads into poverty and is attacked by terrorists.

Hadi bin Mubarak Qahtani, a Saudi

citizen, stated that, "It seems that the richer the king gets, the poorer I become. Instead of watching his people suffer, he should be helping us. He is being corrupted by the self-indulging Americans." Most of the Saudis disagree with their king. Not only are they upset with the difference in wealth, they are upset with his relations with the United States and the western world. To them, the United States represents greed, capitalism, and indecency.

In 2004, Saudi Arabia earned over one hundred sixteen billion dollars in net oil revenue. This was a thirty-five percent increase from 2003. Saudi Arabia is predicted to generate one hundred fifty billion dollars in 2005 and one hundred fifty-four billion dollars in 2006. The monarchy is under incredibly internal pressure to use this added wealth to help the country.

Social Action Paper

What It Is

By *social action,* we mean any activity in which students apply classroom lessons to address real issues in a community, group, or organization (their town, their neighborhood, their school, their family). This could be as simple as a student's attempt to improve her family's diet or as far-reaching as the investigation carried out by a group of high school students on the wrongful conviction of an innocent man, decades past, in another state.

Here's a great example of a powerful social action writing project. At Nathan Hale Middle School in Connecticut, Thomas Dzicek's students, who were studying the Vietnam War, discovered that there was no official memorial to the 612 Connecticut residents who gave their lives in that conflict. Confounded, the kids investigated this oversight, confirmed it, and committed themselves to making it right. Over many months, they researched the lost soldiers, using public records, the Internet, and conversations with the soldiers' neighbors and childhood friends. They also tracked down relatives of the lost soldiers and interviewed them, using a six-item interview protocol to help them gather this information. This tool was also needed, Dzicek says, because kids often became so riveted by the stories they were hearing that they forgot to take notes (Delisio 2002).

There were some emotional moments when the kids met survivors like Ana Pederson, whose fiancé, Robert Mylnarski, kissed her good-bye more than thirty years earlier and never returned. "This is not just an academic exercise, it's reality," Pederson said. "Children learn better by internalizing, and this gives them a better appreciation of freedom and liberty. I'm glad they gave veterans [and their relatives and friends] a chance to talk; a lot of this has been pent up."

In the end, middle schoolers from Nathan Hale wrote biographies of all 612 fallen soldiers, and their writing became part of a traveling memorial that visited many corners of Connecticut. For their work on this amazing project, Dzicek and his students won the International Reading Association's Presidential Award for Reading and Technology (2005).

Now, this Vietnam project may seem a bit ambitious, and maybe a little political, but social action projects can take lots of shapes. The possibilities in our different subjects are wide-ranging. English classes could encourage the reading of literature among young children in the neighborhood. For history, students could promote public awareness of unrecognized local heroes or public figures. We needn't think of social action only as political agitation on controversial issues. For Jeff Hoyer's environmental science students, at Deerfield High School in Chicago's suburbs, a project can be as simple as reducing consumption of a particular resource, like electricity, in a student's home. (More about Jeff's projects to come.)

It's natural to include informative and persuasive writing as an essential tool in such a project, along with writing to report to the teacher and the rest of the class. The form this writing takes is likely to depend on the nature of the project. But the teacher can provide structures to help students make connections between classroom learning and real-world situations and reflect on their significance. And the writing may take place in class in a workshop setting or be completed by students on their own.

When to Use It and Why

We talk a lot as educators about preparing students to become responsible citizens in a democracy. Even some state standards and curricular frameworks around the country sport such language, though it's often forgotten when the state tests are being designed. But does preparation for citizenship refer to skills that get used only after the kids leave us? Don't they need to learn by doing? We send a contradictory message if we imply, "We're telling you about something that's really important for you to do, but we don't really have the time or inclination to do it here in our classrooms." We'd certainly not expect students to train for a sport but never play even an intersquad game.

To carry out and write about social action projects in school, however, is not a simple matter. Students, families, and communities are diverse and have their own sensitivities, and we're not proposing to send the kids out on political campaigns or demonstrations. Teachers shouldn't try to convert students to their own political persuasions. Fortunately, there are ways to engage students in responsible social action that avoid such traps—and writing is a powerful tool in the process. Written words in the service of valuable social activities can give writing real voice, energize students with real purpose, and connect them with real audiences, whose real-world feedback demonstrates what sorts of expression do or do not communicate effectively.

Time is, of course, always a challenge. If students are carrying out a project beyond the school walls, that's where much of the work may take place. However, if you can budget even a few periods for planning the projects, reviewing the plans through quick one-on-one conferences, doing some writing, and then reporting to the class on results, you will be signaling that this work is a truly important part of kids' education.

Play by Play

There are many ways to conduct a school-based social action project and to build writing into it. A few key steps:

- Help students brainstorm possible activities out in the world (or in the school, for that matter) relevant to the topic they have been studying and doable with the time and resources available (e.g., equipment or materials needed, community institutions that focus on the topic the students are studying, and sites such as doctors' offices where pamphlets could be displayed in the waiting room).

- Provide support for the written communication students will use in the project, employing some of the strategies we've described in this book.

- Provide clear guidelines for how and when various steps must be completed and when students will report to you and their classmates on the results.

- Ask students to explain, in their writing, the connections they see between their projects and the curriculum you've taught.

- Be sure to have students reflect on what they've learned from conducting their project—challenges encountered, strategies they used to solve problems, what they'd do differently next time.

Example for High School Science

SCIENCE

Here's how science teacher Jeff Hoyer makes it work for his environmental science class. The projects that Jeff's kids carry out do not stand alone, but are lodged within the larger process of study in the course. One important book students read about the environment and their relationship with it is Aldo Leopold's *Sand County Almanac,* a classic early-twentieth-century collection of journal entries on the author's prairie restoration work, observations of wildlife, and thoughts about man and nature. Leopold is considered by many to be the father of the environmental conservation movement in the United States.

But the kids don't just read the book. Over several weeks, Jeff carries out a variety of activities to immerse them in it. Students respond in writing to various passages and compose their own modern-day analogies to Leopold's thoughts. In circle sessions, students discuss their interpretations of selected passages from the *Almanac.* They write poems after studying Leopold's biography. They develop games and activities to demonstrate Leopold's ideas. And since Leopold developed his own "land ethic," Jeff asks students to write land ethic pieces too, creating individual rationales for the efforts they will carry out later in the course (and, hopefully, in their lives).

Each student in the environmental science class must then carry out and write about a community service of his own choice each quarter. This can involve a wide range of possibilities. Volunteering at an elder care facility is acceptable, for example, because it relates to issues of aging in our population. Some students hold rummage sales, enabling reuse of goods and materials. (Most people forget that recycling is just the last of the conservation steps, after reduce and reuse.) One option is to participate in environmental restoration right on the school's property, where a small branch of the Chicago River and its banks are being restored by students and faculty (learn about this project at www.dist113.org/dhs/Depts/Science/River/index.htm). Some students collect seeds from wild plants in a nearby forest preserve and scatter them in a different preserve to help maintain diversity in those isolated patches of natural growth.

In the second semester, students tackle "Make a Difference" projects that up the ante by requiring them to carry out and document some change in their own lives or surroundings for four weeks. Most choose individual efforts, like attempting to conserve electricity or gasoline. Students proposing bigger campaigns to influence a community or industry must show that they've researched their topic thoroughly and that there's reason to believe their effort will have results. A number of relevant books facilitate kids' choosing: *Fifty Ways You Can Help Save the Planet,* by Tony Campolo and Denny G. Aeschliman, and *Earthscore: Your Personal Audit and Guide,* by Donald Lotter, are two Jeff finds most useful. Individual conferences help the students write up realistic goals. Peer discussions at tables of four further refine and focus the projects. For a week the kids gather baseline data, such as keeping track of and writing down the amount of water they use at their normal rate. In a journal they then record their efforts and compose reflections, with Jeff checking their progress weekly. At the end, students draft evaluations of their experiences and write up and present reports to the class.

Additional activities involve the whole class, as they research and choose among ecological problems in other parts of the world. In 2005–6, for example, the students learned about the health problems due to unsanitary drinking water in the African country of Mali. Only 50 percent of Mali's urban population (and about 60 percent rural) has access to clean water, resulting in thousands of childhood deaths every year from diarrhea and other diseases. By selling fluorescent light bulbs (to encourage conservation of energy) and recycling old cell phones (to reduce consumption of resources), students raised one thousand dollars, which they contributed to the Joliba Trust (www.jolibatrust.org.uk/) to purchase a new compressor for digging wells in Mali. Of course writing fits very usefully into such a project—persuasive pieces about why the class should choose one project over another (including posters and PowerPoint displays on the choices they advocate), emails to organizations that are potential recipients of their fund-raising, pamphlets about the project to inform contributors or purchasers of goods they sell to raise money.

Here is Marina Shifrin's journal reflection after holding a garage sale to raise money for one of the projects.

On our first day Katie and I were surprised about the amount of clothes and other things we had acquired. For our data tables we decided to measure the weight of each thing and then create calculations on how much extra "stuff" people had lying around their house. I think another way we could have gone about measuring everything we had acquired is by prices. Because we live in such a wealthy area, many of the clothes were name brands that once were, and still may be, very expensive. An example is we had a pair of Coach shoes which currently may go for anywhere from 200 to 250 dollars. We sold these shoes for two dollars. This exchange shows that there are many things Americans waste their money on. The amount of clothes we had that still had their price tags on and were in perfectly new condition was surprising. Had the family that donated these shoes invested in a solar panel on their roof instead they may have saved much more energy. We also had four printers, a fax machine and a scanner donated from one family. Surprisingly, all of the printers and scanner were bought during the sale. We were proud of this because had they not been bought, they most likely would have been thrown out and put into a landfill somewhere creating water and air pollution, but now they are being reused. In two days we sold about 1/5 of the clothes and other items we had attained and made around 200 dollars. By donating this money to Give World we will be able to get schooling supplies and many other things to children in India. By giving them a better education we are also spreading knowledge about the environment. We were able to talk to "customers" about what they were buying, where the money was going to, and our motivation for the project. The clothes that were not bought we plan to give to the Salvation Army. Overall, we found this process not only worth all our time and efforts, but we were also able to learn a lot from it. We learned how wasteful people could be but at the same time how resourceful others can be. The garage sale brought about many interesting people with fascinating stories and also gave us the opportunity to share ours.

Interdisciplinary Example

At Byrd Community Academy in Chicago's Cabrini-Green public housing area, teacher Bryan Schultz conducted an extended project that grew out of a brainstorming session he led with his fifth graders on the issues in their lives.

> The intensity was beyond measurement as students called out problems that affect them: "teenage pregnancy," "litter in the park," even "stopping Michael Jackson!" A lot of the problems had to do with the school: "foggy windows pocked with bullet holes," "no lunchroom, gym or auditorium," "clogged toilets" and "broken heaters in the classroom." Before it was all said and done, these fifth graders had identified 89 different problems that affected them and their community, a challenge I had posed to them just an hour prior. (Schultz, in Beane 2005, p. 50)

This led to a major project to focus attention on the needs at the school, which is described in James Beane's *A Reason to Teach* (2005), and which attracted widespread attention, response from Chicago Public Schools, and numerous awards. It was ambitious, all consuming, and politically out there, and we realize that not all teachers would choose to attempt such an effort. But we describe it here because it shows just how powerful a social action project can be, not only in achieving change but in building students' skills across the curriculum and motivating them to read, write, and learn in highly effective ways.

Once they realized that many of their concerns focused on the school itself, Bryan Schultz's students set about documenting its terribly rundown condition. They wrote rough drafts and combined them into a class letter sent to various public officials.

> Responses came pouring in immediately. Phone inquiries, letters, emails, and visits from legislators as well as newspaper and TV reporters kept the students' project flowing with questions, suggestions, and encouragement. . . .
>
> The students' action plan became the epicenter of the entire curriculum for the remainder of the school year. Every subject lost its compartmentalization and became integrated and integral in solving the problem of getting an "equal" school. Reading, writing, arithmetic and social studies were all blended in a natural way. Rather than using basal textbooks the students researched pertinent information about how to solve their problem. . . . Reading flowed into current events as students read and reacted to newspaper articles written about their work. In addition they read about techniques for participation, which "showed us how to do things like survey and petition." The students learned how to prepare documentation including their survey results, photos, and written assessments as they incorporated data analysis and mathematics into their student-driven curriculum to gain support. After taking this documentation to the public, Danisha asserted, "No one who saw our folders could disagree with what we were saying about the school's problems." (Schultz, in Beane 2005, 54–56)

The students' work got citywide and even national attention, as well as local results, with repairs made to the school's bathrooms, lights, and doors. More importantly, the kids saw that they had great abilities and that their efforts at communication could make a difference. Test scores went up, attendance soared, and discipline problems disappeared. As one student, Tavon, commented, "I did not feel school was a place for me. I didn't think it would help me in my life, but this project made me like coming to school. . . . It did not feel like the boring school I was used to."

There were risks, of course. Bryan wondered whether the project would succeed and whether students would grow discouraged if it didn't. Could he really share authority with them as they made decisions about how to proceed? How would the various subjects of the curriculum fit in? But Bryan came to understand how his role had evolved:

> As their teacher, I learned that content can come from the students rather than be driven into them by forcibly preparing concrete objectives in an artificial manner.

Just as students in the more affluent schools are encouraged and rewarded for their insight and creativity, these urban, African American students now could have their voices heard through purposeful action and determination. And in this particular case, their voices were no longer silenced. (Schultz, in Beane and Schultz 2005, 60)

Not all of us get the opportunity to lead a project like this, with these striking results. But it offers possibilities we can aim for and demonstrates how well-executed involvement in a social action project can inspire writing and drive learning that is more powerful than almost anything we can come up with ourselves through clever strategies or instructional tricks.

Textbook Connections

Social action projects provide a natural occasion for students to use their textbooks as they write documents, letters, proposals, or reports on their activities. In fact, this is when a textbook can actually be a useful reference tool, which is what many textbooks are best suited for. In their writing, students can make specific connections with concepts and topics in your course, using references from their textbooks to support their explanations. In Jeff Hoyer's class, students must refer to concepts and passages from their textbook in all of their reports on the social action projects.

What Can Go Wrong?

Jeff observes two challenges that are likely to be common to outside-the-classroom social action projects. First, some students choose unrealistic efforts or goals. For example, a plan to install solar panels on a home would not be feasible within the four-week span of the project, given the construction work required. On the other hand, some projects start off too small and need to be expanded. Turning off the water while you brush your teeth, for example, just doesn't save enough to make a significant difference in a household's water consumption. Jeff finds, however, that between his conferences with students and the peer conferences they hold with one another, most of the problems get resolved before students get too far in the process.

A second issue is procrastination. Being normal teenagers, some kids put off their projects. And since the main activity takes place outside of school, it can be hard to monitor. Jeff's weekly check-ins help. And he has found that specifying grades for each step in the project also reminds students of the need to stay on top of the process:

- 25 percent for the plan and baseline data
- 25 percent for the weekly progress reports
- 50 percent for the written conclusion and presentation

However, Jeff's reading and writing activities lead as many students as possible to immerse themselves in their projects because of their maturing and well-informed beliefs, not because of a grade. One advantage of a more intensive effort like Bryan Schultz's is that there is even less difficulty with this issue.

The other problem that many teachers worry about: that social action projects like Bryan's will raise political questions parents or school leaders won't consider appropriate for school or that they will be seen as an imposition of the teacher's political beliefs on students. Bryan Schultz was prepared to face this. Jeff Hoyer's approach illustrates how students' and their families' values can be respected in the process. It shows, too, how civic responsibility can be promoted without crossing into overtly partisan activity.

Variation

The possibilities are many, but one of our favorite social action projects is based on the book *Fast Food Nation,* by Eric Schlosser. Conducted as a senior project at Best Practice High School in Chicago, this project linked biology, health, economics, and political science with a set of contemporary American issues that included obesity, job safety, and humane treatment of animals. Following a series of activities to support reading and thinking about various parts of the book (such as creating bookmarks on which students summarize passages and write responses to them), students carried out projects aimed at changing people's attitudes toward food. Written communication for these included pamphlets, posters on diet and animal rights, and letters to food service companies and public figures. Social science teacher Mike Myers, now at Northside College Prep High School in Chicago, has broadened his use of *Fast Food Nation* to include other nonfiction texts and to examine a variety of issues and topics related to food in this country.

SOCIAL STUDIES

Learning Fair

What It Is

This major writing activity is based on the format of the ubiquitous science fair but is stretched out across the curriculum. But wait. What pops into your mind when the phrase *science fair* presents itself? Competition? Parent ghost-authored projects? Something ho-hum, old, and overdone?

We'll admit that these events and their derivatives have gotten some well-earned bad press. Go ahead and type "science projects" into Amazon.com's search box; 6,449 results will turn up, including books with titles like *Science Fair Projects for Dummies* and *CliffsNotes Parent's Crash Course Elementary School Science Fair Projects*. Besides thousands of science fair books for sale, we also found within the first two pages of results on Amazon a nifty sea monkeys kit (science project ready) and a cool black-and-white poster of Doctor Robert Oppenheimer; now *that* was some science project! So one problem with science fairs has been that kids often pass the reins of responsibility to eager, overachieving parents, who are the likely buyers of all these corner-cutting books and materials.

However, rather than give up on "parent fairs," it's time to retool the structure. When learning fairs work the way they're supposed to, they're great. When Steve and Smokey helped start a new high school in Chicago in the 1990s, one of the happiest traditions launched was the annual learning fair, where every student created a personal inquiry project, including a paper, a display board, a two-minute presentation, and a handout. On the appointed day, tables were set up all through the gym and auditorium, and parents and community members streamed in to listen, ask questions, and score the kids' projects. This was writing for a real audience at its best; the kids worked really hard and everyone had a ball. It was also fantastic PR for the school.

Sometimes these events can even change the world a little bit. Do you remember reading about twelve-year-old Jasmine Roberts' science fair project? She's the one who tested the ice and toilet water from five local fast-food restaurants. The results? Seventy percent of the time the toilet water had less bacteria in it than the ice did. Yuck! What gave her this winning science project idea? A newspaper article about the contamination of airline drinking water piqued her curiosity and then, when she saw her friends chewing on ice, the focus of her research coalesced. Of course, the advice her father gave her couldn't have hurt either: "Do a project that will have an impact on society" (ABC News 2006).

Not every science project is going to make the nightly news, but when carefully chosen, a fair project can definitely have a real impact upon the student doing the research, and these kinds of projects need *not* be confined to the science department! We've seen great social studies fairs focusing on key persons from history, for example.

When to Use It and Why

A learning fair enables students to study a topic of interest in depth and then share that knowledge with a wider, very public audience. Kids can get their information in a variety of ways, including traditional library and Internet research. But many teachers who use learning fairs also place a strong emphasis on field research—getting out and talking to people, visiting sites, conducting experiments, making use of primary rather than secondary sources. Though the outcomes usually include a paper, learning fairs also require strong visual and oral components. Students must create attractive display boards or demonstrations as well as be able to talk in depth about their projects and answer any questions audience members might have.

Another reason for considering a learning fair is that the skills required of students are authentic; the kids replicate what adults have to do in many job situations. Interviewing relatives and seeing where that information takes them, for example, is very similar to what one has to do when networking during a job search. And just as in the outside adult world, creating a complete final project for a learning fair requires many steps. Students must sequence their research, plan their next steps, and in the end create a final product. In real jobs with real responsibility, employees have to be able to do this. Last, the actual learning fair closely resembles the interview process. Within a limited amount of time, students must convince the listener of their project's worthiness as well as field questions.

The sophomore team at Andrew High School, led by Colleen Ghelfi, Tracy Sukalo, and Lisa Evans, uses their family fair as an avenue for reviewing and extending skills and concepts learned in English, biology, and geometry. It also gives students a chance to investigate their own family backgrounds as well as invite families in to visit the fair, celebrating the research of their own children as well as that of their classmates. We'll use their tried-and-true model to show you the steps involved in creating one kind of learning fair in your school.

Play by Play

Topic Search

Students start by brainstorming a list of family members, living or dead, whom they would be interested in researching. Sometimes students get stuck, thinking that no one in their family is interesting. After all, their family contains no former U.S. presidents, astronauts, or sports heroes. The kids get past that roadblock when they're asked to just think of a relative they'd like to know more about. After some thinking and talking, most kids realize there's a family member whose background they want to explore. Colleen Ghelfi also tells the kids to have two choices in mind because sometimes difficulties arise in the research. If they have a backup all set, they can change course quickly instead of having to go all the way back to square one.

The teachers tell the kids that a finished family fair project will contain the following *polished* components:

- ☞ a well-rehearsed speech about the family member
- ☞ a detailed display that includes an attention-getting display board, family artifacts, photographs, results of genetic research, and a scale model of a piece of architecture significant to the researched family member

ENGLISH

Identifying the Audience

So who is the audience for these projects? Lots of people! In the planning and process stages, the audience encompasses the teachers and classmates. Students discuss their projects, sharing ideas, helping each other with content, and following all of the requirements of the project. Also, besides the public performance, students write a formal paper that is the source of their speech. This paper, as well as all the other process pieces, are checked in or graded by the team teachers. On the day of the family fair, the audience includes the students' families as well as several evaluators: one English or social studies teacher, one science or math teacher, and one former student. Each evaluator examines the project components, listens to the speech, and asks some follow-up questions to see if the student can think on her feet. Colleen, Tracy, and Lisa have found that the student evaluators are the toughest audience members since they know these projects inside and out, having completed the process themselves in the past year or two.

LANGUAGE ARTS

SOCIAL STUDIES

Gathering Information

One of the reasons that most learning fairs become parent fairs is that once an assignment is given, the work is done outside of class, and the big emphasis rests solely on the final product. If you want to have a successful learning fair, you've got to be willing to devote some significant class time to guiding your students through the process. In the case of the family fair, this process starts with helping the kids understand what field research really is. See Figure 9–1 for the summary sheet Colleen uses with her students.

Once students understand that they are going to have to get out and talk to their relatives, they brainstorm a list of initial interview questions (see Figure 9–2). When kids are armed with an initial set of questions, Colleen gives them about a week to complete the interviews. She encourages them to take good notes and also, if possible, create a video or audio recording of the interview. On the day the interviews are due,

Conducting Field Research

Observations and Interviews

- You should plan to make several visits to the person because it will help you learn more about the place, activity, or person by looking at it in different ways.

- Learning more allows you to answer questions you may have had after the first visit.

- Obtain any details you may have missed the first time.

Conducting the Interview

- Plan carefully!

- Arrange your visit by calling ahead.

- Be flexible.

- State your intentions directly and fully.

- Be enthusiastic.

- Bring the proper tools (interview questions, notebook, tape recorder, video).

After the Interview

- Immediately after, reflect on the visit, review your notes, and add to your notes.

Follow-up Visits

- Build on what you have already discovered.

- Develop a plan for your follow-up: questions to be answered.

Questions

- Open—gives the respondent range and flexibility to describe, explain, etc. Requires more than a one-word answer.

- Closed—requests specific information. Sometimes requires a simple yes/no or one-word response.

Figure 9–1 *Field research guidelines*

Family Fair Interview Brainstorm

1. What is the full name of the person who is your Family Fair subject? What is his/her relation to you?

2. What might you want to know more about regarding this person? Discuss the aspects of this person's life you are curious about.

3. With whom will you conduct your first interview? How is this person connected to your Family Fair subject?

4. When do you plan on conducting your first interview? How and when did you arrange the interview date and time?

5. Are there other people you would like to interview who can give you more insight into your Family Fair subject? Name two people here and provide a reason you would consider interviewing them about your subject.

Brainstorm a list of 10 initial interview questions here. Remember, the best questions are those that allow the subject to talk freely but to the point. *Open questions* give the respondent an opportunity to tell a story, reveal attitudes, and provide personal revelations. *Closed questions* ask for specific information. They make very good follow-up questions, so you will probably use them later.

Figure 9–2 *Interview questions*

the class talks about what the students discovered and even watches some of the video interviews. As they watch, they look for emerging themes and avenues that could be explored further. After some discussion, Colleen asks the students to reflect on the initial interview (see Figure 9–3).

Since students will be conducting a second interview, they now need to narrow the focus and think about what aspect of that relative's life they really want to understand. Preparing for that second interview, students no longer use the initial brainstormed interview questions but questions tailor-made for their particular focus. Also, students think about whom else they might interview. Students often realize it might be interesting to get another relative's version of a story Grandma told. Or in order to really find out about their grandpa who has passed away, students need to talk to more relatives than just their mom. Of course, after the second interview, students complete another reflection. Though Colleen officially requires only two interviews, the reflection encourages students to keep thinking about the further investigation they could do if they conducted a third interview.

> ⟲ *Want to Jump Around?*
>
> Looking for information on the kind of reflection described in Figure 9–3? Check out the section on reflective writes in Chapter 4, pages 96–100.

Interview 1 Reflection

1. Now that you have completed your first interview, it is time to reflect upon what you learned. Please write a thoughtful reflection based on the *new* information you gathered from your interview. Do not simply describe the interviewee's responses to your questions, although you can refer to them. Instead, *discuss your feelings* about the interview, what you were surprised to learn, what you found intriguing, the success of the interview itself, etc. Write your response here. Remember, I am looking for a deep level of thought. You may use another sheet of paper if necessary.

2. Think back about your interview. Discuss the area of your subject's life you would like to focus on in a future interview. In other words, how will you narrow your focus, since you can't possibly cover this person's entire life through one project? Explain why you came to this conclusion.

3. With whom will you conduct your second interview? Create five new interview questions to ask this person. These questions should reflect the more narrow focus you have identified above.

Second interview will be with _____

Figure 9–3 *Reflection suggestions for first interview*

While students are conducting their interviews, they are also gathering information for the biology component of the project, which requires them to trace family genetic traits, and their geometry component, which requires them to create a scale model of a building that played an important role in their relative's life. A more in-depth description of these activities can be found later in this chapter.

Once the interviews are completed, Colleen introduces four models that demonstrate different ways to write a character sketch or essay on the life of a person. Once familiar with different ways they might approach their writing, students can begin to think about how they will organize their own information with the help of these prompts:

- ☞ Whom are you featuring in your profile essay?

- ☞ What is the overarching theme or characteristic of this person that you will emphasize in your essay?

- ☞ How will you support this theme? In other words, what type of proof do you have to back up your claims? Describe this proof in some detail.

- ☞ Looking through your interview notes, what are three direct quotes you plan on including in the essay? Write down the exact quotes and explain who said each and why you plan to include them in your essay.

☞ Of the four essays we read in class, which one do you plan on using as a model for your own profile? Why?

Drafting, Revision, and Editing

Once students have organized their interview notes, they begin drafting their profiles, taking time along the way to talk with Colleen and conference with classmates. By the time Colleen reads the final draft, each writer has completed a very thorough self-assessment and had the opportunity to revise weaknesses along the way. Figure 9–4 shows the grading sheet Colleen uses to assess the final product.

In addition to preparing the paper, students also spend class time reviewing the display criteria, planning and talking about what they will include and how they will put the display together. They even map out how they will lay out the information on their trifold display boards, since it's easier to move pieces around on the plan sheet than it is once they're glued to the board.

Sharing the Writing

Though only classmates and the teacher read the essay, this piece serves as the foundation for the speech that students will give to evaluators. Students do not memorize the paper, but they do practice speaking of their relative in an organized way, emphasizing the overriding theme of that person's life and skillfully using the direct quotes they wove into the paper. Besides speaking in detail, all of the students have to be able to talk about their relative in a purely impromptu fashion, confidently answering any questions an evaluator or family fair visitor might ask. Therefore, they have to be thoroughly prepared to explain every detail of their display as well as explain their interviewing process. Students practice "the spiels" with each other, relishing the opportunity to stump their partners by asking some really hard questions.

On the day of the family fair, students stand by their displays, on the watch for their official evaluators, but eager to catch the attention of passersby. These students have a lot of time invested in these projects, and are clearly very proud; they want to tell others about their discoveries. The family fair is a big event that extends far beyond the visiting evaluators. Parents, aunts, uncles, grandparents, and siblings all attend, enjoying the way this fair celebrates the continuation of family history, stories that might otherwise be lost forever. Also, on the day of the fair, students are required to bring in a homemade treat, a favorite family recipe; of course, recipe cards are prominently displayed next to each platter and casserole dish. Though not required, families often reach back into their ethnic heritage. It's not unusual to find guacamole, dolmades, pierogi, Swedish meatballs, and Irish soda bread all residing on the same table.

Profile Essay Grading Criteria

Advanced Development	Developed	Still Developing	Underdeveloped
5–4	4–3	3–2	2–1

These are the *focus areas* for this essay:

_____   The beginning of the essay engages the reader.

_____   The controlling theme is clear and relates to the profile subject in a sophisticated manner.

_____   Vivid and descriptive details are used in the essay.

_____   The writer uses clear and interesting anecdotes that support the theme or focus areas.

_____   The writer uses dialogue effectively.

_____   The pace is informative and entertaining. The writer examines particular aspects of the subject's life and does not attempt to write an autobiography.

_____   The organization is effective and the ending is not too abrupt.

_____   Spelling, grammar, and punctuation are correct.

_____   The title is creative and fitting for the piece.

_____   Overall impression of the essay.

_____ /50
Total

Figure 9–4 *Grading sheet for personal profile*

The Biology Component

Ideally, a learning fair project fits smoothly into the curriculum. In Tracy Sukalo's case, she makes sure that her biology classes are starting the unit on genetics at the same time they begin preparing for the family fair. Here is Tracy's introduction to the biology component of the family fair.

SCIENCE

Family Fair—Biology

This year's family fair will provide you with the opportunity to explore your genetic history. You will be provided with a list of traits and be asked to collect genetic information about your family.

You will then construct a family pedigree and trace your genetic history. Your pedigree will include at least four generations, be properly labeled, and include Roman numerals and numbers to identify each family member. You will also choose one genetic trait and trace its inheritance.

You will also complete two monohybrid crosses. One cross will show complete dominance of an actual trait in your family. The other cross will show incomplete or codominance and will be fictional.

You will receive points for having each part of the project due on a specific date. Be sure to record all of these days on your Family Fair calendar.

The students' first assignment is to create a genealogical chart. Of course, students do come from mixed families, are adopted, and so on. However, even if students may not be biologically related to all of their family members, they can still create the chart and understand the principles of ancestry.

Next, students begin to study a specific phenotype (physical variation) manifested in their family. Students have four choices: tongue rolling, widow's peak, ear lobes, or thumbs.

Now students begin to collect data, tracing this trait within their family with the goal of pinpointing relatives whose traits they themselves have inherited (when appropriate). Tracy even has them imagine the genetic future of their own children, requiring them to use their genetic research for predicting inheritance patterns. This is the second, fictitious monohybrid cross she refers to in the introduction above.

From start to finish, the genetic research project takes about three weeks, but much of the time devoted to it is out of class. All of this study and data collection culminates in the creation of a pedigree chart along with the monohybrid cross charts that illustrate one of the phenotypes. Guiding students in the computer lab for this chart creation takes four to five class periods. Just like the English portion of the final presentation, the charts move from rough drafts to revised, edited, polished products. The students use MS Word to produce the charts, and with the right incentive, Tracy will be happy to come to your school and teach you how to do it!

The Geometry Component

MATH

Lisa Evans' goal is for students to take what they've learned so far in geometry and apply it to the project of researching and constructing an architectural model. Students begin by choosing a structure that has some significant connection to the family member being studied in English class. The choices run the gamut. Some students choose a famous structure (since this school is in the Chicago area, think Sears Tower) from their relative's hometown. Of late, many students have been choosing ancestral homes, even if Grandma sold the old homestead a while ago. Through Internet research, photographs, interviews, and on-site investigation, students determine the measurements necessary to create a model. Students even return to those long-sold homes of their grandparents, introduce themselves to the new owners, and then politely ask if they can come in and measure the rooms. Surprisingly, most of the time the new owners willingly comply!

Measurements in hand, students now can do the math necessary for determining the proportional scale they'll need to use. In other words, if the Sears Tower is 1,729 feet tall (including the antennas), then each foot in a 3-foot-tall model would represent 567.33 feet. Once they have the scale nailed, the kids can start the design and construction phase.

As students build their models outside of class, they periodically report back in class, discussing their progress and examining the geometric principles involved in the construction: surface area, geometric shapes, angles.

As the models near completion, Lisa takes the kids to the computer lab to produce a three-fold brochure using MS Publisher. They spend two days putting together the rough draft, work in class to proofread and revise, and then return to the lab for another two days to polish and perfect their brochure. From past experience, Lisa has found that she needs to emphasize the proofreading element. Students, of course, try to argue that this is geometry, not English, but Lisa doesn't buy the argument. No matter what the content area, the abilities to write, revise, and edit are important skills. Besides, isn't math all about attention to detail? Lisa believes that same

⇝ Want to Jump Around?

Want more ideas about student-created brochures as a public writing activity? Check out Chapter 7, pages 167–173.

attention needs to be applied to the text of their brochures. She has even considered increasing the number of points given to the grammar portion of the brochure rubric. If students do the math, she hopes they'll take their proofreading more seriously.

What Can Go Wrong?

Since this is a big project, acknowledging potential problems is the best way to head them off. First, the project's size and complexity sometimes overwhelm students. Therefore, it's important to break the project into clear steps and guide kids through the process so that they can revise along the way. The big disasters occur when students don't realize their errors until they're far along in the process. And of course, there will always be that one kid who doesn't do anything until the night before. But once again, this problem is minimized by valuing the process as much as the product; the total point value for completing each step of the project should be equal to the value of the final product. If that facet of the grading is made clear to students, waiting until the night before loses its appeal.

The topic of family research can also raise some thorny issues. How does a student complete this project when family relations are strained? How does a student who is adopted complete a genetic family pedigree chart if he knows no true blood relations? The sophomore team treats the family fair as an opportunity for learning, so they pose solutions based on that goal. An adopted child can still do genetic research on her adopted relatives though she is not directly related. A student whose family is weathering some strife can still interview some relatives for her essay, or her notion of family can even be extended to friends who are thought of as family.

Finally, the exploration of family history can lead to some uncomfortable surprises. Colleen described one girl who was doing research on her great-grandmother, who had passed away before she was born. In the course of the interviews, one relative mentioned something that no one had ever spoken of before: during her teens, her great-grandmother had been a member of the female counterpart of the Hitler Youth. That was an emotionally disturbing moment, yet in the end the girl was glad she knew about her great-grandmother's hidden past and did not regret completing the project.

Looking at the scope of this project, it's easy to dismiss it as too complicated and time-consuming to be worthwhile. However, year after year after year, Colleen, Tracy, and Lisa run into former students who still can't stop talking about the family fair. Students enthusiastically give updates on the relatives they interviewed, recall fond memories of the big day, and *always* ask, "Are you still doing it? That was the best thing we did in sophomore team." So is it worth the time and effort? According to all those former students, the answer is a big yes.

How Do I Grade This?

As mentioned earlier, the final family fair grades do not come from the teachers; they come from outside evaluators who are recruited from within the building. Each student has at least three evaluators: a science or math teacher, an English or social studies teacher, and a former sophomore team student who is now a junior or senior. The science or math teacher evaluates the biology and geometry components while the English or social studies teacher evaluates the speech and how it relates to the theme and display elements. The former student evaluates all project aspects since he is familiar with all facets of the family fair project. As an added bonus, this gives the former students a chance to review what they learned in sophomore biology about monohybrid crosses and genetic pedigree! In the end, the rubric scores are added together and averaged to determine a final grade. If there is a disagreement about the final grade, there is an appeals process. However, few students use that option. Considering the continual reflection and revision this process embodies, they are intimately familiar with the expectations by the day the family fair arrives.

Figure 9–5 *Kaitlyn, Kristina, and Steve show off their projects—and their parents—at the family fair.*

I-Search Paper

What It Is

Out of all the public writing projects described, the I-search paper comes closest in format to the traditional research paper, except for a couple of major differences. First, topic choice is as unrestricted as possible since the goal of an I-search paper is for the student to find out about something that truly interests her, something she needs to know more about. The research for this paper mirrors the kind of authentic research adults do in the course of their lives. For example, if you were thinking about buying a new car, you would probably go online to read comments of other owners, *Consumer Reports*–style reviews, government safety records, and more. Armed with knowledge, you would then visit some different dealerships in order to compare prices and options. You'd probably also try to get your local mechanic's opinion as well as that of someone who has already owned the model you're thinking about. Just like adults, kids research the answers to questions they care about when working on an I-search paper.

The second, and probably more important, difference between the traditional research paper and an I-search paper is that it is written in *first person*. The I-search paper is a personal story of research: how the writer became interested in it, what sources proved most useful, and what he found out. This means the I-search can have a chronological narrative structure, which give kids a comfortable and familiar framework to work in.

When to Use It and Why

The best I-search papers are based on a personal curiosity. If the teacher can leave the topic truly wide open, this assignment can happen anytime during the year. On the other hand, if the topic is restricted to a specific area of content study, students will obviously need sufficient background knowledge before generating their own personal questions about, for example, cell biology or the Civil War. In these cases, I-search papers work better after a unit has been completed or toward the end of the semester.

The I-search process is particularly useful because it teaches and reinforces many research skills:

- narrowing a topic
- devising questions that are worth answering
- planning one's research

- utilizing a variety of sources
- judging a website's appropriateness and reliability
- finding useful information and recognizing bias

All of these are not just school skills but life skills.

Play by Play

Topic Search

For a general-topic I-search, students begin by brainstorming, listing all of the things that they know about or that interest them. It's best to have kids start these lists one day, work on them for ten minutes, compare lists with a partner or two, and then put them away. Tell the kids to keep thinking about their lists, trying to think of topics they forgot initially. Two or three days later, have them get the lists back out, add to them, and talk some more. If the lists are getting pretty long, you can move to the next stage of the topic search. Otherwise, put the lists away one more time for some more percolating and then repeat the brainstorming one last time.

Once the lists offer enough choices, have the students review their lists and put stars by the four topics that they would most like to know more about, topics they have questions about, topics where further information would be useful to them. Then for four consecutive days, have partners take turns interviewing each other briefly on one of the starred topics, asking questions like the following:

- How did you get interested in this topic?
- What do you already know?
- What questions do you have?
- Whom could you interview about this topic?
- Where else do you think you could get information?
- How is knowing more about this topic going to help you?

These interviews help the writers think out loud, tapping into their prior knowledge while also helping them think about the search and whether the time investment will be worth it. After finishing up the four quick topic interviews, students return to the items they've starred and rank them 1 through 4, with 1 being the topic that seems to have the most potential. Even though the kids have picked their number one topic, remind them to keep thinking about their second topic choice, as sometimes research leads to dead ends. Instead of wasting valuable time on a fruitless journey, students can go right to their backup choice without losing momentum.

In the case of a content-specific I-search paper, the topic search process has a couple of additional steps. After completing the general-interest list over a few days, students review their notes and textbook, making a new list of content-area topics that interest them. Next, students put the lists side by side and look for connections:

GENERAL TOPIC	CONTENT TOPIC
How will my grandmother be treated for cancer?	Biology of abnormal cell division
Why are people in the United States racially prejudiced?	Segregation after the Civil War
Skateboarding	Mechanics of motion

The point is for students to find a personal reason for researching a specific topic in their content-area class.

Identifying the Audience

The audiences for this paper are the writer, the teacher, and other students. We tell students that they need to think about explaining their information so that anyone would understand it, whether or not she ever played chess, rode a skateboard, or threw a free shot in basketball. Though the style is a bit different than the typical feature article found in a magazine, the paper should still be informative and interesting to a general audience.

Prewriting, Part I

Unlike other writing projects we've described, there is quite a bit of prewriting that takes place before and during the research phase for the I-search. Once students have settled on a topic, they begin their thinking with a double-entry journal–KWL hybrid (see Chapter 4, pages 85–91 and 101–105). The left-hand column is labeled "What I Think I Know" and the right-hand column is labeled "Questions I Have." Students work to brainstorm prior knowledge as well as research questions; they can move back and forth between the columns. As always, remind students that brainstorming means quantity over quality. The longer the lists, the more they'll have to work with. Like the initial topic brainstorming, it's worth sleeping on the KQ notes for a few days, giving time for more ideas and questions to emerge.

Gathering Information

When the KQ notes are complete, students need to reorganize their questions under three or four major questions, creating a two-sided chart that looks like this. In this case, the student was researching dogs.

QUESTION #1
WHAT KIND OF DOG SHOULD I GET?

Which breeds are easy to
  groom?
Like to go for walks?
Affectionate?
Easy to train?
Advantages/disadvantages of
  mixed breed?
Puppy versus adult?
Breeder versus shelter?
Male versus female?

POSSIBLE SOURCES

Interview my vet
Interview workers at local
  animal shelter
Books on dogs
Talk to people who own dogs
Visit pet shop
Internet sites:
    American Kennel Club
    Sites for specific breeds
Programs on Animal Planet

QUESTION #2
HOW DO I TRAIN MY DOG?

Heel, walk without pulling?
Not to bark all the time?
Not to jump on people?
Follow basic commands?
Stay calm around other dogs?

POSSIBLE SOURCES

Interview dog trainer
Interview someone who's
  taken their dog to
  obedience class
Books on dogs
Internet sites on dog training

Nowadays, students immediately want to head for the Internet, Google the word "dogs," and then print out whatever is contained on the first page of the first three hits. However, when you look at the previous chart, it's readily apparent that most of the answers to these questions can also be found via books or interviews. The Internet is still a viable source, but other sources might be more reliable and more specifically target the answers to the questions. Here are some tips for helping kids improve their research.

Books: Talk to your media specialist ahead of time. If you can give him a list of your students' topics, he'll be able to pull a cart, get the photocopy machine repaired, and be ready to direct kids to the stacks as well as offering impromptu lessons on the Dewey decimal system. Also, if the topics focus only on your specific content area, eyeball the cart and see what you can add. Chances are you'll think of other text sources that your media specialist might have overlooked.

Interviews: According to the grandfather of all books on I-search, written by Ken Macrorie (1988), an integral part of the information-gathering process is the interview. A good interview can provide intricate details and personal insight on a topic, and students should be encouraged to seek out those who have information. However, we've found that forcing students to conduct interviews as part of the I-search process has mixed results. Kids are often shy or reluctant to make the phone call, talk to the neighbor, or make the appointment necessary for an interview. Lots of students view adults as too busy to be able to make the time to talk to them. We're certain that sentiment is a combination of some truth mixed in with a lot of excuse. Even when they do conduct the interview, the information they glean is often superficial: "You told me to ask ten questions and I did; do I get the points now?"

Now we're not saying don't bother with interviews, but we are saying that getting some good interviews from the kids will require planning and coaching. If you want to make interviewing a strong component of the research, you'll need to take some class time to talk your students through the steps: how to make contacts, set up appointments, and use good manners when people make some time for the interview. In addition, you'll need to give the kids some class time to write their questions and then role-play some interviews in order to learn how to probe for details or take the interview in a new direction when the interviewee's answers diverge from the planned questioning.

⇒ Want to Jump Around?

For more on planning interviews, see how Colleen Ghelfi coaches her students as they prepare their family fair projects, on pages 225–229. Or check out the "People Research" section of Chapter 7, pages 142–148.

The Internet: Given a choice, students will head straight to the keyboards. That's one of the reasons they need to think about potential sources when they organize their research questions. Otherwise, they'll never focus on the information that's available elsewhere. But even so, those Internet searches will be unavoidable. The trick is for students to leave the computer lab with some really worthwhile information.

Before you take the kids to the computer lab, have them brainstorm potential search words and phrases. Let them share with each other in groups and then discuss as a class. Next, when you take the kids to the lab, make sure the computer projector is set up and ready to go. Rather than immediately letting them loose, ask for someone to volunteer her topic and search words. Have everyone search at the same time with the same words using the same search engine. Once the list comes up, together check out the hits and look at the pages (remember, you'll be projecting the pages as well; the computer is a great way to keep everyone together). Take some time to discuss the reliability of the information as well as its usefulness in answering the questions the volunteer posed. Work through the Internet evaluation sheet (Figure 9–6), talking about each of the answers.

The problem is not always that kids have accessed some hobby blogger's Geocity website of questionable validity. More often, kids land on legitimate sites but somehow manage to print out the pages that provide the least amount of information possible. How do they do it? We guess it's because they don't *read* anything before they print it. The evaluation sheet forces them to slow down and look at the pages more carefully. Just modeling proper search-and-skim techniques is important, but it's no guarantee they'll follow your instructions once the surfing begins. That's why the evaluation sheet is so important. Once we started requiring our students to *fill this out completely before*

Internet Source Evaluation

Name _____   Hour _____

Topic _____   Date Accessed _____

Internet Address _____

Title of Page _____

Title of Site _____

Organization _____

Web Page Author _____

Who is the intended audience for this site? (Consider word choice, content, graphics.)

Does this page provide links to other pages that contain useful information?

List the research questions this site's information helps answer.

What new information or interesting details did you learn from this site, information that goes beyond common sense? *For example, a career site tells you police officers need to know how to stay calm in tense situations. That is something anyone should intuitively know; you* don't *need to go to the Internet to find this out.*

On a scale of 1 (low) to 5 (high), how useful is this information in answering your research questions? Explain your rating.

Figure 9–6 *Internet source evaluation sheet*

printing something, the garbage factor declined significantly. Knowing that the form needs to be filled out *before* they print anything means they'll perform a cursory inspection first and quickly move on if the site doesn't offer much.

As far as the number of sources is concerned, that's really your call. We generally require between four and five *good* sources that make use of a combination of print, Internet, and, possibly, interview information.

Prewriting, Part II

Once upon a time, the next step would have been to create a whole bunch of annotated note cards. As a matter of fact, some people still swear by this process. And that's fine, but if you want the nitty-gritty on note cards, you're going to have to look elsewhere. Once cheap photocopy machines were invented, we gleefully pitched our index cards in favor of a fistful of dimes and some highlighters. Here's how we have the kids organize their information.

1. Students read through the information they've printed out or photocopied with their lists of research questions in front of them. Whenever they run across some important information in the text, they underline it with a pen and jot down some notes in the margin, notes that explain why they underlined, what question is answered, or how they emotionally responded to the information.

2. After all of the reading and note taking is completed, the kids get out four sheets of paper, one for each major question. They write one question at the top of each sheet of paper. Then (here's the fun part) each kid gets a set of colored pencils or four different-color highlighters, color codes the questions, and then returns to the text, color coding what he's underlined, matching each piece of information with the color of the major question it best answers.

3. After the color coding, students jot down notes on each of the question sheets, putting the highlighted information in their own words and including citations so that they remember later where everything came from.

Once this note taking is done, students have a firm grasp of the information and it's all quite well organized. Now it's time to draft the paper!

Drafting

The traditional I-search paper contains these parts in this order:

1. introduction: how I got interested in this topic

2. description of the search

3. what I found out

4. conclusion: how I'm going to use this information and what I still want to find out

This is a good model, but if you want the writing to follow a different format, that's OK. We often omit the description of the search because, if students mostly rely on books and Internet sources, their search stories quickly become rather repetitious: "First I looked up dogs and got over a million hits. Then I typed in 'sheepdogs,' which led me to the National Sheepdog Association of America. That site answered many of my questions and provided several other useful links . . ." Now multiply that little story by sixty students and substitute newts or skateboarding for sheepdogs. Ugh.

What separates an I-search from a traditional term paper is that the I-search has personal value and the prose is written in first person. Before students start their rough drafts, be sure they have a model to follow. Take a look at the sample we've provided, write up a paper yourself, or use a paper from a former student. If the instructions and model are clear, you'll need to use only a little class time for reviewing the model and answering questions. Then, since you've already taken significant class time for the research phase, we suggest having the kids work on their first drafts at home with a specific due date in mind.

Revision

Revising an I-search paper may take a couple of days because focusing on each part within one day is overwhelming for both the writers and the peer editors. On the day the drafts are due, have the kids move into their editing groups and start with the introduction. For each revision meeting, one member reads aloud at a time. Afterward, the group discusses the following specific revision questions and the writer takes notes on her draft.

Introduction

☞ How does the beginning of the introduction grab the reader's attention?

☞ How does the introduction give details about the writer's interest and prior experience in regard to the subject?

☞ How does the writer help readers who are unfamiliar with the topic? How has the writer made the topic appeal to a wide audience?

☞ What are the last lines of the introduction? Do they lead the reader into the next part of the paper?

Question Answers

☞ Which details are most interesting?

☞ Which questions are missing full answers? What information needs to be provided in order to create a more complete answer?

☞ Where does the writer respond to the information with his personal ideas, opinions, or feelings?

☞ Which words have a great sound or create a vivid mental image?

☞ Which information doesn't seem to go along with the question and could be cut?

Conclusion

☞ How does the writer connect the ideas in the introduction with the ideas in the conclusion?

☞ How is the writer going to make use of his research? What will he do next?

☞ What does the final paragraph leave the reader thinking about in relation to the topic?

Editing

The editing of this paper is no different than the editing of any of the others except for the fact that this paper's length will make sustaining attention to detail a bit more challenging. Also, the most common error students make in this paper is the extreme overuse of the word *you* and its kindred, which is the result of them trying to make the paper friendly and conversational. So in addition to having students employ the usual editing strategies described earlier, we always have them read through their papers, putting a big *X* on every *you, your,* and *you're* they find. Then we tell them to determine to whom each *you* really refers. Sometimes a *you* refers to the reader, but many other times the *you* refers to some other third person who needs to be designated: earthquake victim, police officer, college student. Now here are the *you* rules:

☞ If the *you* refers to a third person, replace *you* with the specific noun it was standing in for.

☞ If the *you* refers to the reader, see if you can reword the sentence to eliminate it. Many times you don't have to reword at all; the sentence will still make sense without it. A *you* once or twice a page is OK; more than that is a problem.

Sharing the Writing

It does take time, but after all that work, we really like to have the kids read their papers aloud to the class or turn them into speeches. Also, when students know that they have to read their papers aloud, the products are often better. Even when students are perfectly willing to turn in a paper to the teacher that barely makes sense, they are seldom perfectly willing to read a poorly written, incoherent paper aloud to their peers. As an added benefit, having the kids read their papers aloud will speed up your grading because you'll hear the paper once before reading it. You can even follow along in the paper as the student reads aloud from a second copy and jot comments as you go.

Another way to share the writing is to encourage students to transform their papers into shorter feature articles for the school newspaper. If students have chosen topics that interest them, there's a good chance the topics will interest other teens as well.

What Can Go Wrong?

Like some of the other public writing assignments we've discussed, the biggest problem is plagiarism. As mentioned earlier, the temptation to cheat really affects only the few that skip the process and try to go straight to the final product at the eleventh hour. This bit of ugliness can be almost entirely avoided if you make it very clear that no final paper will be accepted without evidence of having completed all of the preliminary steps. Instead of collecting piles of process material at the end, it is far easier for you to sign off on individual checklists as pieces are satisfactorily completed (see Figure 9–7). This checklist *must* be turned in with the final draft, or the paper will not be graded. Also, making each item on the checklist worth 10 points (150 total) would clearly demonstrate that you value the process as much as the final product.

How Do I Grade This?

Figures 9–7, 9–8, and 9–9 include forms you can use to grade the I-search paper.

Example

As a sophomore, Samantha Lassendrello was intrigued by her friend's pet ferret and was thinking of getting one of her own. Her I-search paper offered her the opportunity to do a little more investigation before becoming a ferret owner.

I-Search Paper—Process Checklist

Name _____   Date _____

Topic _____   Hour _____

ARTIFACT	DUE DATE	COMPLETION DATE	CHECKOFF
KQ chart			
Article 1 + evaluation			
Article 2 + evaluation			
Article 3 + evaluation			
Article 4 + evaluation			
Article 5 + evaluation			
Article 1: underlining, notes, color coding			
Article 2: underlining, notes, color coding			
Article 3: underlining, notes, color coding			
Article 4: underlining, notes, color coding			
Article 5: underlining, notes, color coding			
Major question notes			
Typed, double-spaced revision draft—with notes			
Typed, double-spaced editing draft—with corrections			
Typed and complete bibliography			

Figure 9–7 *Process checklist for I-search*

CATEGORY	4	3	2	1
TOPIC QUESTIONS	Reflect keen personal interest. Definitely require serious research.	Reflect personal interest. Some research required.	Questions are simple, easily answered with minimal research.	Questions are general, reflect little personal interest, little need of research.
QUALITY OF INFORMATION	Interesting, unique details. All questions thoroughly answered.	Uneven use of facts and details. Some questions answered better than others.	Facts and details general or insufficient.	Real detail and research consistently missing.
ORGANIZATION	Example format consistently followed. All paper components present and fully addressed. All paragraphs clear and well organized.	Format followed. Some components more complete than others.	Some components missing or weak. Paragraph structure weak, confusing.	Format not followed. Writing is difficult to follow.
STYLE	Written in first person. Clear voice. Interesting and imaginative. Clear effort made to hold the reader's attention.	Written in first person. Demonstrates clear competence as a writer.	Personal voice inconsistent. Abundant use of *you* and other vague words.	Personal voice is often absent.
DOCUMENTATION	Sources consistently and correctly cited. Works cited page uses correct format and is error free.	Sources consistently cited. Works cited page includes 70 percent accuracy.	Sources consistently cited. Works cited page includes 50 percent accuracy.	Sources inconsistently cited. Works cited page missing key information.
PROCESS	Checklist attached. All project components completed in timely fashion.	Checklist attached. 90 percent of project components completed in timely fashion.	Checklist attached. 70 percent of project components completed in timely fashion.	Checklist attached. 50 percent of project components completed in timely fashion.

Figure 9–8 *I-search rubric*

Performance Evaluation—I-Search Paper Presentation

Name _____   Date _____

Title _____   Hour _____

- **First impression:** confident stance;   no   1   2   3   4   5   Times 1 = _____
  ready to perform

- **Practiced:** no stumbles   no   1   2   3   4   5   Times 2 = _____

- **Voice:** audible, clear enunciation; even   no   1   2   3   4   5   Times 2 = _____
  pace; holds audience's attention

- **Interpretation:** practiced; makes paper   no   1   2   3   4   5   Times 2 = _____
  sound interesting; not monotone

- **Eye contact:** regularly looks at audience;   no   1   2   3   4   5   Times 1 = _____
  face is not buried in paper

- **Posture:** continued confident stance   no   1   2   3   4   5   Times 1 = _____

© 2007 by Daniels, Zemelman, and Steineke from *Content-Area Writing*. Portsmouth, NH: Heinemann.

Figure 9–9 *Evaluation sheet for I-search presentation*

FERRETS AS PETS

Introduction

Ever since I was about ten years old, I've always wanted to know more about ferrets. Who would have known that five years later I would be writing a paper on them? When I was younger, I would always go to my friend Jackie's house, and she had a ferret. Jackie warned me to never pet her ferret. She said that it was mean and would try to bite me if I got too close. Little did I know she was just trying to scare me. As time went on, I did pet Jackie's ferret and soon started to love him. We would give that ferret baths and take him for walks. Ferrets are amusing, energetic animals and most people don't realize what wonderful pets they can make. Who says only a dog can be man's best friend?

The Search

To look for information, I mostly used my computer. Searching on Google, I typed in "ferrets," which brought me to over five hundred hits in an instant. I clicked on the first subject I saw but realized that that site wasn't going to give me enough information because its goal was to sell me a ferret online. Who would want to buy a ferret that gets sent through the mail? That's when I decided that just typing in "ferrets" was making my search a little too broad. Instead I typed in "how to care for a ferret." There weren't as many links this time, but I still had plenty to choose from. Luckily, the first link I clicked on gave me exactly what I needed; it told me how to care for a ferret. The next phrase I tried was "having a ferret as a pet," and I found some good links from that search as well.

When it came time to interview someone, I thought of my friend, Jackie. I called her up and she answered all my questions. Plus, she gave me a magazine on ferrets and told me I could keep it. That magazine told me everything I needed to know about ferrets. Jackie not only helped me with my interview but she helped me with my entire project. Writing this paper has helped me learn all I need to know about owning a ferret. If my mom ever decides to let me own one, she'll be happy with the fact that we saved a lot of money that we might of spent on books about ferrets!

What is a ferret?

There are two kinds of ferrets: the Black-Footed Ferret and the European Domestic Ferret. The two breeds are similar in size, but the Black-Footed Ferret has a different appearance. Compared to the European Domestic, the Black-Footed Ferret's head is much more blunt in shape and its eyes and ears are larger. Its legs and feet are black or dark brown and its crown and forehead also have a dark color. These features are unique to Black-Footed Ferrets. The European Domestic has large front feet that help it in digging. Its tail is wider at the base and tapers off towards the tip. Domestics vary in their coloring, ranging from brown to black and sometimes even white.

Ferrets are carnivorous and feed mainly on rabbits or ground nesting birds, but pet ferrets can eat dry ferret food, easily bought at any pet store. And if dry food is unavailable, they will also eat kitten food. Fully grown, ferrets are almost two feet long; that includes the tail. They love to play in tubes and other semi-tight places. Wrapping paper tubes leftover from Christmas make the perfect ferret toy. A popular myth about ferrets is that they come from the rodent family. They don't. It just so happens that ferrets belong to the weasel family.

How do I become a good ferret owner?

Before jumping into ferret ownership, be prepared with a properly outfitted cage, ferret food, grooming supplies, and plenty of toys. Ferrets also need a litter box. Yes, you will need to train your ferret how to use his litter box. When training a young ferret, never completely clean the box. Once fresh litter is in place, put a little "used" wet litter along with a couple pieces of dried feces on top; these leftovers give the ferret the hint of where to go to the bathroom! Ferrets need regular baths every week or two. Otherwise, the cage as well as the ferret will develop an unpleasant odor. Inside his cage, the ferret needs a warm place to sleep. Put a small blanket in the corner of the cage. A ferret is a burrowing animal and will instinctively bunch up the blanket in order to create a small cozy space for himself. Also, spread another blanket over the cage bottom. This keeps the ferret's little feet from slipping between the cage rungs and possibly hurting himself.

Ferrets are very active animals and need plenty of exercise and attention. One way to give a ferret exercise is to take him for a walk. Pet shops sell leashes made especially for ferrets. The leash wraps around its neck and front legs to keep the ferret from sliding out and scampering off. Ferrets also enjoying running around the house loose, but if you let your ferret out of his cage make sure there are no places for him to hide. Ferrets love to crawl into all the places that a human cannot reach. Also, an unsupervised ferret might leave little "presents" in places that are difficult to clean.

What would be considered a safe environment for a ferret?

What's so scary about sofas, mattresses, and refrigerators? These pieces of household furniture pose potential hazards to a pet ferret. The number one hazard in a home is the reclining chair, whether a person is sitting in it or not. The hidden cranny of a recliner looks perfect for a ferret nap, but it may be crushed when the chair is opened. Another ferret hazard is rubber bands or other items left on the floor unnoticed. Ferrets tend to eat soft rubber and plastic that can lodge in the intestines. A ferret can die of an intestinal blockage without the owner ever realizing what happened. The third biggest household hazard is medicine or chemicals. Quite often, women leave their purses on the floor, and a curious ferret will investigate. Ferrets might eat loose pills and can even open medicine bottles without childproof caps. Just like when families baby-proof a house to keep their infants safe, families need to ferret proof their homes as well. A final hazard to ferrets is toys. Ferrets like to chew, so make sure they play with toys that cannot be chewed apart. Latex rubber cat and dog toys are the number one cause of gastrointestinal blockage, the leading cause of death for ferrets. It may sound like owning a ferret requires a lot of work, but these are just some common sense examples of what you need to watch out for in order to keep your pet safe.

What are some ferret behaviors?

It's hard to tell whether a ferret is happy or sad. Ferrets have unique ways of expressing their excitement and anger. When ferrets jump and dance around, people jump to the conclusion that the ferret is upset or frustrated. Actually, dancing is an expression of pure joy and excitement for ferrets, so just sit back and enjoy the show. Many ferrets enjoy it when you join them in the dance, chasing them or letting them chase you! Ferrets have a reputation for stealing and stashing everything they can get their little paws and teeth on. Anything that isn't out of reach or too heavy to drag is fair game. To prevent putting your ferret in any danger, let your ferret run loose in an area free of nooks, crannies, and furniture.

When a ferret is angry or scared, it will usually not be active and will definitely not want to be touched, so don't try to pick it up or play with it. An angry ferret often needs food or sleep. Make sure a ferret's food bowl is always full. Don't worry about over feeding it; ferrets will eat when they want and only what they need.

Conclusion

Learning about ferrets, I have a better idea about the type of pet they can make. Before I did this project, I had no idea that ferrets "danced" when they were happy. I also didn't know that they are known for stealing things. I've always wanted to own a ferret and doing this project has only made me want one even more. If it weren't for my parents, I would own a ferret right now. For anyone who is thinking about getting a pet but doesn't want something as big as a dog, I recommend a ferret. These animals are small enough to keep in a cage, but you can still give them baths and take them for walks just like you would a dog. Some people think that a dog is man's best friend, but I feel that if you love and nurture any pet from the time you get him he will grow to be your best friend.

Works Cited

"Ferret Behaviors." *Ferrets* 23 Sept. 2001: 25.

"Ferret Essentials." *Ferrets* 23 Sept. 2001.

"Ferret Food for Thought." *Ferrets* 23 Sept. 2001.

"Ferrets." *Ferrets.Com.* 28 Sept. 2003 <www.ferrets-ferrets.com>.

"Home, Safe Home." *Ferrets* 23 Sept. 2001.

Leidig, Lisa. "My Ferret Won't Use His Litter Pan." *The Ferret Store.* 2 Oct. 2003 <wsww.neeps-inc.com/newletter/litter.html>.

Novakowski, Jackie M. Personal interview. 7 Oct. 2003.

Works Cited

ABC News. 2006. "Fast Food Ice Dirtier than Toilet Water." http://abcnews.go.com/GMS/ONCall/story?id=1641825&page=1. Accessed October 23, 2006.

Beane, James. 2005. *A Reason to Teach: Creating Classrooms of Dignity and Hope: The Power of the Democratic Way.* Portsmouth, NH: Heinemann.

Delisio, Ellen. 2002. "Students Remember Connecticut's Vietnam War Heroes." Education World. Accessed September 2, 2006, from www.education-world.com/a_curr/curr377.shtml.

Macrorie, Ken. 1988. *The I-Search Paper.* Portsmouth, NH: Boynton/Cook Publishers.

Putz, Melinda. 2005. *A Teacher's Guide to the Multigenre Research Project: Everything You Need to Get Started.* Portsmouth, NH: Heinemann.

Roadmap to Success (website). May 11, 2005. "Plato Learning Sponsors International Reading Association Presidential Award." Plato Learning, INC.

Romano, Tom. 1995. *Writing with Passion: Life Stories, Multiple Genres.* Portsmouth, NH: Boynton/Cook.

——. 2000. *Blending Genre, Altering Style: Writing Multigenre Papers.* Portsmouth, NH: Boynton/Cook.

CHAPTER ten

Writing for Tests and Assessments

Tests are everywhere in school—tests in classes, state tests, tests for college entrance. Sometimes it seems as if these exams are choking out the very teaching and learning they are supposed to measure. Citizens want to know how a school is performing. Colleges want to know if a student is prepared to do the work that will be assigned there. And most teachers use tests to determine what students are learning day to day. All understandable needs. Yet tests provide quite limited information. Like a photograph, they offer a snapshot, a moment in time, seen through the narrow tunnel of one lens. A college applicant may score outstandingly on the ACT, but his actual achievement may depend much more on what else is going on in his life and his head.

Some tests are more meaningful, more revealing of students' actual learning, more "valid," as testing experts say, than others. And tests do not stand alone, but profoundly influence what and how we teach. Some tests encourage teachers to race through content never slowing down to help students think deeply about the material, thus encouraging memorization of endless data bytes promptly forgotten once the test is over—or sometimes even before. In contrast, a well-structured test can actually promote new learning even as the student is in the midst of it. Still, the best measures of student learning are almost always more expensive, more time-consuming, or both.

OK, so it's complicated. But is writing a good tool to find out what students have learned? In many ways, yes. A piece of student writing can go well beyond what a teacher can discover from a multiple-choice exam. It can invite students to develop and share their thinking, rather than just choose among disconnected bits of information. Math teachers have always insisted that students show their work and explain their process, rather than present only a final, mysterious number. Even some state tests include constructed-response questions that ask students to explain their ideas rather than just darken bubbles. The quality of information that we get from essay tests, however, will depend as much on the quality of the prompts and the ways we've previously taught students how to approach them as on the student's knowledge.

Essay tests can be crudely designed and misused. So how can we design the most effective writing prompts for our classroom tests? How can we ensure that essay prompts focus on the most important ideas and values we teach, and lead students to demonstrate what they've actually learned? How can we help students respond successfully, so they access as much of their real knowledge as possible? And how can we prepare students to do well on writing tasks in state and national standardized tests?

Before we dive into the how-to, let's get clear about the inherent limitations of tests, whether they include essays or not.

The first limitation: The very purpose of writing on a test differs from that of most writing in our lives. The student is writing only to demonstrate what she knows, rather than to inform or persuade or entertain anyone about anything. It's an artificial situation. The cute remark by writing teacher Peter Elbow that we've mentioned before in this book bears repeating: If you are a student yourself, try writing a request to your teacher for a contribution to your political campaign and see how you feel when you get an *A* but no check (1981, p. 220). The reward is an external prize (or just as likely, the avoidance of punishment) that fails to connect students to our subjects. So when we complain that kids care only about grades but not the real meat of what we are teaching, we need to recognize that the testing situation we put kids in only reinforces that flawed approach to learning.

The second limitation: The audience for a test essay is very limited—either the teacher himself, who already knows what the student is telling him, or some distant test grader the student will never meet. It's like playing tennis with a pro when you are a bare beginner—you can expect to lose. And it doesn't help much to include in the prompt "Pretend you are writing a letter to . . ." The kids know who is really going to read it.

Actually, many smart teachers solve this issue by assessing oral presentations (usually written out in advance, of course) given to panels of outside visitors that often include other students. If the panel is interested and asks good questions, the words do inform someone about something. But yes, this strategy does eat up a lot of time.

As if artificiality is not trouble enough, here's *limitation number three:* Usually, you get only what you ask for. The student may respond to your essay question but not discuss other things she knows about the topic. Or if the student does not know much about it, we're simply encouraging fake writing—BS, to put it bluntly.

And limitation four: The tasks you can assign for a test cannot always be realistic ones. Sure, a swimming coach can have lifesaving students actually jump in the water, pull in a thrashing "victim," and then write about it after they've dried off. (Steve in fact vividly remembers just such an experience from his teenage years—the teacher flailing in the water seemed huge, and of course did not resist with his full strength.) But a science student can't go back and rerun an experiment or observe a plant's growth on test day. Similarly, with the writing itself, an essay test allows only minimal time for planning or revising. It's not like writing workshop, or the work of real writers as they draft, let things rest, and come back to the task (as happened with writing this very sentence).

And one more—limitation five: A test captures only one moment in time. At best you can see what the student knows, but not the value that has been added. Did he get a lot from the unit, or was it material he already knew before it started? It takes a portfolio of work, with written reflections by the student, to observe that.

Better Essay Test Design

So after all these qualifications, how can we design solid classroom essay test prompts that invite students to dig more deeply into real learning? How do we make sure that the prompts focus on key concepts in our subjects? And how can we make the test itself more of a learning experience for young people? Here are a few suggestions.

Focus on the Big Ideas That Should Stay with Students Long Term

There are many ways to concentrate on the big ideas, some direct, and some more indirect. When Dorne Eastwood works with her seventh-grade math students on graphing, she wants them to understand that a graph is not merely about plotting points for a variable to form a line. The line as a whole tells us something, and Dorne wants her students thinking about that. So she borrowed an idea from her graduate school teacher, Miriam Sherin, at Northwestern University, and presented students with the following task on a test:

> A, B, and C are swimmers in a race, and the graph tells how they swam the race. You are the announcer calling the race from start to finish. Write out

how you would call the race as it is taking place. What is happening for each swimmer?

MATH

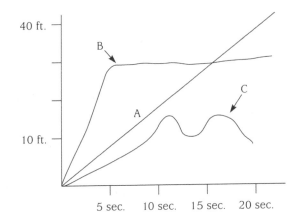

The kids loved writing to this prompt and invented all sorts of explanations for what was going on. Here's how a typical student would call it:

And they're off! A is swimming a good steady stroke. B is dashing ahead, almost halfway down the pool. C is a little behind. Wait a minute! B appears to have stopped dead in the water! Something must be wrong—maybe he's got a cramp. Looks like they're throwing him a life preserver. A is still working steadily down the pool. And what's happening with C? He just stopped and started heading backwards. I think he just lost his swimtrunks and is going back to get them. . .

Dare we introduce the F word—*fun*—into essay tests? Meanwhile, the students are actually learning more about the larger concepts embodied in graphing. They're applying what they've learned in class to a new situation. And they're getting practice making inferences.

> *Dare we introduce the F word—fun—into essay tests?*

Of course, prompts like this create much more thought-provoking tasks. One key strategy is to simply move questions up the hierarchy of thinking skills. That trusty old tool, Bloom's taxonomy (the cognitive part), is actually a pretty useful guide:

- ☞ **Knowledge:** the recall of data or information
- ☞ **Comprehension:** understanding the meaning of something
- ☞ **Application:** using a concept in a new situation

- **Analysis:** seeing the parts and organizational structure of something
- **Synthesis:** putting ideas together to form a whole
- **Evaluation:** making judgments about the value of ideas

Instead of asking students just to summarize or restate material, try creating a higher-level task that asks them to attempt one of the thinking activities farther down the list. Of course the prompt should require students to support their ideas with information from the material they've studied, so their responses concretely use what they've learned.

Make Tests a Part of the Learning Process

Hilary Quagliana and Niki Antonakos go still further and integrate essay test writing with the very fabric of their teaching. Since their yearlong focus is to teach students to analyze and interpret the significance of historical events, they simply make test essays one more step in the process. Early in the year when teaching students how to use outlines to develop thinking, for example, they have students draft outlines on the question, "How did geography influence the development of China?" Then on a take-home test, the students must develop several essay body paragraphs from the outline. Instead of leaving the students at sea, or just hoping their in-class lessons are taking hold, the teachers provide specific tips and guidelines, based on the needs for improvement that they see in the outlines. All of this leads to deeper thinking. For example, one of the tips begins as follows:

> Thesis: Make sure your thesis has a significance. Simply saying "The geography of China impacted China socially, economically, and politically" is not enough. This thesis includes the topic, an opinion, but it does not include a "so-what." It makes an observation, but it does not make an argument. *How* did the geography impact China's political, economic, or social systems? Did it cause the Chinese to be behind in development, or does the way the Chinese dealt with the environment show the Chinese culture's resourcefulness and imagination? Did the geography cause China to advance more quickly or more slowly than other cultures? These are all questions to consider when revising your thesis.

Build in More Time

Hilary Quagliana explains, "I often find that take-home tests, rather than in-class writing, provide a better way to assess students' analytical thinking and writing abilities. Giving them time to draft, edit, and revise outside of class rather than asking them to quickly regurgitate in class provides a more accurate picture of their writing abilities at that moment in time." And if the prompts are more thought provoking and promote actual learning, it's easier to justify additional in-class time for them as well.

Use Oral Presentations to Widen the Audience and Make Writing a Teaching Activity

Oral presentations increase the value of essay responses by connecting writing with a live audience beyond the teacher—as long as you ensure that the audience is engaged and learning from the presenters and not just sitting passively. You might not be able to bring in an outside panel of adults just to hear presentations at the end of a unit, but the rest of the class can be expected to take notes and taught to ask probing questions. You can collect the written versions to double-check for anything you might have missed during the talks. While this structure consumes time, it needn't drag on endlessly.

At Addison Trail High School, English teacher Amy Ferraro and history teacher Chad Pohlmann partner in an American studies program and frequently use oral presentations instead of written tests. For presentations in an immigration unit, for example, students link information on their own families to material they've studied, and they may also include music, dance, poetry, food, flags, and interesting family memorabilia. With sixty kids in a double-period hundred-minute block, these teachers solve the time problem (and avoid listener fatigue) by running the presentations "museum style." First, kids work in pairs, presenting to each other with a rubric to guide peer evaluation. While the teachers circulate around the room, each viewing and assessing thirty presentations one at a time, some partners continue to rehearse. Some kids— usually about eight to ten—watch the ones they are most interested in. And those who wish can start reading on the next assignment. No one is bored or wasting time. The process generally takes two block periods, or four fifty-minute periods. Most presentations are five to ten minutes long, though some that attract great interest run longer. The teachers calculate that if they had to do with less time, they would hold the kids to five minutes each, condensing the total to just three fifty-minute periods. And here's a winning bonus: while this is longer than a traditional single-period test, there's no grading the tests at home or going over them later in class.

What makes oral presentations worth the extra time? They not only widen the students' audience but also encourage the creation of understandable explanations that inform listeners. Audience questions help the writer-speaker realize when her account is helpful and when she needs to explain further. And her responses to the questions bring out additional knowledge that might not have been elicited in the written piece itself.

ENGLISH

HISTORY

Try Lab-Type Tests

Labs needn't be just for science classes. Suzanne Brion, eighth-grade English teacher in Saline, Michigan, ended the past school year with an interdisciplinary project titled "Read and Write Saline." In addition to having kids study various historical documents, Suzanne used a small grant to rent buses just before exam day and take the students around to various historical locations, including Underground Railroad sites (which most students knew nothing about) and the salt flats for which the town is named. Her final exam for the semester was an open-ended in-class essay in which students wrote about what they learned on the tour. This was an open-book exam: students could use the trip itinerary and the notes they took along the way.

Ask Questions That Require Students to Reflect

If we want to know how a unit or project has advanced learning and obtain responses that reflect the value added rather than just the kids' present level of knowledge, well . . . *let's ask them.* We should include questions about how students' thinking has changed. Suzanne Brion's interdisciplinary project, "Generations," connects family history with U.S. history, and especially with immigration. It includes research on government, political events, science, art, and so on, divided among student teams, and an I-search study of each student's own family history. The project ends with in-class reflection on several interconnected questions:

SOCIAL STUDIES

- ⇌ What sacrifices did some immigrants make? What did you learn about sacrifices *your* ancestors made?
- ⇌ How do you imagine they would have defined "a better, freer, nobler life"? What is your definition of "a better, freer, nobler life"?
- ⇌ How do you plan to repay your debt of gratitude to your ancestors for their efforts/sacrifices/lives?

By the way, we hope it's clear that on questions like these, it's just about impossible for students to plagiarize, even on an open-book or take-home test.

Teaching Students How to Respond

If tests with essays and extended responses have become such a big part of school, it stands to

⇌ Want to Jump Around?

I-search papers are a great way to turn the dreaded research paper into one of your students' richest and most enjoyable learning experiences—for them and for you. To learn more, go to Chapter 9, pages 236–252.

reason that we should teach kids how to navigate them. Not only are we helping young people succeed, but we are making the tests more valid. This is not "teaching to the test." When students handle essay tests more fluently, there is less interference from struggles with the writing, so they can better show us what they know. Here's how good teachers accomplish this.

Have Kids Practice Through Pair Discussions

In her fascinating book *Writing to the Prompt: When Students Don't Have a Choice,* Janet Angelillo (2005) describes her work with sixth-grade English teacher Mary Ellen Lehner to help students engage more meaningfully with assigned topics. She and Mary Ellen approach this through paired conversations, starting with ordinary, everyday topics. Each student asks his partner to talk about an unfamiliar topic. The teacher models first and then helps the kids brainstorm strategies for responding. How can the student connect the question with ideas or information she *does* know about, in order to have something meaningful to say? Students begin to view this as a game. That way, even if an essay question may approach a topic differently than the student would think about it, she is comfortable with the challenge.

Help Students View Test Essays as They Do Computer Games

Angelillo shows kids that computer gaming and test taking draw on the same kinds of skills and attitudes. After students practice with personal topics, Angelillo and Lehner help them to focus similar effort on questions about the material they are reading, again using paired discussion for the students to try it out. While even good students testify that it's confining to elaborate on someone else's ideas rather than their own (these are teenagers, after all), this approach helps alter their mental framework and provides them with tools for the task.

Have Kids Practice Using Engaging Daily Life Topics

Amy Ferraro, at Addison Trail High School, presented students with Frank McCourt's list, from *Teacher Man,* of the various types of students in his classroom:

> . . . the mouth . . . the clown, the goody-goody, the beauty queen, the volunteer for everything, the jock, the intellectual, the momma's boy, the mystic, the sissy, the lover, the critic, the jerk, the religious fanatic who sees sin everywhere, the brooding one who sits in the back staring at the desk . . . (2005, p. 20)

She then asked, for a timed, in-class writing task, that each student decide what type he was and write about it. While this wasn't a subject-area topic like the causes of the Revolutionary War, it still allowed students and teacher to address many of the challenges posed by a timed writing task. And the kids wrote with great eagerness. As Amy explains, "Because the kids were already confident about the topic, they didn't have to worry about getting the answer 'right' so they were able to focus on organization and other elements of their writing. They were able to have fun with it. It was introspective and even turned into college application essays for several students."

Help Students Review Previous Test Efforts

How often do we sweat over comments on students' papers and tests only to see them wadded up and slam-dunked into the wastebasket? Hilary Quagliana, whose work using writing to teach history we've described earlier, created the chart shown in Figure 10–1 to help students actually learn from their previous efforts before the next test. It's just one of life's little lessons: when you want something, it's a good idea to ask for it!

Want to Jump Around?

Most of the brief in-class writing strategies described in Chapter 3 make excellent prewriting tools for students to gather their thoughts before drafting an essay test answer. Brainstorming, drawing, clustering, and mapping are all tools for quickly generating, recalling, and organizing ideas. And if you've used some of these regularly in class, students just need a little reminder to employ them in a test situation.

Use Rubrics

Testing experts love rubrics. Many teachers swear by them. They can be very useful. Or they can drive you and the kids crazy and lead you down paths you don't really want to follow. First, what is a rubric, exactly? It's simply a chart that itemizes various characteristics of writing (or other work) and indicates various levels of quality for each item and the number of points at each level. The widely used 6 + 1 Traits model, for example, looks like this:

TRAIT	A: 45–50 PTS	B: 40–44 PTS	C: 35–39 PTS	D: 30–34 PTS
Ideas/content	[Details in these boxes are based on type of writing.]			
Organization				
Word choice				
Sentence fluency				
Voice				
Conventions				
Presentation				

We have to admit that though the 6 + 1 Traits are popular, we're not excited about them. Look how little they focus on the ideas, the real meat of the writing. What are some of the things you may like or find troubling about rubrics?

World History—I   Name: _____

Quagliana

Writing Workshop: Focus on *OLD* Focus Questions

Let's face it—sometimes you don't read the comments I write on your essays, right? And even if you've taken the time to read the comments I have given you, really using them to improve your writing can be a daunting task. So, follow the steps below to help you use the comments from your previous focus questions to improve the writing you'll do for the final exam.

1. Read through each of the comments I made on your previous focus questions.

2. As you read, keep a list below of the main strengths and weaknesses I noted in each essay. If you do not have each of the focus questions listed, consider the ones you do have.

FOCUS QUESTION	STRENGTH(S)	WEAKNESS(ES)
How did geography influence the development of China?		
How did the combination of people, products, ideas, and modes of transit create the first global exchange/marketplace?		
How was the Ming Dynasty a combination of traditional Chinese values and foreign influences?		
To what extent did local cultural forces combine with Islam to make the Ottoman and Mughal Empires distinct civilizations?		

3. Review your chart. Do you see specific comments repeated in either column? List those repeated comments below.

Strengths	Weaknesses

4. What focus question did you think was your strongest? Why? Answer this in the space provided below.

5. Now, do some specific goal setting. In your final exam focus question, what will you try to continue to do from your "Strengths" column? What is one area you really want to try to improve upon from your "Weaknesses" category? Write those below.

Be sure to refer to this as you write and revise your final exam focus question!
Turn this sheet in with your focus question next week.

Figure 10–1 *Reflection sheet for writing workshop*

- **Advantages:** Sharing a rubric with students in advance lets them know what you consider important in writing a particular essay. At its best, a rubric says to kids, "These are the ingredients of good writing." In that sense, they are a big step ahead of the intuitive/subjective A's and F's that have traditionally been assigned to writing. It can guide kids to study appropriately and to think about how to present information through their writing.

- **Disadvantages:** The rubric can put you and the students in a straitjacket. What if a really smart kid develops some good, relevant ideas in an area you hadn't anticipated? How do you give her credit if it's not on the rubric? Or what if the narrowness of the rubric leads all the students to say nearly the same thing? How do you keep yourself from simply no longer paying attention after reading the first ten papers? How do you tell when one student is copying off another?

- **When a Rubric Is Useful:** This sort of contradicts the previous bullet, but if the rubric is kept short and simple, it can focus students on just a few aspects of the writing to improve those and not try to solve all their weaknesses at once.

- **When a Rubric Becomes Impossible to Use:** Do you ever look at the huge charts produced by some states and districts and just grow dizzy trying to make sense of the dozens of little squares filled with tiny type swimming before your eyes? It's doubtful that students can really learn from these, either.

We have just a few key suggestions to make rubrics work for you as a real tool for helping students write well on tests, while avoiding some of the pitfalls.

1. **Involve students in creating the rubric.** The discussion will help kids understand the qualities of good essays, review the concepts you want them to learn, and highlight writing strategies they'll need in order to do well on the test. In fact, discussions of assessment criteria provide a great learning tool whether you're using a rubric or any other means of evaluation. And don't be surprised if the kids come up with ideas and criteria you hadn't thought of yourself.

2. **Keep the number of criteria in the rubric fairly small.** This will help the students focus on just a few key ideas and skills at a time, increasing the likelihood that students will learn from the test experience. It will also make evaluation easier to handle, so you won't feel overloaded and give up on essay tests.

3. **Make the content criteria broad and conceptual, and maintain a balance between content and writing skills.** If criteria are very narrow and

focused on small facts, the essay test reverts to a memorize-it-and-spit-it-back event. Instead, steer kids to back up their arguments with specific evidence by asking for that in the rubric. And if you include just a couple of writing skills that you and your fellow teachers have emphasized, you'll be communicating their importance and observing students' knowledge of them without creating an impossible paper jam.

4. **Build in flexibility.** We mentioned earlier the concern that some good writing might not fit anywhere in your rubric. Or suppose a kid has worked really hard to conquer something that stumped him all year and you want to give him extra credit for it. The solution is simple: always include an extra blank line in your rubric for unexpected outcomes. Unintended consequences abound in the world, and while many are unfortunate, some are happy events. Shouldn't we consider this in our assessments? And discuss it with the kids—it signals to them that you're always open to and watching for the surprises that make life interesting.

Essays on Standardized Tests

Do standardized tests help our kids learn? No. Do they provide usable and timely data to guide teachers' instructional decisions? No; the results come back too late and are rarely specific enough to pinpoint teaching that's needed. Do they lead schools to actually improve? Debatable. Do they reflect what students are actually learning? Depends—when teachers teach narrowly to the tests, they can get score increases. But are the skills examined in state tests the most important ones for kids to learn? Some of them, maybe; however, few state tests look at students' ability to ask questions as they read, for example, one of the proven cognitive strategies good readers must use. And do the tests even focus on the skills and concepts in the standards that the tests are supposed to advance? In our book, *Best Practice: Today's Standards for Teaching and Learning in America's Schools* (Zemelman, Daniels, and Hyde 2005), we documented the troubling disconnect between the high-level goals in many state standards and the low level of thinking actually required on the tests.

Well then, are the tests going away anytime soon? No way. So we need to find ways to help our students do well on them, while we protect good innovative instruction and not abandon deeper learning in our curriculum. Let's outline some strategies for strengthening students' writing for standardized test essays and extended responses.

Strategy 1: For most of the year, students should read widely in your subject, and write for assignments that ask them to think, elaborate on their ideas, and make connections between material you teach and the outside world.

The more students are comfortable with and skilled at explaining their thinking on paper, the better they'll do at writing those test essays. But the benefits even on the tests go well beyond that. We quoted the following studies from the Consortium on Chicago School Research earlier, but they're so crucial that we'll state them once again. In classrooms where assignments asked students to develop arguments, draw conclusions, elaborate their understanding, construct knowledge rather than just state information, and connect topics with their own lives or situations outside of school, Chicago students made one-year gains 20 percent greater than the city average on the Iowa Test of Basic Skills (Newmann et al. 2001). And in classrooms that featured high levels of interactive instruction, students gained 5.2 percent more than the city's average growth on the ITBS in one year; in contrast, students exposed to high levels of didactic instruction (i.e., lectures) gained 3.4 percent less than the city average growth (Smith et al. 2001).

> *We needn't, indeed we shouldn't, abandon good, thoughtful writing assignments in response to pressure about standardized tests. On the contrary, they'll not only help prepare students for writing on the tests but also help increase scores in general.*

The clear message: We needn't, indeed we *shouldn't*, abandon good, thoughtful writing assignments in response to pressure about standardized tests. On the contrary, they'll not only help prepare students for writing on the tests but also help increase scores in general. Need we say more?

Strategy 2: Be sure you and your students know the expectations about content and presentation, as well as scoring of the tests.

Students need to learn how to analyze a test question to understand what the test people are asking for. You can review sample test questions that have been released for public access along with the scoring guide used for the essay portion of the test. Sample student responses with the scores that the test makers considered appropriate can also be very handy.

To see how this would work, let's take a quick look at the Illinois Standards Achievement Test for mathematics at eighth grade. The test includes two extended-response items. The Extended Response Mathematics Scoring Rubric focuses on three areas:

- **Mathematical Knowledge:** Knowledge of mathematical principles and concepts which result in a correct solution to a problem.

- ☞ **Strategic Knowledge:** Identification and use of important elements of the problem that represent and integrate concepts which yield the solution (e.g., models, diagrams, symbols, algorithms).

- ☞ **Explanation:** Ability to translate into words the steps of the solution process and to provide a justification for each step. (2005, website page)

To a nonexpert, the difference between the first two can be fuzzy. But once kids look at a few of the student samples and the comments that explain the scores they received, the distinction becomes clear: strategic knowledge means the readers are looking for a problem-solving strategy such as a set of equations, a tally chart, or even a guess-and-check process, which is OK if it's used systematically.

And here's what the test graders expect in the writing of the explanation itself:

> Explanation is defined as a student's ability to translate into words the steps of the solution process and to provide a justification for each step. Therefore, to do well on this dimension, a student must describe not only what steps he or she chose to solve a problem but must also describe why he or she chose those steps. Though important, the length of the response, grammar, and syntax are not critical elements of this dimension. (2005, website page)

Looking at the grades on the student samples, however, it appears that the test makers reward a certain degree of conceptual thinking, but it's OK if the student does not think more broadly about problem solving or mathematical concepts. In three top-graded explanations, the sentences were mostly of the form, "I did ___ so I could find out ___."

In their book, *Writing on Demand,* Anne Ruggles Gere, Leila Christenbury, and Kelly Sassi (2005) offer an organized set of steps that can guide students in analyzing test prompts on more humanities-oriented topics. They pose these questions, which we can teach the students to ask themselves as they read a test prompt:

1. What is the central claim or *topic* called for?

2. Who is the intended *audience?* [That is, what sort of audience does the question ask the student to imagine, if any—rather than the actual test graders?]

3. What is the *purpose* or *mode* for the writing task?

4. What *strategies* will be most effective?

5. What is my *role* as a writer in achieving the purpose? [A role the question asks the student to imagine, not her actual role as an anxious and weary test taker.] (2005, 67)

Strategy 3: Go back to viewing test writing as a kind of computer game.

Janet Angelillo lists the skills required for playing computer games that are also relevant to test writing. Some of these are

- being ready to engage with a topic as an intellectual exercise
- being alert and quick to respond
- searching the mind to bring knowledge and information forward
- considering many possibilities, selecting some, and discarding others
- deciding on the type of game or response needed (2005, 14)

Angelillo is talking, of course, about the more complex and sophisticated games that teenagers play these days, not the Pac-Man that started this craze. Kids don't merely play these games, but, as Angelillo says, "Young players can 'get lost' in them, the way many adults remember getting lost in books when they were young" (2005, 13). We can easily picture asking a class of ninth graders to talk over and brainstorm their own list of such skills. The teaching activity, then, is to demonstrate for students by thinking aloud on a sample test question in your subject area and showing kids just how the mental activity of attacking an essay test question resembles playing a computer game. The students can then practice this kind of thinking in pairs on another such question.

You might worry that this is trivializing the content you are trying to teach—or that you are just encouraging and endorsing a bad habit that eats up time when students should be studying. But the games are here to stay, and perhaps we should start using them and the skills they teach, rather than fighting them (for a passionate argument on this, read the chapter on games in *Everything Bad Is Good for You,* by Steven Johnson [2005]).

OK, so have we solved every problem that can be encountered in making writing for tests a more meaningful and productive exercise? Certainly not. But perhaps you can adopt some of the strategies used by the really smart teachers we've quoted, so that test essays actually help kids learn, lead them to show what they can do, and let you see their real thinking, rather than just yield a bunch of dots on a Scantron page.

Works Cited

Angelillo, Janet. 2005. *Writing to the Prompt: When Students Don't Have a Choice.* Portsmouth, NH: Heinemann.

Elbow, Peter. 1981. *Writing with Power.* New York: Oxford University Press.

Gere, Anne Ruggles, Leila Christenbury, and Kelly Sassi. 2005. *Writing on Demand: Best Practices and Strategies for Success.* Portsmouth, NH: Heinemann.

Illinois State Board of Education. 2005. "Extended Response Mathematics Scoring Rubric." ISBE website.

McCourt, Frank. 2005. *Teacher Man.* New York: Scribner.

Newmann, Fred, et al. 2001. *Authentic Intellectual Work and Standardized Tests: Conflict or Coexistence.* Chicago: Consortium on Chicago School Research.

Johnson, Steven. 2005. *Everything Bad Is Good for You: How Today's Popular Culture Is Actually Making Us Smarter.* New York: Riverhead.

Smith, Julia, et al. 2001. *Instruction and Achievement in Chicago Elementary Schools.* Chicago: Consortium for Chicago Schools Research.

Zemelman, Steven, Harvey Daniels, and Arthur Hyde. 2005. *Best Practice: Today's Standards for Teaching and Learning in America's Schools, Third Edition.* Portsmouth, NH: Heinemann.

Closing Thoughts

Well, that was our best twenty-five activities for using writing in content-area classes. We didn't hold any back. But we know that *you* will come up with tons of great variations and whole new activities that we never thought of. So why don't we stay in touch? You can always find one of us at www.walloon.com, where we will continue to park new handouts and materials for your use.

Remember at the beginning, where we said this was the first book that all three of us had written together? Well, we have arrived at the end, and the friendship has survived coauthorship. We still enjoy teaching, planning, and hanging out with each other—especially when Bill Steineke's wine cellar is open for business.

We had a great time making this book for you. We hope it has seemed sensible, practical, and maybe even (can you use the F word in a professional book?) *fun*. Teach away—and write on!

Santa Fe, NM
Evanston, IL
Brookfield, IL

Index